# Little Bird of Auschwitz

**Alina Peretti** graduated from Wroclaw Technical University in Poland and trained as an architect, working in the Sudan, Senegal, England, France and Switzerland. She later became a tour guide, taking visitors all over the world, including to Auschwitz, but would never go back through the gates herself. She now lives in London with her husband Peter.

After graduating from The London School of Economics, **Jacques Peretti** became an investigative journalist. His award-winning television series include *The Men Who Made Us Fat*, *The Super Rich and Us*, and *Trillion Pound Island*. His first book *The Deals That Made the World* is now a paperback, and his podcast series *Edge of Reality* available as an audible original.

ALINA and JACQUES
PERETTI

# Little Bird of Auschwitz

How My Mother Escaped Death and
Found Our Family

HODDER

First published in Great Britain in 2022 by Hodder & Stoughton
An Hachette UK company

This paperback edition published in 2023

4

A CIP catalogue record for this title is available from the British Library

Paperback ISBN 9781473646445
eBook ISBN 9781473646438

Typeset in Plantin Light by Hewer Text UK Ltd, Edinburgh
Printed and bound in Great Britain by Clays Ltd, Elcograf S.p.A.

Hodder & Stoughton policy is to use papers that are natural, renewable
and recyclable products and made from wood grown in sustainable
forests. The logging and manufacturing processes are expected to
conform to the environmental regulations of the country of origin.

Hodder & Stoughton Ltd
Carmelite House
50 Victoria Embankment
London EC4Y 0DZ

www.hodder.co.uk

*For Juta, Kazhik, Pavel, Olga and Michael*
*– who never got to tell their story*


*Don't be sad, don't be angry, if life deceives you. Submit to your*
*grief – your time for joy will come, believe me*
– Pushkin

# Contents

### Alina Peretti, 25 June, 2021

'My son Jacques is telling my story. I always wanted to tell it myself but never could. Maybe my English wasn't good enough. I never had the courage. I never imagined for a second it would be written down.

Even when Jacques was little, I told him stories of our family in the war. He always asked more questions, wanting to know every detail. He never asked what people did when they found out I'd been in Auschwitz. They'd say, 'Are you Jewish?' and I'd explain that there were lots of nationalities in the camp: Poles, like us, French, Italians, even Germans. The camp was only one part of our family's story. A big part, but just a part. The beginning of my journey in life, not the end.

Maybe me telling Jacques about Auschwitz, so young, did have an effect on him – we had a woman who came to our house once, she was German. Jacques was six or seven. She was a cleaner, and one day she saw this spider, and started killing it, really grinding it into the ground with her foot. Jacques watched this from the corner of the room, and then said to her when it was finished, 'Is that what the Germans did to the Jews?' She handed in her notice, saying to me, 'Is this what you teach your son?' and I said he came to that conclusion himself. But it became an obsession of his – wanting to know what happened to our family. Now we have told the story together. Perhaps this is my last chance to tell it. What do I feel? I feel proud that we've done it. And that it deserves to be told.'

# Introduction

It is a story I heard hundreds of times as a child. It begins with snowbound forests and wolves. Then the Nazis make their dramatic entrance. A dog is shot. A piano is played. Uncle Kazhik steals a gun and joins the army, aged fourteen.

The Jewish ghetto burns and the Warsaw Insurrection is crushed. Jewellery is hidden in underwear and sewn into the hems of clothes, bartered to stay alive. My grandfather has a love affair. The frozen ocean is crossed by sleigh, and a plane drops from the sky. A sister is taken. There's a firing squad, and then the train arrives at Auschwitz.

I have spent my life investigating stories that I thought were important, whilst sitting in front of me all the time was the most extraordinary story I have ever heard: my mother's. I have decided to tell it now because my mum has dementia. It is a race against time to beat her memory loss, fighting an enemy more relentless than the Nazis.

As Alina's short-term files are erasing themselves, her long-term memory of her odyssey through war grows ever sharper. She might not know where her glasses are, but can tell me every feature on the face of the German doctor who gave her 'medicine' in the concentration camp.

This book is the result of a year of conversations together. It is my mum's story, told as much as possible in her own words, describing what she experienced. It is one also told by thousands of families separated by momentous events: millions of people who together faced incredible danger, the lottery of who would survive, and bittersweet reunion with those who did. It is an experience that resonates once more with a world that has lived through a pandemic.

For my family, the war was a catalyst, which forced them to confront secrets they had concealed from one another for years: jealousies, infidelity and a dramatic double life kept hidden, then prised open and revealed by war. Ours is the tale of a family taken to the darkest place in history, who found one another in that darkness, and forgave. If it had not been for the trauma unleashed by Hitler, there would never have been this redemption and forgiveness.

Writing this book has also been a way for me to understand my own prickly relationship with my mother. A woman whom I had not called 'Mum' once my entire life, and who never wanted to be called it. I refer to her as 'Mum' in the book as my own form of wish fulfilment; something never possible in reality.

Why did she never want to be called 'Mum'? I had assumed it was because of events in her early childhood, some of which I knew about, but it was nothing to do with that. I discovered it was for one single unspeakable reason, buried in Auschwitz.

In researching the book, I have asked Alina to recall terrible memories she had pushed to the back of her mind for eighty years. It has been an experience simultaneously cruel and cathartic. I have interviewed her several times about the same event, eking out more detail, which has been difficult for her. These remembered scenes have been given minimal dialogue, based on what she remembers being said, or was told to her by her siblings, on the occasions she wasn't present.

In revisiting these events, Alina has opened up about her relationship with her own mother, Olga, for the first time, revealing why she hated her so much and unquestioningly adored her father (and why that was such a mistake). I understand now why Alina still flinches when she hears the word 'mother' and how difficult it must have been for her to have been a mother to me.

At the heart of this story is a family who were strangers to one another. That is the case with every family to some extent, yet very few are forced to confront the secrets they hold from one another as the bombs fall in the tumult of war. To my mother, these events – and the secrets they revealed – are as vivid as if they happened yesterday.

Michael, Alina's mysterious father, lived two lives, constantly 'away', hiding the truth of who he really was and what he did. His duplicity, it turned out, was multi-layered, concealing not only a love affair but involvement with the underground Polish resistance. Michael was at the heart of decision-making that would change the course of history. He lived a double life for good reason: to keep his family alive.

According to my mother, her three siblings, Pavel, Kazhik and Juta, hated her. I always thought it was because they suspected her of being adopted. In writing this book, I discovered that her brothers and sister were in fact selected in Nazi-occupied Warsaw to be reprogrammed as 'New Aryans' – ethnic Poles chosen to become model Nazis. I now know what that really entailed, and from whence their hatred stemmed.

My family's perilous journey through war is filled with decisions that defy comprehension. Why, for instance, did my superstitious, tarot-card-obsessed grandmother abandon her children to face the advance of German tanks alone, only to change her mind and embark on an insane plan to save them? How did my mother survive a firing squad and cross a continent to escape death, only to find herself back in the inferno of the Warsaw insurrection? These are questions my mum has been waiting eighty years to find the answers to.

Auschwitz looms throughout, the inevitable destination. Auschwitz has quite rightly been a Jewish story. This is an account of Auschwitz as my mother, grandmother and aunt – three of the 13,000 non-Jewish Poles deported from the Warsaw uprising – arrived at its gates. By November 1944, the camp was collapsing, the Germans hastily destroying evidence of the Holocaust as Russian gunfire flashed on the horizon.

The gas chambers were being broken up, the bones of the dead smashed with hammers. New prisoners, including Jews, were forced to collude in the eradication of any evidence of genocide; then they were killed themselves. My family rode the chaos of the camp's last days as it imploded. Death was no longer industrial, but arbitrary and quixotic, at the hands of SS guards desperate to cover their tracks and leave no witnesses. My family were ethnic Poles, *Dungervolke* (or 'shit people'), and their fate was intertwined with that of their Jewish neighbours, who had arrived on the same cattle trains from a burning Warsaw.

For my mum – Alina – the missing piece of her own story in Auschwitz is what happened to her sister, Juta, there. I had suspected that the reason no one in the family ever wanted to know the truth was because it was too shameful. What actually happened to Juta was both more terrible and poignant than I could ever have imagined.

For this part of the book, I have relied upon the account that Juta herself gave in two letters she wrote to my mother and grandmother whilst all three were in the camp, between November 1944 and January 1945.

Juta was picked from the queue by an SS guard at Pruszków, the Auschwitz sorting camp, for 'special duties'. Two alternative fates befell women who spoke German, as Juta did, chosen for special duties. One was to work as a translator for the Polish prisoners being given orders by German guards, and the other was to work as a prostitute for the SS officers in the 'Dolls' House' of Block 24, nicknamed 'Puff'. Sometimes these two fates were fatally connected.

For the account of what happened to my family during the Jewish ghetto uprising of 1943 and Warsaw uprising of 1944, I have relied primarily on extensive conversations my mother had with her brother Kazhik in Lodz in the 1950s, and later in Paris in the 1960s. Kazhik was a child combatant and told me some of what happened himself when Alina and I visited Poland in the late 1970s, shortly before he died. These conversations also inform the narrative.

The story of my grandfather Michael's life in the Polish underground movement during and after the war was told to my mother and uncle partially by Michael himself, but mostly by Michael's lover, Marta, after he was imprisoned as an 'enemy of the state' by the Polish communist government in 1951. Marta described their secret life together in wartime London: how Michael organised 'bandit' terrorist missions against the Nazis and arranged for Olga and Alina to escape from Siberia. Marta also confessed why she betrayed him after the war.

My mum has lived over seventy-five years of life freed of Auschwitz. But those years between the ages of eight and thirteen, as she was tossed across Europe on the storm of war, overshadowed everything she did subsequently, for better and for worse. Alina has gone on to live an extraordinary life because of, not despite, what happened to her and her family. She describes it as 'a gift', making her who she is. Alina went on to become an engineer and architect, travelled the world and learnt six languages. Most extraordinary of all, given what happened to her in the camp, she became a mother.

Like so many of those who survived, Alina – my 'mum' – is one of the most generous and least bitter human beings I have ever met, and that is because, as the poet George Herbert advises every person on earth, 'Live well, it is the greatest revenge'. A lesson she learnt herself from the story you are about to read.

## The Basiak Family

Michael Basiak (Polish businessman) and Olga Bialonoga-Szahovska (Russian aristocrat) meet and marry in Paris, in 1920.

They have four children:
Pavel (adopted 1923, died 1944)
Juta (born 1926, died 1945)
Kazhik (born 1930, died 1980)
Alina (born 1931, *pictured*)

*This is the only photo that exists of any of the
Basiak children. It was taken on Alina's sixteenth birthday.*

Kazhik marries Mirka Adamiak in 1960 and has one son, Martin.

Alina marries Peter Peretti in 1965 and has one son, Jacques.

# *Prologue*

*19 July 1998, Oświęcim, Southern Poland*

It is sweltering hot, and excited tourists pour from giant, air-conditioned buses, shuffling expectantly through the *Arbeit Macht Frei* gates in T-shirts and shorts, their camcorders at the ready.

One of those walking up to the gates is Alina Peretti, my mother. It isn't her first time at Auschwitz. In 1944, she came here as a thirteen-year-old girl with her sister, Juta, and mother, Olga to be put to death.

Alina had tried to go back on several occasions after the war – stepping off the train and always getting as far as the car park – but she was never able to walk through the gates. She could never bring herself to do it. This attempt in 1998 is her fourth.

She has it all planned out in her head. Alina will avoid the crowds, the displays of piled-up shoes and hair, the gas chambers and crematoria. Instead, she will head to a deserted area at the back of Auschwitz I, the place where she believes it all happened.

When Alina gets to the gates, she stops. Just as she has on three previous occasions. Something prevents her from crossing the threshold into the camp. She looks ahead for a moment and then turns around, walking back to the car park. As she does, she overhears a young woman with a yellow umbrella, wearing Gucci wrap around sunglasses, speaking to a small group she is about to take into Auschwitz.

'There is a lot of controversy about what happened here,' says the guide breezily. 'It could well be that as many as a million Jews were killed, but there's no evidence to say it really happened.'

'Excuse me?'

'Yes, madam?' the guide replies, looking a little affronted.

Alina steps over to join the group.

'Can you please repeat what you just said?'

'I said, madam, that it's believed by many that it might not have happened.'

'Well, you see. Here's the thing. I need your badge number now.'

'Excuse me?'

'Your badge number, please.' My mum is a polite person, but quite direct. 'I can tell you why it is my business. My sister was murdered here.'

There is a low-key, collective gasp from the group. Perhaps this is part of the tour? They stare at the guide. The guide stares at my mum. Alina feels the need to say something to break the awkward silence.

'By the Nazis . . . she was murdered by the Nazis.'

In that second, in her mind, my mum is faced not by a tour guide in sunglasses, but a fully signed-up Holocaust denier. A *bona fide* enemy of civilisation. In her head, she is back in 1944.

'You, madam,' she tells the guide, 'are a liar.'

Alina walks briskly to the car park information office and reports her. A security guard is dispatched to find the offending woman, who denies she has said any such thing, is not a proper guide anyway but on a 'private tour', and counter-claims that Alina was 'verbally abusive'.

My mum explains why this woman should never again walk through the gates of Auschwitz, earning a living by denying what happened to her sister. Or the 1.1 million people who were murdered there.

The guide is banned. Someone in authority at Auschwitz has listened to a prisoner.

My mum walks out of the office and bursts into tears.

To this day, she has never been able to walk back through the gates that she first went through aged thirteen.

# I

## Three Weeks Before War

*10 August 1939, Warsaw, Poland*

The Basiak family arrived on holiday only twenty-two days before war was declared. It was the hottest summer anyone could remember. Eleven months of the year, Olga and her children lived 400 miles away, deep in the Prypec forest near the Russian border. Each summer, they would come to the city for a month to stay in an apartment that Olga's husband, Michael, had bought in 1933. This year, Michael wasn't with them. He rarely came to Warsaw with his family and was always away 'on business'.

The flat was at 49 Krolewska Street, a five-minute walk from the pleasure gardens of Ogród Saski ('The Saxon Garden'), with its boating lake and café selling waffles and hot chocolate. It was in Srodmiescie, a well-to-do area like Regent's Park in London. They lived on the second floor of an elegant five-storey property.

The flat was laid out like a Parisian apartment, with a wrought-iron balcony and a cool breeze blowing through in summer. The rooms were high, and filled with rococo-style furniture. There was also a baby grand piano for Juta to keep up her practice; she planned to apply to the Paris Conservatoire de Musique the following year.

The four children arrived with great excitement in Warsaw. The Polish capital had wide boulevards criss-crossed by trams. Hundreds of people darted in and out of big department stores laden with expensive-looking bags, and there were brightly coloured shops selling umbrellas, cigars and toys. It seemed amazing to my mum that you could have a whole shop dedicated to selling only toys.

There were more cars in Warsaw than Alina had seen in her life. Her father, Michael, owned a Ford – the only one in a fifty-mile radius – but because they lived in the forest, the nearest petrol station was in Lvov, three hours' drive away. When they ran out of petrol, it was pulled home by a horse.

In Warsaw, the children were in heaven. On the boating lake, they spent hours rowing or sailing miniature wooden yachts. There were theatres and concerts to attend, silent films starring Harold Lloyd and horse-drawn carriage rides across the wide bridges of the River Vistula.

Kazhik, Pavel and Juta adored the city, but Alina rarely went out exploring with them. Olga asked her daughter one day why she didn't like spending time with her brothers and sister. Alina said she was happier to stay in the apartment by herself and could her mother talk about something else?

Olga was Russian and from military stock. Her father, Anthony Bialonoga-Szahovski, was a general in the Tsar's army. Olga told her children proudly that they were 'White Russians', aristocrats who continued to pledge allegiance to the Tsar, even after her family lost its entire fortune in the Russian revolution.

Olga had two brothers, Peter and Vladimir. In 1916, Vladimir was made a personal bodyguard to Tsar Nicholas II, one of the elite Cossacks whose job was to protect the supreme Russian emperor round the clock. This is the only photo that exists of Vladimir (front row, right) taken with his fellow Cossack guards. They did everything from taste the Tsar's food to check for bombs under his carriage.

When the revolution came and Vladimir was executed along with the Russian royal family, Olga's mother hid a tranche of the family's diamonds, gold and jewellery in a box located under the floorboards in a house outside St Petersburg. Before she died, her mother told Olga where the fortune was hidden and Olga, aged nineteen, retrieved it.

The Russian aristocracy that escaped the revolution fled to Paris, where they recreated their social world of glittering parties and debutante society balls. Olga met Michael Basiak, a successful Polish architect, at one such event. Michael was leaning on a bar in his black-tie dress suit nursing a large vodka. He looked bored, and very handsome. Olga asked him to dance.

Michael made little effort to impress the besotted Olga. He was tight-lipped about his job, but did tell her that his expertise was in building railway stations and bridges, which he constructed in France, England and as far afield as China. He was away, Michael said, a lot.

That wasn't what he really did. It was a cover story. When Michael failed to go to Warsaw for the holidays in August 1939, nineteen years after he'd first met Olga and lied about his true occupation, he had even more important reasons for not telling Olga the truth. He knew he was abandoning his family to a war starting in less than three weeks, because he had to attend to more important business.

Michael played the part of a successful businessman to a tee. In 1929, he avoided the Wall Street crash by sinking the money he'd made into a big house in the middle of a Polish forest. The nearest village was so small and remote, it didn't even register as a name on a map. Once married, Olga imagined that Michael would keep her in the aristocratic manner to which she was accustomed. Instead, he parked his Russian wife in his big, gloomy house in the forest, surrounded by nothing but cows and mosquitoes.

Olga sat for much of the day in the same embroidered day chair, mournfully turning tarot cards. Sometimes she never got out of bed at all, drinking tea and eating incredibly sweet *halva*. She was depressed. Michael's solution was to extend his travelling abroad for months on end. After a while, he stopped even telling Olga he was going.

They tried for children, but failed. In 1923, they adopted a boy, Pavel, at Olga's insistence. Then, against the odds, they had three of their own children in quick succession. A daughter, Josepha (known as 'Juta') in 1926; a boy, Kazhik in 1930; and a year later, my mother, Alina.

Pavel, the oldest, was tall and gentle. He was too big for every room he walked into, and had an air of vulnerability. No one ever talked about him being adopted, but it soon became an issue with the children that one of them had been. Speculation was rife between them and the candidate for the 'adopted one' changed weekly, prompted by Kazhik. No one ever accused Pavel, perhaps because they knew deep down that he *was* the adopted one, and would not survive being singled out.

As soon as he could walk, Kazhik was obsessed with war (his

name was an abbreviation of Kazimierz, meaning 'destroyer of peace' in Polish folklore). He loved play-fighting and would order his older brother Pavel to be his army, building forts in the forest and hiding supplies from the kitchen cupboard in a den for sieges. When he was seven, Kazhik got his first real gun and shot squirrels and rabbits in the forest. Pavel and Kazhik fished, hunted and learnt to cook in the wild. By the age of ten, the boy knew how to survive.

Michael didn't recognise much of himself in his younger son. He said Kazhik must have inherited 'the army gene' from his mother's military family. Kazhik ran amok through the house, playing practical jokes such as hiding dead animals in Alina's bed, but he knew better than to mess with Juta.

Kazhik stayed clear of his older sister. Juta had a forbidding air and could stop her brother dead with a single, withering stare. She was a beautiful and exceptionally gifted pianist, with what Olga called 'perfect piano fingers', but Juta's beauty was a curse, drawing unwanted attention from boys in the nearby village. She created a detached, condescending air as a protective shell, calling the boys '*slodka swinka*' (sweet little pigs).

However, Juta had a soft spot for her little sister, Alina. She taught Alina the piano, a kind of neutral ground for them both, and Alina – though useless at playing – tried her best. Juta, nearly a teenager, played complicated dolls' tea parties with Alina, who hated dolls. Juta was becoming too old to play, but she was insistent.

On the rare occasions their father was home, the sisters fought to sit on his lap. Michael pretended to have an invisible crankshaft in the middle of his forehead, and the girls would take turns to wind it up so he would tell a story. Should Juta lose the fight for their father's attention, she feigned boredom and would waft away to read a book, or brush her long hair. Alina came to believe that Juta was manipulative, and would get whatever she wanted in life.

The Warsaw apartment off Saski Park, four weeks before it was dive-bombed by Nazi Stuka bombers, was blissfully quiet. My mum woke up groggy at around eleven, because she had been up all night reading books. She loved Pushkin's poetry and translations of Robert Louis Stevenson. The doors to the balcony were flung open to let the breeze through the apartment. The other children were already out, in Saski Park or swimming in the river.

Alina stayed indoors. She avoided her siblings, because ever since arriving in Warsaw, by her own admission she had begun behaving in the most horrible way. One morning, as they were all eating breakfast, Alina bit Kazhik's arm without warning, drawing blood. Alina could not understand why she did it; perhaps it was attention-seeking, she really had no idea. There was no provocation.

Olga sent Alina to her bedroom.

'You are a horrible child,' she told Alina in front of her brothers and sister. 'Egocentric.'

'I hate you,' she told her mother. 'I hate you all.'

After the biting incident, the children ganged up on Alina when Olga was out shopping. Alina was sitting in a window chair reading, when she looked up to see Kazhik and Pavel standing over her. Juta was there too, which felt like a minor act of betrayal. Juta's hair was in blonde pigtails and there was a smile on her face, which was very odd, because she never smiled. Kazhik spoke first, as if it was a speech he'd been preparing for some time.

'You are not one of us,' he said.

Alina looked up blankly.

'You were adopted. You don't look like us.'

Juta brought over a small hand mirror and gave it to Alina.

'Look at yourself,' Kazhik said. 'We're all blonde and you are dark, so you can't be one of us.'

There was silence, as if they were waiting for Alina to bite one of them again.

'Our parents found you on the church steps,' Kazhik continued, itching for a response. Alina pondered the statement.

'Which church?' she asked, eventually.

Kazhik looked panicked and glanced at Juta for back-up.

'The Russian church,' Juta said.

'Prove it,' Alina replied. 'Prove I'm adopted.'

Pavel had stood awkwardly to one side the whole time. He was scared for Alina, but more worried they would turn on him. Though Pavel was sixteen and Juta thirteen, it was the nine-year-old Kazhik who was in charge and spoke for the group. Pavel was pleased he was being included in their gang and not lumped in with Alina. He felt bad for his sister, but wasn't going to stand up for her. He knew he was the adopted one.

The scene was a portent of things to come. When war came, the price for failing to prove you had the right kind of blood flowing through your veins was to be sent to a concentration camp. Pavel was the adopted one, but at Kazhik's prompting, it was decided Alina was 'guilty'. When Olga returned, an anxious daughter confronted her mother.

'Am I the adopted one?'

'Read your book.'

Olga said it was none of Alina's business, and was never to be mentioned again. She neither confirmed nor denied the question. Alina believed in that moment that her mother didn't love her. She was sure Olga didn't really love Juta either. Olga idolised her boys, and perhaps she was jealous of Juta's good fortune at being so beautiful and intelligent. Towards Alina, Olga felt nothing.

Over the next week, the mood darkened in the apartment. Olga began snapping at Alina for 'moping around'. She would fly into a rage, then go silent without warning. When Alina asked her one morning if they were going together to the big department store in town to buy new shoes, Olga slapped her across the face. Alina went to the bathroom mirror and saw a deep purple blotch spreading slowly under the skin.

One evening, soup was prepared for the five of them by their housekeeper, Hela, a thin, intense woman with scraped-back hair, who smelt vaguely of bleach. Hela kept the entire house running, but was never thanked or paid enough for it.

Olga spent the day with the curtains drawn in her bedroom, turning tarot cards furiously until they predicted the future she wanted. When they sat down to dinner, Alina asked if father would be joining them in Warsaw for their holidays.

Olga leant across and grabbed Alina's hair, pulling a big clump out and holding it like a trophy in front of her. Alina felt the hole in her hair in disbelief.

'Ask me about him again and I will throw you across the room.'

Alina felt shame for the first time in her life. Her response was to stand defiantly in front of her mother and enunciate her next words as calmly and precisely as possible.

'Where. Is. My. Father?'

Alina used the singular possessive, as though Michael was her father alone, not the other children's.

Olga stood slowly from the table, pushed back her soup and lunged at Alina, throwing her to the ground. Olga then hit her daughter repeatedly on the back of the head as she cowered on the floor. Olga was in thrall to her tarot cards, which had told her before dinner that Michael had another woman in London, and this was where he was now.

'You want to know if you are adopted?' she shouted at her daughter.

The children sat in silence, looking at their mother and sister on the ground.

'You want to know, Alina?'

Pavel looked down into his soup, the looming shadow of his face darkening the gloomy liquid.

'You're not the adopted one, Alina.'

My mother felt a guilty pang of relief, but it soon evaporated.

'You want to know why?'

The children sat on the edge of their seats, Pavel sank back defeated, sure that he would be revealed.

'Because whenever I see your face, Alina, I see your father's ugly features, and that's why I despise you so much.'

Back in their country home, the children had acres of woods and fields to roam in. The house was a sprawling, Chekhovian idyll; large rooms with worn leather chairs and threadbare carpets, and huge, inherited paintings hanging on the walls. They had dogs and horses in the stable. The children didn't go to school, but were tutored instead by a pretty local woman, whom Olga suspected was having an affair with her husband.

When Michael returned home from his mysterious business trips, Olga would start on him in a wild and passionate way. The rows would be long and cacophonic, with crockery thrown plentifully.

'Look at the cards!' she would scream, the sound echoing through the forest. 'You have been with a blonde woman. The cards will tell me her name!' She had no proof, but the cards were all she needed. When she turned them over, Michael was always guilty.

The constant rows had turned the children against their mother. They worshipped their largely absent father and hated Olga. When he returned, he took the boys shooting and showered all his children with presents. He sat with a doting daughter on each leg, telling them bedtime stories. In these times, Olga was once more in her husband's shadow.

Olga was angry not just at Michael, but because her whole world had collapsed. She had been pulled from her glamorous life in Paris and dumped in a remote Polish forest, alone with four young children. The fact that these children now hated her for being so enraged about this trap, only made her more angry.

### 18 August 1939, Warsaw

Two weeks before the Germans invaded Poland, a silver sugar bowl was passed across the table. It was filled to the brim with white cubes and Kazhik was trying to stack them on top of one another to make the tallest tower in the world.

No one could remember the touch-paper for the incident, only the aftermath. Alina and Kazhik argued about who should pass the bowl. A struggle ensued and it was thrown across the room, accidentally smashing the side of Pavel's head, who was sitting minding his own business in a corner. Pavel sustained a deep cut on his temple, which was visible to his dying day; the long gash left blood all over the apartment, turning it into an appalling crime scene. Kazhik had thrown the bowl, but Alina was blamed.

Olga called the children into the drawing room. Alina pre-empted an attack from her mother by begging for forgiveness; she said it was all her fault. Olga stopped her abruptly mid-sentence with a raised hand. She told Alina that she had ruined everything. The holiday was over and they were all to return immediately to the house in the forest.

Kazhik stood up straight as a soldier and confronted his mother. He said he wasn't giving up his holiday because of his sister. He was nine years old, but talked like the man of the house. He was staying in Warsaw.

Pavel and Juta stood loyally behind him. Pavel was about two foot taller than all the other children; he was sixteen and hardly spoke, but he made it clear from his body language that he was behind his little brother's decision. If Kazhik was staying, he was staying. Juta said the same. Alina sat on the carpet, watching this pincer movement against her mother, and wondering what this would mean.

Juta asked politely if she may speak. She had piano lessons coming up, she said, and wasn't giving them up to go home. In truth, she hated the countryside. Juta was thirteen and Alina suspected she had a boyfriend in Warsaw. One night, Juta confessed to her younger sister in bed that she had been kissed by a boy down at the riverbank. Alina knew this was Juta's real reason for staying, but she didn't say anything.

Olga could sense the power shift. She had a choice – cave in to her children or put her foot down and bend them to her will. In truth, she couldn't wait to get back to the country either. Olga hated being in Warsaw, because it reminded her of her old life of society balls, sparkling friends and the dizzying whirl of Paris. She preferred to be back in the forest with the curtains drawn, robotically turning her tarot cards as if to confirm all this misery had been preordained. Juta had a secret agenda for staying and Olga had one for leaving.

'It's been decided,' she said.

'What's been decided?' Kazhik replied contemptuously.

'Alina and I will return alone immediately. It's the only way to keep the peace.'

Olga laid out her plan for the formal separation of the children. Kazhik and Juta were to stay in the apartment in Warsaw, looked after by their oldest brother, Pavel. He seemed utterly bewildered at the idea, as if he couldn't believe Olga was putting him in charge. Kazhik patted Pavel on the arm with fatherly reassurance.

Hela would come and help them with cleaning and groceries. 'We can live on her bloody awful dry German biscuits,' Kazhik said. It was his way of lightening the moment. He was happy, because he had won.

Olga said a small weekly allowance would be telegraphed to the bank for them to live on. They would receive a weekly phone call from the huge bakelite telephone that hung like a coffin on the wall in the country house, checking they were fine. And that was that.

In the morning, Olga and Alina were gone.

### 1 September 1939, Warsaw

Two weeks later, the Second World War started. Olga and Alina were back in the country minus the three oldest children, the consequence of the sugar-bowl incident. In the forest, Alina knew nothing of the events unfolding on the outskirts of Warsaw, as the locals prepared for harvest, the birds continued to tweet and leaves rustled in the wind. There was no distant rumbling of tanks, nor trudging of soldiers' boots. Simply my mum, aged eight, playing alone in a meadow.

In the west of Poland, the Germans advanced quickly over the border. They executed at will. Wehrmacht soldiers were told to save their bullets, greeting old women holding bunches of flowers by hitting them in the head with the butt of their rifles.

Kazhik was the first of the children in Warsaw to find out. A single shell dropped out of the cloudless blue sky, and scooped out three floors of an apartment block two streets from their flat. It was an amuse bouche for what was to come.

Stuka bombers dived vertically, screaming through the hot, thin air, followed by a mind-boggling sight for a nine-year-old boy – explosions approaching steadily from the far end of the street. Craters appeared magically like advancing footsteps from an invisible Titan, marching towards Kazhik, who was rooted to the spot.

Kazhik would have lied if he said he wasn't excited. He had been waiting his whole life for this moment. The imaginary war he had been fighting against trees in the forest, throwing pebble grenades and machine-gunning with sticks, was now real. War was happening in three dimensions before his uncomprehending eyes.

Hitler had prepared a special fate for Warsaw. He told the advancing army that they were to grind the Polish capital to dust. History was to remember Warsaw only as a memory. The rest would be blood and rubble. Wave upon wave of molten metal rained down on the city. Kazhik ran back home, dodging the explosions, where he found Pavel and Juta cowering with Hela under the kitchen table with a young woman from the flat opposite, who had come to check on them and found herself trapped.

It would be three days before any of them ventured beyond the kitchen table and out of the flat to find food and water, by which time the Nazis had marched victoriously through the centre of Warsaw in full uniform, demanding that the Polish onlookers bow their heads in deference. The Polish capital was now a city of Germany.

Many advancing Wehrmacht were conscripted soldiers with little interest in sadistic acts against the Polish population, but within this advancing army was a shard of glass. The *Einsatzgruppen*, created by Hitler's most loyal and terrifying lieutenant, Reinhard Heydrich, nicknamed 'The Blonde Beast'. Heydrich had invented the yellow star of David worn by Europe's Jews and was to become the self-proclaimed 'architect' of the 'Final Solution'.

If the SS were the all-seeing eyes of the Nazi octopus, the *Einsatzgruppen* were its tentacles. In Warsaw, they were ordered to kill all anti-German 'elements' and begin reprogramming Poles as model citizens of the Third Reich. Heydrich said

Warsaw was to become a textbook example of 'Nazification', quoted in textbooks for a thousand years to come, and children like Kazhik, Pavel and Juta were to become the first subjects of this experiment: 'New Aryans'.

Kazhik, Juta and Pavel faced war without parents. Olga was back in the countryside with Alina. Their father was in Paris, but he wasn't there to fix a bridge. Michael had a secret he had kept from Olga and his children for over a decade. Something he couldn't tell anyone.

Michael was a political dissident, an 'enemy of the state'. In the 1930s, he had been a vocal critic of Poland's autocratic leader, General Pilsudski, which marked his card as a subversive. Pilsudski was a hero to millions of Poles for helping create the Polish state in 1919, but as the years went on, and especially after Hitler rose to power in Germany, Pilsudski began to play with fire. He viewed Russia and Germany as twin evils, and his strategy to save Poland from what he believed to be the two snakes of Stalin and Hitler was to court the smaller snake of Hitler. It was a fatal miscalculation.

Over a million Jews who had escaped persecution in Eastern Europe and fled to Poland in the early 1930s now feared Pilsudski would appease Hitler by condoning anti-Semitism in Poland. The intimidation and killing of Jews in Poland's towns and villages became commonplace once more, as it had been 300 years before.

Michael denounced Poland's drift towards fascism. This put him on Pilsudski's radar, and in danger. In 1935, the secret police began a file on him. They produced surveillance reports and had Michael arrested three times, imprisoning him without charge in the Bereza Kartuska prison. He always managed to get out.

When war was declared, everything changed. The old regime of Pilsudski collapsed and former enemies of the Pilsudski government like Michael saw their chance. Michael became a member of the Polish government-in-exile in Paris. It may have said 'Architect' in his passport, but he had been leading this double life for over a decade.

Michael made no bones about it. He was prepared to sacrifice everything for Poland, even his family. The government-in-exile wanted Poland freed of both Nazism and Communism. They called themselves the Home Army, the *Armia Krajowa*, or AK for short.

With his background in engineering and architecture, Michael was pivotal in their plans to attack the Nazi infrastructure. He pinpointed weak spots on railways, dams, power stations and telephone exchanges, and the resistance bombed them. Michael did far less building bridges than blowing them up.

Olga despised Michael's political convictions, but had no idea how deeply involved he was with the AK. Her tarot cards told her he was up to something, but she had always assumed it was other women. What Olga also didn't know was that Michael had lied to her about his name. It wasn't Basiak, but Sobanski. A powerful, land-owning Russian family, who had fought the Tsar, and his persecution of Jews and kulaks. The Sobanski dynasty were put to death by the Tsar, and Michael's great-uncle Ludwik was sent to a Siberian labour camp; but the Sobanskis reaped their revenge, playing a key role in the Bolshevik revolution.

Olga always suspected Michael was keeping the truth about his family origins from her, but her tarot cards failed to reveal the full extent. Olga believed she was the Russian aristocrat, but Michael was the real thing. The money he had inherited from the Sobanski fortune was the reason they could buy a huge house in the Polish forest. Not building stations.

Michael also happened to be a very dangerous man. Something Olga would soon find out.

# 2

# The Forest

A jeep pulled in to the village and two Gestapo officers stepped out. They walked through the square to the café. My mum would go on a Saturday morning and eat *lane kluski* (a milky breakfast soup with spaghetti floating in it). This Saturday, she was at home.

Tables were arranged with checked tablecloths, men drank alcohol though it was still early morning and families ate *pierogi* (dumplings) and *lane kluski*. The café had a smell of furniture polish and linen that had been left in a drawer for years.

The two Gestapo officers knew the drill. One stood by the door, guarding the exit should anything go wrong. The other did the interrogation. They surveyed the room with curiosity.

The scene could not have been more perfect for an atrocity. A group of children ate breakfast. A table of farmers drank vodka. An old man played the piano. He happened to be quite a personage in the village; the retired organist of Oliwa Cathedral in Gdansk, one of the finest examples of cathedral piping in Europe dating back to the sixteenth century. On Saturday mornings, he relived his glory days hammering out Polish folk songs on the upright piano in the café.

The Gestapo officer stood for a moment, weighing up the alternative ways this could go. His boss back in Berlin, SS Commander Heydrich, had drilled into the *Einsatzgruppen* and Gestapo the principle of human submission: get the condemned to sign their own death warrant. Provoked, they will retaliate, which means when you shoot them, it's their own fault.

The café did not respond in the way the lead Gestapo officer expected. People ignored him. They carried on eating, the old men chatting and drinking. The organist played his old folk song. No one even acknowledged the two Nazi officers were present, or more accurately, they had not yet learnt to show their fear.

The Gestapo man walked calmly up to the piano, removed his pistol from its holster and shot the organist in the middle of his forehead. He fell neatly backwards, a perfect compliant 'C' shape on the floor.

He had a question.

'Where is the country house?'

Silence. Not even the children had the presence of mind to scream.

'Come on, hurry up now. I don't have all day.'

There were no formal introductions. The gun was the introduction. Welcome to Germany.

My mum wasn't there, as she had a temperature that morning – a heaven-sent infection. Had she been, she would have known where the 'country house' was, because that's where she lived.

The Gestapo men got back in their jeep and headed up to the country house. They drove through the woods, the silver birches rustling musically in the breeze. The family dogs were pleased to see visitors and went wild, barking and chasing the jeep the length of the dusty drive. The jeep stopped and the Gestapo officers climbed out.

Alina was first to greet them. She ran into the garden, expectant that whoever these people were, it would be exciting. Since returning to the country from Warsaw, Alina had been bored.

'Hello, little princess,' the Nazi said. 'Is your father here?'

'Oh, he's in Paris.'

'Indeed. Can we by any chance speak to your mother?'

'Of course.'

But she was already there, standing behind her daughter. Olga was short and stout, and staring straight at the Germans.

'This is a beautiful house you have here, *Frau* Basiak.'

They knew her name, they knew her daughter's name, they knew everything.

'We will be staying here from now on. You and your family have two hours to remove your valuables. Prepare an itemised list of furniture, carpets and so on, and the Third Reich shall reimburse you for any requisitioned goods.'

It was a speech he had given a dozen times at identical properties since war started. As he spoke, an Alsatian called 'Rex' – my mum's dog – jumped up for a pat. The Gestapo officer pulled out his gun and shot him in the head. He didn't even look at the dog as he did it, putting far less effort into the whole action than lighting a cigarette.

By the next morning, the Germans had gone.

Then the Russians came.

The disappearance of the Germans was perplexing to my grandmother, but perfectly logical. The Nazi-Soviet Pact of 1939 stated that the Nazis would invade Poland from the west, the Soviets from the east; the two armies meeting at the River Bug.

Olga's house in the forest was east of the River Bug, so the Soviet army should have got to it first, but Olga was later told that a rogue battalion of Field Marshal Gerd Von Rundstedt's *Heeresgruppe Sud* (Army Group South), the XIX corps, ignored orders. So the Nazis had got there first.

Whoever these errant soldiers were, Berlin was furious. German intelligence had discovered that the Prypec region was full of partisans. If anyone was to have a guerrilla war and be massacred in the mosquito-infested forest, it should be the Soviets, Hitler said. So the German army retreated.

Then the Russians arrived. They entered the village on a Monday, but unlike the Nazis, did not shoot any old men or dogs. Soviet soldiers picked fruit, sat on the grass and eyed the local girls. The Russian commander walked through the orchard, up the dusty path the Nazi jeep had driven down, and knocked politely on the door.

His speech had a familiar ring.

'This building, grounds and stables are now the property of the People's Army of the Soviet Union,' he told Olga. 'Is the master of the house present? I require him to countersign this document.'

Olga told the commander that her husband was in Paris.

'He's an architect, you see, building a train station.'

Olga had been frantically turning tarot cards ever since the Nazis left, trying to predict the next few days. As a result of her intense psychic efforts, she now believed she had conjured up a magical force field that had successfully enveloped the forest. It drove the Nazis away, she told Alina, and would now repel the Soviets.

Behind her back, Olga held a tiny pebble in her left hand, which she rubbed between her thumb and middle finger as she spoke. The Russian commander looked at Olga. He slapped his thick, sweating neck, leaving behind a dead mosquito with a bloody smear.

'You are Russian,' he said factually.

Olga stood perfectly still and said nothing.

'What did you say your husband does?'

'He's an architect.'

'What is he doing in Paris?'

'Building train stations. I told you.'

The Russian commander smiled and shook his head regretfully, as if disappointed by a small child.

'You are lying, *Pane* Basiak.'

Olga rubbed the pebble furiously between her fingers. Her hands were greasy with sweat, making the stone slippery. She ordered Alina to go and play somewhere, but her daughter ignored her, standing still and staring fixedly at the Russian.

'Your husband is working with the government-in-exile,' he said calmly, brushing dust from his sleeve. 'The traitors planning to overthrow our leader, Joseph Vissarionovich Stalin.' Alina noted the full use of Stalin's name. It stuck sharply in her memory like a thorn under a fingernail. She had never heard the name before.

Olga had never spoken of Michael's political activities, of which she knew very little, let alone to a Russian soldier who would shoot her and her daughter if she said the wrong thing. All she did know was that Michael wanted to help poor people, whatever that meant. However, she had little choice but to elaborate now.

'Michael is a socialist,' she said. 'Like you.'

The Russian smiled again. 'Yes, he is. But the wrong kind of socialist.'

Michael's family, the Sobanskis, supported the 1919 Bolshevik revolution, but were Mensheviks, a rival faction to Lenin's. Even though they were socialists, Mensheviks were decreed enemies of the Soviet state by the Bolsheviks in the power struggle between the two factions. In 1935, Stalin staged a trial and executed the Menshevik leadership. Had Michael been in the countryside that day, he would already have a bullet in his head.

'We know all about you, too, *Pane* Basiak,' the commander continued, enjoying his role as the bringer of bad news. 'You are a White Russian. A Tsarist. Your family are also enemies of the Soviet people.'

Bees buzzed in the meadow, the Russian soldiers lay casually in the long grass, watching their commander coolly interrogate this evasive aristocrat.

'You really have quite a family here, don't you? Traitors of Russia hiding like beetles in the forest.'

Olga dropped her pebble, which lay damp in the dust.

'Where is your jewellery?' he asked, changing tack.

'I have no jewels.'

'I will ask you again. Where is your jewellery?'

'Where are your gold roubles?' a voice piped up from the field. It was a teenage soldier with black teeth, lying in the grass with his uniform unbuttoned. He was grinning boastfully at his other teenage comrades as he shouted at Olga, revealing the gaping cave of his mouth.

'*Gde zoloto! Blyat?*' he shouted. ('Where's the gold, whore?')

'I have no jewellery. I have no gold,' Olga said calmly, ignoring the boy and staring straight at the commander.

'Search the property.'

The soldiers ransacked the house. They broke open wooden chests, upturned drawers onto the lawn, broke vases and threw a wardrobe from the bedroom window, smashing spectacularly on the ground below. They found nothing, because they hadn't looked in the right place.

This was because a week after returning from Warsaw, Olga had stayed up all night hiding her fortune. She cut open the seams of clothing: winter coats, dresses, waistcoats and corsets, and stuffed the heirlooms she had been given as a young woman – roubles, diamonds and gold, and cash of various denominations – zloty, dollars and bankers' drafts – into every fold, crease and hidden lining of her clothes.

Olga broke up the tiara she had worn for her coming-out ball in St Petersburg aged sixteen, and hid the individual stones behind a false fabric panel in her fur coat running the length of the back. Her plan was to use her small fortune as a portable cash machine. Bartering and bribing survival for her and her daughter whenever required. Olga was not as stupid as either her husband or children imagined. She was preparing for war.

The Russian soldiers found none of it.

After they had finished smashing things, the teenage soldier with the black teeth who had called my grandmother a whore mockingly held up one of Olga's dresses to his sallow body, oblivious that its lining was crammed with the very jewels they were looking for. It was the one and only time that day when Olga allowed herself a barely perceptible smile.

There were few options left to the Soviet commander, stonewalled by this Russian aristocrat. He winced and swatted another mosquito, a small insect punished for the failure of his idiot soldiers to find the fortune.

This was how he saw it: shoot the woman. Or shoot her daughter. Then shoot the woman. Better still, threaten to shoot the daughter, find out where the gold and jewels are, then shoot both of them. The commander mulled it over. He decided to go for none of the above and instead try a new tack.

'Your husband is Jewish, isn't he?'

*No reply.*

The local villagers had suspected it for years. 'Why would anyone want to come and live here?' they muttered. 'What's their game?' or 'These rich city people,' they would say in the café, 'they're Jews fleeing the pogroms.' Locals called Michael 'the Jewish king' of the forest. When he helped them with medical supplies and penicillin, they called him 'the Jewish doctor'.

'You're very lucky it's us and not the Nazis who came to your house,' the Russian commander said flatly.

*No reply.*

'Is this your daughter?' he said, pointing at Alina.

*No reply.*

'I will kill her, unless you tell me about your husband.'

The air was punched from Alina's chest, but she didn't move. She knew if she made any kind of movement, she would be dead.

'I told you,' Olga said coolly. 'He's an architect.'

The Russian commander was being outplayed. He stood in a god-forsaken forest, and needed to decide what to do with this stupid woman and her child. They had no gold and no information. They might as well be shot, but he was also worried about his career, and the consequences of doing something wrong.

Someone in the NKVD would want to talk to such a woman. He knew that. They had given him her name, so clearly she was someone of note to the secret police. If the commander took an executive decision to kill her, it might recoil on him like a cheap gun. Better to push the problem on.

'Pack your belongings together,' the commander ordered Olga. 'You're going home.'

'This is my home,' she said.

'No,' he said. 'Your real home.'

*30 September 1939, Lvov Station, Eastern Poland*

On the platform, it was pandemonium. Hundreds of Poles were being herded by Russian soldiers onto trains. Some consisted of cattle trucks with straw and a bucket; others were made up of first-class carriages with lamps and velvet seating.

Olga assumed when the Russian commander said her 'real home', he meant St Petersburg. The commander ordered a young soldier, a teenager with a thin moustache and appalling acne, to escort Olga and Alina to the station, where a superior would decide if they were to be sent on to NKVD headquarters on the outskirts of Moscow, or just killed.

The commander gave the boy soldier a letter explaining that the woman and the girl were informants. In all probability, he never believed Olga and Alina would get to Moscow. They would be killed either in Lvov, or in transit. Either way, the problem would not be his.

On the platform, the boy looked hopelessly around for the commander's boss. Sensing his bewilderment, Olga took her opportunity. She gave him some roubles from her coat and told him to look the other way so they could escape. It was more money than the boy had ever seen in his life. He nodded gratefully. Olga took the commander's letter and dropped it contemptuously to the floor like a tissue.

Alina said she wanted to return home to the forest, but Olga told her they could not take the risk. The Russians could still be in their house, she said, and even the Nazis might return.

'What about Warsaw?' Alina asked. They could find Pavel, Juta and Kazhik and bring them home.

'Don't you understand, Alina? There is no home now.'

Olga surveyed the scene. Crowds swayed on the platform like densely packed corn blowing in a wheat field, pushed this way and that by contradictory Russian orders. The idea of anyone knowing where a train was going seemed ridiculous. All the trains appeared to be heading to the same place, though no one would say where it was.

Someone knew. He was standing in a glass box above the station overlooking all platforms. He was young, bald and wore small round glasses, peering down impassively on the mayhem and unmoved by the chaos he was orchestrating.

Free of the boy soldier, Olga and Alina decided to board any train, no matter where it was going. They joined a melee of Polish and Ukrainian families being pushed into the carriage of an old-fashioned train, like stuffing into a mattress. Once on board, there was a surprising amount of space and they spread out, sitting on boxes and suitcases. Olga asked a neatly dressed Jewish doctor with an air of calm about him where they were heading.

'I'm afraid I have absolutely no idea,' he said, smiling ruefully.

For the first four days, they seemed to be going in roughly the right direction for St Petersburg, 1400 kilometres away. The train followed the road, crammed with mile after mile of people walking. Millions across Europe were doing the same thing, moving slowly without a plan towards a place that might once have existed: somewhere they hoped might provide a bolthole from the coming storm.

From the open window, Alina watched families pushing anything that had wheels on it: prams, old dinner-service trolleys, and wheelbarrows piled high with valuables – paintings and candelabras, shoes, hen-boxes, clothes horses and the odd grandparent perched on top, dressed for church.

The train passed charred villages burnt to the ground and still smouldering. The result of Nazi or Soviet attack. Other towns were perfectly intact, people going about their daily business as normal.

The station names became increasingly unfamiliar. Gone were places Olga had heard of, such as Kiev and Kursk. They clearly were not going to St Petersburg or Moscow. They headed further and further east, past Kazan, Izhevsk and Perm, out onto a flatter, sparser, completely unpopulated plain without a tree in sight. The train rumbled doggedly on. After a week, all food ran out. The doctor offered Olga and Alina bread and pastries, and some stewed fruit in a jar, which they accepted gratefully.

My mum made a bed in one corner of the compartment, but it was now too cold to sleep alone, on account of several wooden slats in the floor having fallen out. Olga and Alina huddled under Olga's fur coat for warmth. To anyone else, it may have seemed miserable, but to Alina it was exciting.

Olga was able to barter for food with roubles. They picked up sausage and dried reindeer meat, passed through the missing slats at stations, or when the train stopped to take on more coal. Hands would appear through the floor, locals doing a roaring trade from this ceaseless caravan of Polish trains heading east.

The other refugees on board were a random collection of Ukrainians, Romanians and Russians. No one had any idea where they were going and barely talked. The doctor was the exception. He was called Rafael. Olga made friends with him on the basis of their shared memories of St Petersburg in the 1920s.

Rafael had studied in Paris, where Olga first met Michael. The doctor was quiet and appeared kind. He asked about Olga's family, and what had happened to them. Olga told him about Pavel, Kazhik and Juta. Rafael heard many terrible things, he said, about what was happening in Warsaw, but chose not to share them. He listened sympathetically to Olga and said he hoped she would find a way to reunite with her children.

Alina sat gloomily by herself, watching the tracks speed past through the missing slats in the floor. She didn't like her mother getting this unwanted attention from a stranger.

'What do you think of him?' Olga asked Alina breezily, when Rafael was asleep.

'You already have one husband,' Alina replied.

One morning, the train stopped without warning near a small lake. A number of small wooden huts were arranged in rows, with rolls of fencing on the ground in preparation to be put up. As far as the eye could see, there was nothing. No trees, no buildings, no mountains and no people. They were in Siberia.

The little man in the glass box at Lvov station had been the regional Soviet commissar, responsible for transporting over a million captured Poles to Siberia. Following Stalin's purges of the 1930s, millions of Russians were sent to these barren wastes to till the soil, never to be seen again. The Polish evacuees were next.

The Tsar was first to use this unpromising province – minus 50° in winter, baked dry in summer – as a dumping ground for 'undesirables'. Stalin then industrialised exile to Siberia: political prisoners, petty thieves, homosexuals, writers and intellectuals, prostitutes, single mothers, aristocrats, the mentally ill and disabled. All were sent to plough the ground by hand or rough implement till they keeled over.

With a war to fight and virtually no one left to exile to Siberia, Stalin needed new people to farm the vast plains, which is why Alina, Olga and Rafael found themselves on a train there. In less than two years, more than half the captured Poles sent to Siberia, half of whom were women and girls, would be dead too.

Their arrival was not as expected. They were greeted by a ramshackle bunch of men stumbling out of a hut, as though rudely interrupted from a drinking session. They were in various stages of undress. One was wearing a hunting coat and vest, another had nothing on but long johns and heavy boots and one was in a big green army coat customised with home-made patches made from garish, torn-up cushion material. They looked less like an army platoon than a band of travelling minstrels.

The passengers from the train looked at one another nervously. The Russians appeared rollickingly drunk, and they were. An old commander with a neatly trimmed grey beard and a bright red face ran over to Alina, Olga and the refugees.

'Welcome! Welcome!'

He pointed at the dozen or so children hiding behind their parents.

'Come! Come!'

The commander took the children to a supply hut, where they were each given a safari hat: a 'welcoming present'. Weeks before the glacial Siberian winter was due to set in, the children ran laughing around the camp throwing safari hats in the air.

The purpose of the fences laid on the ground was supposedly to prepare them for the work to come. The worried newcomers imagined they would be instructed to begin digging, but instead the Russian soldiers prepared a vat of mint tea.

Hundreds of gulag labour camps were strung out across the desolate landscape. Olga and Alina were lucky. In other camps, ambitious young officers worked new recruits to death as soon as they arrived. Here, the commander and his platoon, who had survived several winters in Siberia by evading scrutiny from their superiors, were keener on avoiding war or any trouble.

Most of the prisoners from the train were Poles who'd had their homes taken. They were well off, and the guards deferred to their superior social status. They gave them decent food and rarely asked anyone to do any work, unless it was practical to the camp: fixing a roof or cleaning out the latrines. War and revolution had not erased the old class pecking order.

Within the first week, an old soldier died. His comrades buried him and stood round his graveside; one of them was sobbing. The old soldier had been at the camp for twelve years, first sent there in the late 1920s to oversee political prisoners exiled by Stalin. Olga and the other prisoners watched the ceremony at a respectful distance.

They slept in a hut with a wood fire stove and bunk beds. The women and children in one, men in the other. A week or so after the old soldier's funeral, the commander shook Olga awake in the middle of the night.

'*Kwik, prosza pani. Pomigite*,' he whispered in a mix of Russian and pidgin Polish. ('Hurry, madam. Help, please.')

Since arrival, Olga had become an unofficial translator between the soldiers and prisoners. She knew Russian and Polish, and the soldiers deferred to her authority. The commander would probably have given over control of the camp to Olga had she asked.

A young Ukrainian woman, he said, was giving birth in one of the other huts. She was in considerable distress; the commander had no idea what to do, and he needed Olga's help. Olga shook the sleep from her eyes and focused on the commander's ruddy face.

'How far gone?'

'Three hours.'

Olga had never seen a baby being born. Her own children had been delivered by local midwives at home, with hot water and clean towels, whilst she lay close to unconscious on morphine, oblivious to what was happening to the lower half of her body. Olga did not know what to do, but imagined the tarot cards might help.

She turned them over in the hut and they augured well. Olga scooped a handful of pebbles from the ground outside and made her way with the commander to the hut with the screaming woman inside.

She was on her back on a lower bunk, pouring in sweat and making fast panting sounds, interspersed with short whistles and moans. Her feet were pressed hard against the upper bed. Other women crouched around her. One explained to Olga that although the woman's contractions had started, the baby hadn't moved. Olga had no idea why everyone was deferring to her authority in this matter.

'There is a doctor here,' she said. 'In one of the male huts. His name is Rafael. I think you should get him quickly.'

The commander nodded and waddled quickly off.

Olga began placing the pebbles she had picked up outside around the bunk bed and on the pregnant woman's distended belly. They glistened in the candlelight. Olga did this with such calm and confidence, the woman stopped moaning and became momentarily entranced by the strange ritual. Olga completed the ceremony by putting a small stone on the woman's chest and another on her forehead.

'Lie very still,' she commanded. The woman did as she was told.

Olga hummed a Russian orthodox liturgy she had learnt as a child in church. It sounded like a profound incantation. The people in the hut were entranced, convinced they were listening to a magical mantra.

By the time Rafael the doctor arrived, the baby was born. A healthy, strong boy bellowing loudly. A whisper went round the hut and soon round the whole camp.

'*Khoroshaya ved'ma.*'

'She is a witch,' they said. 'The good witch.'

# 3

## Siberia

*January 1940, Siberia, Russia*

It was Olga and Alina's first winter in the Siberian labour camp and extraordinarily cold even by Siberian standards. Temperatures below minus 45° meant that eyeballs froze. Blizzards heaped ten feet of snow and ice onto the roofs of the huts. They were told by guards they would be dead from hypothermia within five minutes of going out.

It was rumoured by prisoners in the camp that Russian soldiers were using the stiff bodies of the newly arrived as draft excluders, piling them against doorways and windows to keep out the cold. Olga and Alina never saw it and from what they now knew of the bumbling commander, they believed him incapable of such behaviour.

In the depths of winter, Olga's hut became a sanctuary for both prisoners and their Russian captors. With her new-found reputation as a 'good witch', Olga found herself an unexpected hit. Her whole life she had been in the shadow of someone else: her Tsarist military father, and then her 'do-gooding socialist' husband. 'Such a humanitarian, he abandoned us to the Nazis on the eve of war,' she told her daughter.

In the Siberian camp, Olga was her own person for the first time and in her element. She read palms and the lines on people's faces, invariably divining long lives and dozens of children. She read strangers' tarot cards. If they augured bad luck, she lied, saying the future looked rosy. They would soon leave the camp, she predicted, and the war would end well for everyone, even the Nazis and Russians.

Soldiers wanted to know if they would win card games on which they had staked huge amounts of their savings. Several men and women had begun illicit relationships in the camp and they wanted to be told if their infidelity would be discovered by their spouses. 'Of course not,' Olga would say, stroking their hands reassuringly and asking for more money.

Olga's favourite ruse was dangling a watch chain in front of her subject. Depending on which way it circled, Olga could tell them the trajectory of their entire life. She divined everything, from specifics, such as if there would be enough newspaper to wipe their arse in the latrines next week, to whether they would ever see their lost children again. Olga never used the watch chain on herself. She was too scared of what it would reveal.

Alina was sceptical of her mother's powers. 'Do you think it's responsible to be telling people these lies?' she asked her one evening, as they shared some fresh bread that the soldiers had baked for the prisoners.

'I'm not lying to people,' Olga said. 'I'm giving them hope.'

Prisoners and soldiers missed their families, Olga said. Most had no idea if their loved ones were even alive. They didn't want the truth, Olga told her daughter. They craved escape, and wanted drama.

Olga created a darkened space in the corner of her hut. She lit a candle and burnt dried herbs. Customers risked being frozen to death as they fought through the blizzard outside for an audience with the good witch in the third hut from the end. There was a hefty charge to see her, and the cost went up with demand. It was plain economics.

The camp was awash with barterable goods. Six months after arriving, Red Cross parcels began appearing. Olga's entry-level price for a 'consultation' was some bread and lard. This soon escalated to cheese, even chocolate if you wanted a séance with a dead loved one. If you needed *la pendule* (the watch chain pendulum), then a wad of money was required. Or even better, soap.

People were clearly addicted to Olga's tarot cards, Alina realised. But *la pendule* was Olga's true calling: the stage on which she shone. Some people came twice a day. Prisoners and soldiers alike knew their fate was already written in this war. If they were going to die, they wanted to know the details.

Even though Alina was highly sceptical, Olga persuaded her to be part of her show. 'Do it so I can take a rest,' Olga pleaded with her daughter, feigning tiredness. 'There's simply too many people coming, daughter. Help me.'

'What do I say?' Alina asked, terrified she would muck it up.

'I'm sure you have the gift, as I do,' Olga replied, smiling. Alina couldn't tell if her mother was being serious or not. The gift of taking people's money? She said nothing.

As Olga's 'assistant', Alina did what she had seen her mother do. She shut her eyes and took a melodramatic deep breath. But instead of predicting salvation, she painted lurid pictures of revenge for her fellow prisoners. She could see the Nazis and Russians burning in hell for what they had done to Poland, she said. Depriving them all of their beautiful homes and wrenching them from their families. The prisoners muttered their approval, and handed over bread and chocolate.

The Russian commander burst into the hut, incandescent with rage. His usually benign countenance was contorted with anger. The ginger hair sprouting from random areas of his face was prickling with indignation.

'What the hell has your daughter been telling the prisoners?'

Olga needed to act quickly. She offered the commander a VIP service to calm him down: a Ouija board so he could speak to his dead brother killed in the revolution.

Placated, the commander hesitantly sat down and placed his hands on the wooden board. Olga knew the brother's death was the poor commander's weak spot. After some minutes of the glass moving around the board, Olga told the commander his brother was fine in the afterlife and a hell of a lot better off than here. Death was nothing to be feared in the Siberian camp. The commander left much happier than he had arrived, his face restored to its normal purple.

Such a connection to the spiritual world was comforting to the Soviet soldiers. Mystics were a valued possession in war, and could ward off everything from dysentery to enemy attack. The Russians, a people guided by faith-healers, witch doctors and aspiring Rasputins, took Olga and Alina's presence very seriously. No one, least of all the commander, wanted the bad luck that might come from displeasing her.

For Alina's part, those months playing a clairvoyant in the Siberian hut were the happiest she had ever spent with her mother. They were working as a team, keeping up the spirits of a small band of lost souls stranded on a tiny island of huts, surrounded by an ocean of ice. The prisoners and Russian soldiers were as one. They both feared the war beyond. Rescue from Siberia was no rescue at all.

*July 1940, London, England*

France officially fell to the Germans on 25 June 1940, and the Polish government-in-exile hastily relocated across the Channel to London. Michael moved with them.

Resistance groups across Europe were congregating in London – French, Czechs, Poles, Dutch and Norwegians – clandestinely meeting in pubs like the French House in Soho and in cramped Lyons Corner Houses, condensation dripping down the windows as they plotted. Spies were everywhere and these resistance groups could not trust anyone, least of all the British government.

Michael had heard nothing from Olga for almost a year. The last time they had spoken was in early August 1939, when he phoned her to say he was being called on urgent business to Paris – a structural fault with a bridge, he said – and as a result, he would not be able to join the family at the apartment in Warsaw. He had tried to warn Olga that war was coming, but she had put the phone down on him. Now, when Michael tried to phone from London to the flat in Warsaw, where he believed Olga must be staying, the line was dead.

Michael knew there was a strong likelihood his entire family had been killed. Perhaps, he told himself, if they were not in the apartment, then Olga would have taken them to a place of safety. He preferred to hold on to this thought rather than the first.

In London, he was given a contact in the *Zwiazek Walki Zbrojnej*, the ZWZ, one of the first Polish resistance groups operating an underground intelligence network in Poland for the government-in-exile. The ZWZ could get information on the whereabouts of practically anyone they wanted in Poland. The London office dispatched an operative on the ground in Warsaw to the flat at 49 Krolewska Street. Another was sent to the house in the forest.

The news took three weeks to get to Michael. The telegram sat in front of him on the table of his rented flat in King's Cross. It was a miserable space, close to the stinking train terminus, from which thick black smoke belched from the coal-powered steam engines night and day.

He tore open the envelope. It was brief. The message said that 49 Krolewska Street, the entire residential block near Saski Park, had been destroyed. The house in the country was burnt to the ground: 'FAMILY PRESUMED DEAD'.

Michael sat and poured himself a whisky.

*January 1940, Warsaw*

The telegram was right in one regard. The country house was now a pile of blackened timber remains on the ground, incinerated with petrol by the Russian soldiers who had shouted obscenities at Olga. A fit of vandalism prompted by failure to retrieve the woman's fortune promised to them by the commander.

The apartment block near Saski Park was another story. Though bombed, it was largely intact. The top two floors had been crunched together by a single Stuka strike, but the family's apartment on the second floor was virtually untouched. The bomb had broken a vase.

Generaloberst Franz Halder, the commander of the attack, told Hitler during the first salvos on Warsaw that the city was not strategically important. They could bypass it easily and advance towards Russia. Hitler exploded, his eyes popping out of his head with rage. He told Halder that the skies needed to darken, millions of tons of shells rain down on Warsaw, people drown in blood.

So nine German divisions pounded the city for twenty-five days, killing 25,000 civilians in the first wave alone. Hitler's plan was to grind Warsaw into the ground, eviscerate every inch, burning the living and the dead together. Then start the city again.

Once the bombing was over, the Nazis marched triumphantly through defeated Warsaw in full ceremonial uniform, announcing themselves as conquering Romans. Hitler's aim was simple: to remove and kill Warsaw's Jews, then destroy the 'ethnic Poles', or *dungervolke*. This translated as 'shit people' – people who were made of shit, said Hitler, had come from the shit of the boggy marshes of the East and would return to the shit when gone. The 'Germanic' Poles of Warsaw were, Hitler said, a different matter. A new city would then be built on the old footprint, and the surviving population of Germanic Poles would be

'Nazified', with non-Jewish children like Kazhik, Pavel and Juta reprogrammed as New Aryans.

In Olga's absence, the children were looked after by Hela, the housekeeper. Hela had known the Basiaks since 1933, when they bought the flat. She had cooked, cleaned and humoured my family for nearly a decade, and never once been given a pay rise. No one even knew where Hela lived, because no one asked her. She had a husband and two children in the working-class district of Wola, which had seen the worst of the Nazi destruction.

Over the years, Hela had developed her own rewards and perks structure from the Basiaks, lifting money from the house-keeping when she needed it. Hela knew Olga's abandoned children needed help now, and in helping them, she would keep herself and own family alive.

Hela picked up leaflets that came through the door informing Warsaw's inhabitants of the new Nazi 'rules'. They were to inform immediately on any 'undesirables': Jews, political subver-sives or resistance members. Anyone in the street caught with-out identification papers or after curfew would be arrested or executed.

*Lapanka* was the name given to the round-ups carried out by the death squads, who rode Warsaw's wide boulevards in open trucks, often followed by an SS officer in a low-slung Citroën Traction, the same car used by Al Capone. Anyone 'rounded up' by the *lapanka* was either shot on the spot or thrown into the back of the truck and shot later. Collected corpses were then piled up at street corners as an example to a recalcitrant neighbourhood.

This was to be Warsaw life under Nazi rule. A new routine calcified in the ruins: shopping only at designated grocery stores, including those under new ownership, taken over by 'Aryan Poles' from 'deported' Jewish shopkeepers; Saturday morning cinema matinees bookended by rousing Nazi news-reels; and all schoolchildren to be taught in German.

Hela took it upon herself to secure Kazhik and Juta places at a new kind of exclusive school created by the war. Such schools were called *komplety* in Polish and sat in private houses without the Nazis' knowledge, often with no more than a dozen or so privileged children learning subjects like art, geometry, Latin and French literature. They were hard to get into, cost a fortune and the one Hela had in mind for the children was on the nearby boulevard of Senatorski.

The *komplety* schools were secret cells of learning. Some were set up by enterprising parents in their homes, who asked other families to join the school through word of mouth. Germans did not know, or were not supposed to know, they existed. These affluent families wanted their children to continue being educated as sophisticated Europeans (regardless of what Europe might be like once the Nazis had conquered it). *Komplety* soon proliferated amongst the wealthy bourgeoisie of Warsaw, hidden away, and often moving location for fear of being discovered by the Gestapo. Everyone else went to the local school, overseen by the Germans.

Hela could not afford to pay the fees for the *komplety* on Senatorski, but she knew Olga would have wanted her children to go there. The monthly allowance promised by Olga had never materialised (since she and Alina were sent to the labour camp in Siberia), and the meagre funds Olga had left Hela were running out fast.

Then Kazhik had a brainwave: why don't we sell off items in the apartment to rich people? Hela organised it. As the children sat in the kitchen, strangers dressed up for the occasion in Homburg hats, or wearing pearls and fur coats, walked around the flat inspecting the Basiak family belongings. Starved of their peacetime shopping experience at Warsaw's most expensive store, Jablkowski Brothers, these rich Warsaw residents – mainly parents from the school – offered cash for furniture and paintings. Hela overcharged them hugely and got enough to pay for three terms at the *komplety*.

Kazhik was convinced Hela was royally 'ripped off' by these 'vultures' at the fire sale of their belongings. She had given away paintings, he said, for next to nothing. 'She has no idea what they were worth!' he told the other children. I'm not so sure. I think Hela sounded quite wily and did a pretty good job.

The *komplety* on Senatorski was run by Madame Graminski, a Warsaw ex-socialite. She was tall and haughty, wore immaculate make-up with a button red mouth, and an expensive hound's-tooth Chanel suit she had bought before the war. Madame Graminski was proud of her elite school, which had already moved location several times in the chaos of Warsaw, and would do anything to keep it open.

She was a pragmatist and though she despised the Nazis, had a business to run. In order to curry favour should she be raided, she hired a retired German soldier, a veteran of the First World War with a limp, thinning wire-brush moustache and a chest of medals, to informally monitor lessons. Though he was originally from Bavaria, he had somehow ended up living in Warsaw. The old soldier seemed ambivalent about the Nazis, but Madame Graminski figured that if the Gestapo ever raided the school, the presence of this relic from the trenches might come in useful.

Juta and Kazhik were duly enrolled in Madame Graminski's *komplety*. Pavel was too old to be officially a pupil. However, Madame Graminski took pity on this ungainly man-child and gave Pavel odd jobs such as cleaning and even decorating around the school. Before long, Pavel was upgraded to caretaker's assistant, taking orders from the old soldier with the limp. Pavel was proud of his job and was at work before the children had woken, scrubbing the floors till he could see his perpetually uncomprehending face staring back.

Kazhik and Pavel were taught by the First World War veteran to be young soldiers. Guns were strictly banned at school but the old Bavarian, who boasted he had skewered a hundred Frenchmen at Verdun with his bayonet, did the next best thing, showing the boys how to run through an enemy using a broomstick in the yard. Pavel was big and awkward, but Kazhik looked the part: blonde and blue-eyed, with an appetite for war. His survivalist skills, honed in the forest, impressed the old soldier. Kazhik was by name and birthright, 'the destroyer of peace'. Hitler could not have dreamed of a better convert to the Aryan cause.

Juta, along with the handful of girls of the school, sat primly in class learning needlepoint and reciting the bible, as the boys pretended to bayonet invisible adversaries. Had they gone to the free school, where ordinary, unprivileged Poles went, they would have been taught a Polish variation of *Kinder, Kuche, Kirche*, the core Nazi values for women in the Third Reich: 'Children, Cooking, Church'.

The fact these strange Basiak children had no parents and no past made them an oddity to the well-to-do parents of the komplety, but strangely perfect as prototype Aryans. Kazhik was the most enthusiastic Nazi-in-the-making. He mimicked the shout of a *lapanka* officer as he herded classmates in the playground, using the same commands – '*Raus! Schnell! Raus!*' – that he heard the real *lapanka* shouting in the streets.

If Kazhik was a model soldier, Juta became a blonde, clockwork doll, useful to the school.

One afternoon, there was a terrible commotion as a Gestapo Citroën pulled up unexpectedly outside. Madame Graminski was terrified that someone had informed on her. Three officers got out and knocked curtly on the door; she was surprised they didn't smash the door down. Instead they came in, sat in the drawing room and were given tea.

They had been notified by a passing patrol, they told Madame Graminski, that beautiful music was being played at the house, and were curious to see who was playing. Madame Graminski had no idea if this was a trick, and merely a prelude to her and the schoolchildren being executed. So she played along and had the bright idea of sending Juta in to play piano to the Gestapo officers, to buy time and keep them amused.

Juta recited Chopin, playing each note with cold, steely precision. The Gestapo applauded politely and nodded approvingly. They had enjoyed themselves: a brief cultural interlude for them before going out into the street and shooting more Poles.

Kazhik was sarcastic about the incident at dinner that evening. 'You saved the school with your performance today,' he said, mocking Madame Graminski and the old soldier with the limp, fawning over the Gestapo officers. Juta said nothing and ate in silence.

After dinner, the boys went into their bedroom and shut the door behind them. They took out two rusting bayonets that they had bought from an old shop in Mokotow, in preparation for the fighting to come, and began to oil them. They never told their sister or Hela what they had hidden in their room. The Nazis who controlled Warsaw had not factored into their programming of 'New Aryans' a generation of young Poles, that once these children knew how to use bayonets, they could be used against Nazis.

*April 1940, Warsaw*

Life at school continued as normal, until one night the flat-fronted townhouse in which it was located was destroyed in a bombing raid. In the morning, the handful of privileged children who attended gathered respectfully outside the smoking ruin. It was more than a month before Madame Graminski found another private house that was suitable. In the meantime, the children were enrolled in the state school down the road.

Their new school was a chaotic and ramshackle affair. Polish teachers, mainly women who had worked diligently at the school before the war, continued as best they could without books or any resources, teaching what they had always taught. Their new German masters demanded lessons be conducted in the German language, but this was quickly ignored without any Nazis present to enforce it. Children arrived, milled around in partially bombed or dismantled classrooms, sometimes learning something, often not.

No one appeared to be in charge and there was no timetable or curriculum. However, there was one teacher who was keen that Poland's new conquerors, the Nazis, be treated with respect. His name was Kacmar, and he was a stooping colossus of a man with thick, greased-back hair. Though originally a Polish chemistry teacher, he had always been pro-Hitler, and now the Germans were in charge, he felt lessons should mirror this world-historic shift – a new dawn for the Polish people, and a chance for the next generation to grasp their destiny.

Kacmar wanted the children to learn about the 'glorious Teutonic triumphs of the past'. Medieval knights with black crosses on their armour had ridden across central Europe in the twelfth and thirteenth centuries, Kacmar said, striking fear into their enemies. These brave soldiers liberated 'Germania', the common ethnic homeland of Germans and 'Germanic Poles'. This shared past of Poland and Germany, he told the children, was their 'true heritage'.

When the Basiak children arrived in the school, Kacmar thought it a good opportunity to set about putting all his pupils straight on a few matters.

'These neighbours you have lived with,' he said, looming over the children in his tiny classroom like an optical illusion, 'these

Jews and Slavs. They are not your real neighbours. We Poles and Germans share a thousand years of shared chivalric blood against the common enemy of Jews and Slavs.'

They would not have received better Nazi propaganda from the Germans themselves. Kacmar was a huge anti-Semite and a key part of his education programme was teaching the children how to be anti-Semitic. This was a novelty to Kazhik and Juta, children from the countryside, who had never thought of Jews as being any different from them before. They were excited by these new revelations about the Jews, things they had never imagined possible.

Jews drank the blood of babies, Kacmar said. They were partly rodent, and some of the most talented changed shape. Kazhik and Juta had never been in an educational establishment like this before, and it was almost like being in a Nazi finishing school.

As the rest of Warsaw cowered in fear of the *lapanka* death squads, roaming the streets and executing arbitrarily to instil fear in the population, Srodmiescie and the wider district of Mokotow – where the state school was – became a prototype for an 'Aryan' district. The affluent non-Jewish residents, many with private wealth tied up abroad, were seen as prime candidates for 'Nazification'. They were left alone by the Gestapo to live their life much as they had before the war, so long as they informed on any Jews or 'undesirables' they came across.

When Madame Graminski's school reopened three months later, the children moved back. Hela realised she had miscalculated the money. Even with the sale of more belongings, she could not keep paying the extortionate fees. This was largely because she had pocketed half the money from the furniture sales for herself; recompense for looking after this ungrateful family. If the fees were not paid, Madame Graminski warned Hela, she might inform her new friends in the Gestapo that the children were parentless Jews, and have the Basiak apartment confiscated.

Running an illegal school, she was not really in a position to inform on anyone. But now the Gestapo had visited once and left her alone, she felt she might have some leverage with the Germans. Madame Graminski did not want to expel the Basiak children; she liked them. Kazhik was very popular with his classmates, and his chance to shine was on 'prize-giving' day.

Children were awarded medals for their academic achievements, as excited parents stood in fur hats and jewellery, tea cups in hand. It was all a bit strange, as the school had not been functioning again for more than a few weeks.

The old soldier handed out the gongs. 'Congratulations!' the old Bavarian said warmly, as he grasped each child by the arm and gave them a prize for best handwriting or French diction. Being his favourite, Kazhik was given an iron cross from the old officer's own collection of First World War medals. It was going mouldy with verdigris. Kazhik was unclear what he had done to deserve such a special honour; most probably it was for his enthusiastic bayoneting practice with a broom handle. The old Bavarian's voice cracked with emotion as he pinned it on Kazhik.

'*Herzliche gluckwunsche kleiner soldat!*' he said. ('Congratulations, little soldier!')

Kazhik was ten years old.

Pavel watched with the parents. He had never found anything he could do properly in life or felt happy with. As assistant caretaker of the new school, however, he excelled; there was not a task he could not do. He kept the coat pegs clear, shone the floors and replaced the sawdust in the small courtyard at the back. He locked up at night when everyone else had gone home.

Before the caretaker job, he was lost in the world. Now he was no longer merely the brother of 'brave Kazhik' or 'the beautiful, talented Juta'. He had purpose. That is not to say he was not easily led. Pavel still deferred in most things to his younger brother, the supremely confident Kazhik. It had always been that way.

Pavel was also given an award: for being a first-class care-taker, which was his job anyway. He was happy nonetheless to receive it.

'*Große bruden!*' the old Bavarian guard said, beaming at Kazhik as he pinned the award on Pavel. ('What great brothers!')

Kazhik and Pavel smiled at one another, and the boys ran home triumphantly.

Their route looked different from normal. A huge red wall topped with barbed wire had sprung up through the heart of the city. Kazhik and Pavel were now officially going home on the 'Aryan' side of Warsaw.

On the other side of the new red wall was 'the Jewish ghetto'.

## *October 1940, London*

The Blitz was in full swing, but Michael was oblivious to being blown up. He kept looking at the telegram, imagining that if he glanced another time, it would magically say something differ-ent. It never did. His family had been killed. What was the point in believing anything else? He was a realist. He never believed the fatalistic mumbo-jumbo that his wife went in for.

Michael could not bear to be in his cramped rented flat in King's Cross, so he walked the streets, wandering through a landscape continuously rearranged by the Luftwaffe raids. His own death never occurred to him. It felt irrelevant. What more could the war do to him than had not already been done to his wife and children?

He went through the scenarios: if they had stayed in Warsaw, the Nazis would surely have killed them, he thought. If all five of them had made it back to the country house, then the Russians would have done the job. That was the reality. Michael had no one left in the world. His parents were long gone, and now his own family were dead too.

He knew very well what the Soviets were capable of. Reports were arriving daily to the Polish government-in-exile of fresh atrocities. In the village of Grabowiec, Russian soldiers walked into a hospital and massacred the patients, turning their guns on the doctors and nurses. At the Battle of Szack, the Soviets were beaten against the odds by inferior Polish numbers and forced to abandon their tanks. They wreaked revenge on the local population, then machine-gunned a stray division of surrendered Polish infantrymen in the woods with their arms in the air.

The Nazi-Soviet pact was still going strong. Stalin and Hitler distrusted each other, but the heads of their respective secret police forces, Adolf Eichmann and Lavrentiy Beria, got on like a house on fire. They had a common enemy, the AK Polish government-in-exile, and both adored torture, especially if the goal was extracting names of AK agents in London.

On 20 February 1940, the Nazi and Soviet secret police arranged to meet to coordinate strategy at the picturesque Polish mountain village of Zakopane, all wooden chalets and pretty churches. Beria's second-in-command, Gregory Litvinov, was invited by Eichmann to dinner in the grand mansion overlooking the town, commandeered by Nazi high command so they could enjoy the beautiful panoramic views over the valley.

The mansion also had a cellar for torturing local political dissidents with branding irons and hooks. As Litvinov and Eichmann drank their pre-dinner aperitif, they would have been able to hear the distant screams of captured AK agents having their eyes gouged out.

In London, Michael knew this would be his fate if he was captured. Had his family been alive, it would have been theirs too.

# 4

## *The Telegram*

Hela knew what was going on, and had warned the boys in advance to avoid the west gate of the ghetto wall. It was here that groups of Jews had begun to be executed by firing squad every morning and night.

There was something else at the bottom of the west gate. A sluice through which a thick, coagulating stream of blood seeped slowly out to the pavement on the other side: the bloody slabs on which the brothers skipped excitedly home from school.

Warsaw was made up of six distinct districts. One east of the river Vistula and five west. Praga, east of the river, considered itself better than the rest of the city; it didn't even have a bridge to the other side until the turn of the nineteenth century. Its culture was strongly Catholic and conservative, and its name derived from the Polish verb *prazyc*, meaning to burn or roast.

The Zoliborz, Wola, Ochota and Mokotow districts lay on the other side of the river. Srodmiescie, at the northern end of Mokotow, where my family had their apartment, was affluent and liberal. Wola was where Hela lived; a densely populated working-class area, fiercely independent and patriotic. Zoliborz, to the north, was where the professionals lived: doctors, lawyers and bank managers in big houses behind iron gates. Ochota, in the centre, was bohemian and academic; it was also where Marie Curie had conducted her experiments into radium.

Before the war, Warsaw was known throughout the world as the 'Paris of the North' for its sophisticated internationalism, epitomised by the Polish tango performed at the famous Adria restaurant, where Eugeniusz Bodo danced nightly for audiences from all over Europe.

Adolf Dymsza was a transvestite and star of Warsaw's most celebrated cabaret, *Qui Pro Quo*. Dymsza became Poland's most famous drag act, starring in numerous farces and slapstick films. What his audience didn't know was that after the Nazis occupied Warsaw, Dymsza also secretly helped Jews escape the ghetto.

In the mid-1930s, Warsaw was a destination for foreign musicians under-appreciated in their own country. Duke Ellington and Louis Armstrong travelled from the States to play to rapt audiences in Warsaw's jazz clubs; Gershon Sirota, 'the Jewish Caruso' repaid the compliment, singing in New York.

Jews flocked to Warsaw in the nineteenth century, fleeing the Tsarist pogroms. In 1816, the Jewish population was only 15,600. By 1900, it had grown over twenty-one times to 337,000.

The city gained a reputation for tolerance and each of the five districts emphasised a different facet of its progressive triumphs. In 1932, Marie Curie had opened her Radium Institute. Kazimierz Proszynski invented the film camera in Warsaw, Josef Kosacki the mine detector; everything from Vitamin B to the periscope was developed and manufactured in the Paris of the North.

Jews were at the heart of Warsaw's artistic culture and the greatest symbol of assimilation was the huge synagogue in Tlomackie Square, holding 2,400 people. In 1939, at the outbreak of war, 340,000 Jews lived a fully integrated life in Warsaw, spread out across a vibrant, multicultural metropolis. It all stopped in 1940.

The sixth district of Warsaw was the old town. It was directly opposite Praga on the west shore of the river and thrived as the beating heart of the city for a thousand years. On 2 October 1940, just over a year after the Nazis took over, the German Governor of Warsaw, Ludwig Fischer, decreed there would be a new quarter, 'the Jewish Ghetto'.

The Nazis had already begun creating segregated pens for Jews across Poland. Not only in big cities like Warsaw, Krakow and Lodz, but in country market towns and small villages. The ghettos were designed to stigmatise and alienate the Jewish population from their neighbouring Poles. The ghettos were step one of the 'relocation' lie that would end with the concentration camps.

Warsaw's Jews were told to move immediately to the cramped narrow streets and buildings of the old town. At the same time, 113,000 gentiles were shipped out of the old town to the 'Aryan' side, where Kazhik, Pavel and Juta lived. Many Jewish families tried to stay hidden on the Aryan side helped by the neighbours, but were soon discovered and either shot or transferred to the ghetto.

On 15 November 1940, the ghetto was officially sealed off from the rest of the city. All exits in the wall were locked and the completed structure was topped with barbed wire. Anyone caught harbouring Jews outside the ghetto was shot. Jews discovered beyond its confines were either killed on the spot or forced into the ghetto.


*November 1940, London*

Michael sat in his flat, turning the folded telegram over in his hand. The words offered finality, but no proof. There was one word he couldn't stop staring at: 'PRESUMED'. A new plan began to take shape in his head.

Michael called for a meeting with his superiors in the AK, led by President-in-exile Wladyslaw Raczkiewicz. Six men sat round a table. They wore heavy wool suits and carried the weight of a nation on their shoulders; they could give Michael five minutes. Michael said he needed to find his family. He was told by each in turn that it wasn't an option; his work in London – to help liberate Poland – was too important. If he wanted to find his family, they said, contact the Red Cross. They had a 'Wounded, Missing and Relatives Department' near Moorfields Eye Hospital in Old Street.

'Go there,' Raczkiewicz said. The meeting was over.

The following day, Michael navigated his way through the wreckage created by the previous night's bombing. London was a great smashed mouth, with new teeth missing every morning. Giant holes appeared in City Road as he walked up from King's Cross. Makeshift ambulances ferried the fresh dead, whilst children made their way to school through the rubble, excitedly picking up any shrapnel they found, to be traded in the playground.

At the Red Cross HQ, Michael was told to wait. An hour later, a man with far better things to do told Michael that he was looking for a needle in a haystack with his family. The chances of finding his wife and children, even if any were still alive, was a million to one. Volunteers could run searches on anyone in the world, but only if they were in a Red Cross hospital, or a prison camp supported by the Red Cross.

'If that's the case,' the man said, 'then your odds go down to ten thousand to one.'

The haystack that Michael was looking in was made up of millions of people walking the roads of Europe and Russia; refugees with no paperwork. They were 'non-persons' – *pustoye mesto* in Russian. A woman behind the front desk said she would take the names of Michael's family, but could promise nothing.

Between 1939 and 1941, 200,000 Polish civilians were killed by the advancing Germans and Russians, often with no one ordering the massacre. It just happened. They killed roughly half each. If the Russians rolled into town and you were not immediately deported to Siberia, the results were a lottery. Sometimes the soldiers were nice, stroked the dogs and ate the fresh Polish bread. Other times, they lined up the population in the pretty main square and fired their guns till no one was moving.

In the middle of this lottery were the refugees: the *pustoye mesto*. What Michael did not know was that Olga and Alina were already in a Red Cross camp or, at least, one to which they were delivering food parcels. Within a matter of days, the 'Wounded, Missing and Relatives Department' contacted Michael and told him that two of the five names he had given them matched their records: Olga and Alina Basiak. They were alive and in a camp in Siberia.

Michael met a man in a café in Bloomsbury. He handed over a large wad of bank notes in an envelope. The man said it would take time to arrange their escape.

It took eleven months.

*The conversations with my mum over the last few months researching this book have helped her through a difficult time.*

*Though her memories of the war are pin-sharp, and her conversations with her brother about what happened in Warsaw are as vivid as if they happened yesterday, her short-term memory is beginning to falter.*

*My dad and I are begrudgingly beginning to accept that these are her first unsteady steps into the cave of dementia. Those who go into this cave with their personality intact gradually fade from view, descending into the darkness step by step.*

*There is always a founding incident prompting 'diagnosis' of dementia and Alina's happened on a Wednesday evening. She cooked a beef stew, and the following morning, the oven was still blazing away. The stew was a blackened disc at the bottom of the pot.*

*'What happened to the stew?' My dad asked my mum.*

'What stew?'

My mum's first tests were at the doctor's. Simple questions were asked: What is your name? When were you born? What did you have for lunch? Count backwards from ten. What is the name of your son?

My mum laughed at the questions, but she was nervous and frightened. The easy questions, she said, were impossible to answer and the impossible questions, easy.

'How do you feel?' the doctor asked.

'I know that one, I feel great.'

For a year before the stew incident, Alina had been having TIAs – transient ischaemic attacks, or 'mini-strokes'. She would be in the street and suddenly she would be struck dumb like a statue, unable to speak, unaware where she was, or who either my dad or I was. These would last for about ten minutes and then she would be back to normal, with no memory of what had happened.

TIAs are a common early sign of vascular dementia, a slowing of the blood supply to the brain, and the second-most common form of dementia after Alzheimer's disease. It was diagnosed that these mini-strokes were a prelude to dementia.

But an MRA revealed my mum had not been having TIAs at all. She had developed epilepsy in her late eighties and these were epileptic fits. Drugs prescribed would control the epilepsy, but could not slow the dementia. Losing her memory was a train onto a vast, flat landscape. No one could stop the train, and the destination was inevitable.

## October 1941, Warsaw

By April 1941, the Jewish ghetto in the centre of Warsaw held nearly half a million Jews. More than 400,000 people were crammed into an area of barely 3.4 kilometres. On average, that was over seven to a single room. Soon the population of this densely overcrowded prison began being deported on trains to what was euphemistically called 'the east'.

Kazhik, Juta and Pavel saw none of this from their apartment off Saski Park, although they lived only five minutes from the red wall. At the end of their street, the ghetto started; they were near enough to hear the shootings and smell the corpses, but they carried on a normal bourgeois life.

The district of Mokotow had been allowed to function as a model example of successful 'Aryanisation'. Inhabitants were reprogrammed to live as loyal citizens of the Third Reich: to abide by the same rules as Germans and absorb Nazi values into everyday life, which included informing on anyone suspicious.

Resident attitudes towards the ghetto fell into three categories: ignore and pretend it wasn't happening; actively welcome the Nazi occupiers; or secretly plot to rise up against them. The Basiak children and their housekeeper appeared on the surface to be in the first category. Hela shopped for food in the local grocery store, buying fresh bread and fruit, which were still readily available. The children bought clothes in one of the three Warsaw department stores still allowed to stay open by the Nazis.

They bought everything on 'chit' (credit) or by selling more furniture from the apartment. Hela moved from room to room, searching out more valuables. She began with the gold mirrors and the red velvet chaise longue that had been given to Olga and Michael as a wedding present. Once the spare linen and porcelain had gone, she moved on to upholstered chairs and the full dinner service, complete with heavy silver cutlery. She then dismantled the grand chandelier in the principal dining room.

Hela was able to sell most of it to the rich parents from the school, who gave her a good price. They would come to the apartment and pick through the family belongings as the children sat in the kitchen; they were used to the drill by now. Kazhik cursed the return of these vultures and told Hela that soon there would be nothing left. She told him brusquely that it was necessary if they were to eat.

Everyone in the school knew this suspicious family had money problems, but after nearly three years attending, the Basiak children were beyond reproach. Juta was the star of the school: smarter, sparkier and more beautiful than any other pupil. She was an incredible pianist, spoke German proficiently and could read French. She was a natural linguist.

One morning, Madame Graminski announced that the Nazis were going to make another visit to the school. The highest-ranking SS officers in Warsaw had been told about Juta's virtuoso piano playing. They were to come and see 'fine young Aryan Poles' being educated, even if it was at an illegal school that was not officially supposed to exist. The old Bavarian soldier agreed with Madame Graminski that Juta should reprise her first concert for their esteemed guests, playing the piano brilliantly again, this time for the SS.

On the appointed day, four SS guards walked respectfully into the drawing room and sat politely in a line on chairs. Behind them were seated two lines of parents wearing fur coats and pearls. The SS were like movie stars to the parents – they had jet black, slicked-back hair, with crisply ironed uniforms and highly polished black boots; they exuded power and menace.

Juta walked in wearing a white dress, clutching her sheet music, and sat primly on the piano stool. She had been waiting her whole life for a moment like this: an audience she hoped would be cultured enough to appreciate how clever and talented she really was. Juta began with Chopin's *Nocturne,* then his *Polonaise* and *Prelude in D.* The music trickled from her fingers, a waterfall of notes tumbling into the room and evaporating magically in the dust and sunlight.

The three SS officers listened intently. They seemed transported. Their eyes, which had overseen the burning of babies and garrotting of old women, were transfixed by this confection of purity they saw before them.

Juta's final note hung in the air for an eternity before the applause began. The clapping of the parents was clipped and polite, but the SS officers got to their feet and stood beating their meaty hands ecstatically for a solid minute, beaming their approval. The fact they had spent twenty minutes listening to Chopin, the music of a man who was everything they despised – a Polish patriot and homosexual, who despised fascism – was entirely lost on them.

The SS officers came over to congratulate Juta.

'Your name?' the oldest SS man said, in German. He looked the most superior.

'Juta, sir.'

'Beautiful, Juta. Sublime music.' A thought occurred to him and he smiled. 'Do you know Goethe?' It was such an odd question, it seemed to come out of nowhere like a test of some sort.

'I do, sir,' Juta replied slowly, her mind whirring. There was an awkward pause as the Germans waited for Juta to say something entertaining.

'*Es ist nichts schrecklicher al seine tatige unwissenheit,*' she said eventually. ('There is nothing more frightful than ignorance in action.')

It was the first thing that came into her head; it was the only Goethe quote she knew. There was silence. Juta repeated it. She looked into each of the Nazis' eyes, lingering deliberately on their faces as she spoke. The SS officers studied Juta with curiosity, like an exotic bird in the zoo. The Goethe quote hung in the air like a bad smell.

'Indeed,' the oldest one replied.

His temples were greying beneath his death's head cap. The SS officer stared unblinkingly at Juta for what felt like an age. He seemed to Juta to be trying to look into her soul; but though his eyes drilled into her face, he saw nothing. The SS officer's stare bounced off something hard and impenetrable within.

He broke off his stare. 'Indeed,' he said again, flatly, for want of something better. People rarely withstood the SS officer's glare without revealing something of themselves. Juta appeared on the surface to be the perfect Aryan convert, reciting Goethe and playing Chopin contritely, but something was not right about her. He turned on his heel and left.

The Basiak children seemed to have landed from space. They had no parents and no relatives in Warsaw. No one ever suspected them of having connections to other human beings; least of all to the AK resistance movement being organised in London by their father, Michael.

In practical terms they were alone. Michael assumed his children were deceased, and for their part, the children had long given up hope that their father was alive. Kazhik was a young man of formidable stature. A handsome eleven-year-old who looked closer to fifteen, hugely affable, self-assured, and adroit at making the crippled Bavarian monitor believe he was a perfect Aryan in the making.

To Madame Graminski, who tolerated the Nazis but secretly despised them, Kazhik looked the model young Nazi. Like Juta, he was useful for PR purposes. When the Gestapo came to visit the school again, however, he never saluted *Sieg Heil* as the other children did; he stood with his arms by his side and said nothing. Meanwhile nineteen-year-old Pavel steadily gained the trust of Madame Graminski and took over full caretaker duties in late 1941. He was given the keys to every door and cupboard in the school, except one.

One night, Pavel, who never had ideas of his own, had an idea. He whispered it to Kazhik as they lay in their bunk beds. Next day, they met in the alleyway behind the school at 5 p.m. as they had agreed the night before.

When the coast was clear, the boys let themselves into the school with Pavel's key and began rummaging for what they could steal. It began with books and pens, but they soon discovered army knives and bayonet blades procured for junior squad drill, but never used.

There was one room to which they had no access. Only the old soldier had a key. One morning, when he was drinking his 11 a.m. coffee and smoking a cigarette, Pavel stole it from his jacket and made a plasticine imprint. That night, he had a duplicate made in a hardware shop on Szarotki.

The following evening, the brothers let themselves back into the school and crept up to the locked room; there was no one in the building, but they still wanted to make no noise. They knew what was in there, but the expectation was killing them.

Pavel opened the door. It was a common store room. From floor to ceiling were wooden shelves stacked with the obligatory paraphernalia of a functioning school: fire extinguishers, a folded canvas stretcher, the moth-eaten cushioned top of a dismantled wooden horse. But on one entire wall was what they were looking for. Dozens of small cardboard boxes with the same purple insignia on the front. Live ammunition shells, kept by the old soldier in case of an emergency.

Taking a couple of the boxes each night, the brothers found that the Bavarian soldier with the limp never even noticed any had gone. He was so lax, spending his afternoons smoking, or reminiscing to anyone who would listen about the First World War, that he never bothered to check.

Within a couple of months, Kazhik and Pavel had amassed boxes and boxes of bullets that they kept under the floorboards in their room of the apartment. They had a plan, and were methodically putting it into action.

# 5

## The Smuggler

*15 November 1941, Siberia*

Just over a month before Christmas, a Russian with an impressive moustache and a coat made of the pelts of stoats and squirrels arrived at the perimeter fence of the Siberian camp, semi-buried in snow. He knew where the camp was, because he had been there many times before. He was a human smuggler.

Smugglers took anyone who would pay enough money across thousands of miles of war-ravaged Europe: they arranged Jewish families' passage to America, helped resistance leaders evade Nazi arrest and Nazi spies escape the Allies. They worked for anyone if the bill was paid. If the journey was proving too perilous or time-consuming, smugglers were known to kill their human cargo and move on to the next job. In 1941, there was plenty of work.

'Where are they?' the smuggler asked the Russian soldiers. He knew this camp well. The soldiers gestured to the hut where the commander was settling in for the night with a jug of potato vodka.

The smuggler was a huge man, covered head to toe in animal skins. My mum had seen people like him before, laying traps in the Polish forest. He wore layers of grease and fur because it was the best way to keep warm; over time, the pelts melded together as a second skin, glued to the body with sweat. Trappers and smugglers smelt to high heaven: a memorable sickly-sweet mix of ancient body odour, long dead animal and fresh alcohol.

The smuggler took out a dirty envelope breaking at the seams and handed it to the soldiers. It was to be the first of many such transactions on this journey. The envelope had already been on its own epic voyage from London, handed from one smuggler to the next over seven borders. Now it was in the hands of the purple-faced commander of the gulag, who counted it fast and smooth, like a bank teller.

'It's not enough,' he said simply. 'Not enough for the good witch.' He handed it back. The smuggler reached into a side pocket of his animal-pelt construction, pulling out a second ragged envelope with a pre-prepared sum inside. He handed it over without saying a word. The commander counted the money, and this time he nodded positively, gesturing out of the frozen window to the third hut from the end. The smuggler barged in without ceremony, sending a blast of cold air into the room.

'Are Olga and Alina Basiak present?'

About thirty people put their hand up.

'Us,' Olga said.

Alina was awestruck. The man in the animal skins stank of a whole field of dead cows. He was called Stefan and he was there to escort them, he said, to neutral Sweden. Alina didn't want to go, but Olga said they must. For nearly two years they had been in Siberia, safe so long as they kept warm and read tarot cards for the soldiers. Stefan was about to deliver them into the force-twelve gale of war.

His plan, he said, was to reunite them with Michael in a Red Cross camp near Stockholm. Alina couldn't take it in. Her father was alive; not only that, he had paid to save them, and sent this stinking man to deliver them to freedom.

She had a thousand questions for him – Where was Michael? What about her siblings? – but Stefan had no interest in answering, even if he had known. She jumped around him like a puppy dog, trying to get his attention. The smuggler didn't even notice she was there.

The journey, Stefan told Olga, would be treacherous. One route was to go over the top of Finland via Murmansk, then through Norway and across the three-nations border-point near Kilpisjarvi. Olga listened intently, but had no clue what any of it meant. This option had one thing going for it, continued Stefan – an absence of Nazis. It also involved crossing thousands of miles of frozen tundra. Even when they got to the vast plains of Northern Sweden, Olga and the girl still had a thousand kilometres more of exposed ice plain to cross back down to Stockholm.

An alternative was to make their way across the border to Nazi Germany, then into neutral but German-occupied Denmark; crossing at the narrowest point of the Oresund, from Elsinore (the castle in *Hamlet*) to Helsingborg in Sweden.

The last stretch was two and a half nautical miles, easily traversable by rowing boat, but that was in peacetime. In 1941, the Oresund was one of the most perilous channels of water in the world. The Gestapo shone searchlights across the strait in the dark, machine-gunning rowing boats as regular passenger ferries continued to cross with Danes and Swedes on board.

Nevertheless, it was a tempting option from a distance point of view. Two and a half miles of unnervingly still water used by thousands of evacuees fleeing the Nazis. It was hugely risky. 'Capture or death', Stefan said, 'are almost guaranteed.' Another route was required.

Stefan fumbled about in his rucksack and pulled out more envelopes. Forged identification papers. Without the right documentation, there was no point in leaving the Siberian camp, he said. Even having immaculate paperwork was no guarantee against . . .

'Don't tell me,' Olga said, 'capture or death.'

In September 1940, the German-Jewish philosopher Walter Benjamin attempted to travel to America with perfect forged papers. His first step was to get to Spain, crossing the border at Port Bou, after having successfully scaled the Pyrenees. Spain was a gateway to America by plane or ship, and hundreds of refugees used Port Bou as the bridgehead to freedom. But on 5 September 1940, the day Walter Benjamin chose to cross, the Spanish changed the visa requirements.

Benjamin was with a group of refugees led by two experienced smuggler-guides. Their perfect forged papers were suddenly out of date and they were immediately placed under house arrest in a nearby hotel. In a frenzy, Benjamin paced his room, terrified that he had missed his chance. In his suitcase, he had morphine tablets hidden in a concealed compartment. Benjamin's choice was stark: hold out till morning and see what the Spanish authorities would do – most probably hand him over to the nearest Nazis – or kill himself.

Benjamin saw no way out. He swallowed the pills and died in his room. The following day, the entry requirements reverted back and the other members of Benjamin's party of Jewish émigrés travelled on safely to Spain and freedom.

This was the high-stakes poker game my mum and Olga were now embarking on. Stefan had good, but not foolproof, forged papers, and the Nazis were expert at spotting forgeries. To stay one step ahead of the forgers, the Germans continuously changed the way papers were authenticated, forever altering the serrated edging and watermarks.

In Paris, a man called Adolfo Kaminsky helped émigrés stay a step ahead of the Nazis. Kaminsky, an Argentinian Jew, had narrowly escaped being sent to Auschwitz and his miraculous getaway inspired him to help others by using chemistry skills he had picked up as a child.

In his basement, Kaminsky set up an underground lab for forgeries. He worked on removing the blue Waterman ink distinctive to Nazi identity papers. By using lactic acid, he found he could erase the Waterman ink perfectly, leaving the paper as good as new to print on. This simple discovery was nothing short of the Enigma Code breakthrough for forgeries, saving the lives of tens of thousands of people by giving them a blank canvas to print on.

Kaminsky's forgeries did not come into general circulation with émigrés until winter 1941, weeks too late for Stefan to obtain them for my mum and grandmother. Fortunately, the Polish government-in-exile in London had another useful contact to help obtain immaculate papers.

Winston Churchill had just created the so-called 'Ministry for Ungentlemanly Warfare', which was run by a Polish master forger called Jerzy Maciejewsky, a genius at producing fake passports, IDs and visas for British spies from his lab in a country house in Harlow. Maciejewsky was a true patriot, and forged papers for the AK too.

*I am walking with my mum to the post office to buy some envelopes, appropriately enough.*

'*Did Stefan tell you where he got the forged papers from?' I ask.*

'*No. But I remember him being impressed by what he'd been given. He even had duplicates made. My mother asked him if we would be stopped, and he said the papers were as good as he'd ever seen.*'

Stefan was faced with the dilemma of the safest route from Siberia to Sweden. He thought the Oresund crossing would be too risky. The best way, he finally decided, was to use the port of Tallinn in Estonia as their 'keyhole' into Stockholm. It was not a long crossing and equally dangerous in its own way, but less watched. His task now was to find someone willing to take them across.

The first leg of the journey took two days and two nights by train. Alina was scared, almost for the first time since the Russian commander had threatened to shoot her in the forest, back home. They were on an old passenger train and each carriage had a berth for six people, with bunk beds that came out of the wall, unlocked by a key. It was filled with people like them carrying false papers, crammed against one another in the airless compartment.

When they arrived at the station to board, the scene that greeted my mum and Olga did not augur well. Thousands of people were fighting chaotically to get on the same train. Theirs was the only one leaving. People had jammed the narrow corridors of each carriage. The doors were locked to stop any more boarding, so instead, people were clambering desperately through the windows.

There was an expectant, almost thrilling hum on the platform that became familiar to my mum: the buzz that precedes blind panic. Everyone in the station believed the same thing: if they did not get on this train, there would not be another. There was an unspoken sense that the war was going up a notch and chaos was just around the corner.

Stefan asked Olga if she had any gold or money. She shook her head slowly, no. Stefan asked again, and waited for the right answer. Olga turned her back and rummaged for a small jewel she had hidden in her underwear.

With a tiny emerald in his huge bear paw, Stefan walked up to the railway guard and bribed him to find them a space on the train. The bribery was hardly covert. There was an orderly queue of people with cash, jewellery and other barterable valuables waiting to speak to the guard. One person had a live chicken. Bribery was a reliable system of transaction. Everything had its price, and everyone knew what the price was. In war, when someone promised to do something for nothing, you were suspicious of their motives.

The train was even more chaotic than the platform. There were sixteen where six should be in one compartment; people were so close together, limbs were preposterously intertwined, and arses were pushed against faces. Alina was disgusted by all the farting and belching. She was glad she was pushed tight against her mother and not a stranger. In one corner, a man was fondling and harassing a woman; people pushed up against the couple were eating food, uncaring. Alina didn't know where to look. In the next compartment, a Russian guard had the whole space to himself. He lay stretched out, smiling, and his gun had its own seat.

Alina didn't feel secure, so Stefan reluctantly got the three of them to another carriage. It was far quieter. For some reason, the crowds had entirely missed one six-berth compartment, and one man sat in there alone. He seemed keen to be by himself, but could see the young girl's distress and nodded that they could join him. His name, he said, was Joseph.

An hour into the journey, Olga tried to make small talk, but Joseph was having none of it. He stared glumly out of the window. Finally he began to explain to Olga that he was travelling to Tallinn by himself.

'Why alone?' Olga asked.

'Because my family are dead,' he said, 'and it was all my fault.'

Joseph had been living in a small village near Lwowek Slaski, in western Poland, one of the first areas to be overrun by the advancing Nazis in 1939. There were two other Jewish families in the village besides him and his wife. They knew what would happen the moment the Germans came and so Joseph organised to have them all hide in his cellar.

'Surely you would be discovered once the Nazis came?' Olga said.

The cellar was a really good place to hide, Joseph said. There were big heavy cabinets that could be pulled over a trapdoor, so it was possible to hide down there without anyone ever finding them. There was enough space in the cellar for three families, and there was electric light, so you could feasibly stay down there for months as long as you had food and water.

The problem was having someone retrieve these essentials and bring them back. Joseph took pity on the other families and decided to be their lifeline; he would go out and get the food. They would have done the same for him, he said.

'So what happened?' Olga asked.

When the families moved in to the cellar, his wife was heavily pregnant with their first child. Joseph felt he had no choice but to make him and his wife live down there as well. She ended up giving birth in the cellar. Everyone knew this baby was going to be a threat to them all, because she would cry for hours, but what could they do?

Joseph would go up and collect food for all the families and bring it back. He would be careful never to buy too much, and would vary where he got it from so as not to raise suspicion. By this point the Nazis were in full control of the village. They allowed normal life to carry on and the market traders continued selling fruit and vegetables in the square. The Nazis' only interest was to root out *Untermenschen* – Jews and other 'degenerates' – to be shot or sent to one of the Jewish ghettos being created in the nearby towns.

They did this with periodic sweeps through the village: door-to-door searches of properties and outbuildings. The Nazis used dogs, but mainly relied on local inhabitants to give them information. Anyone discovered harbouring an undesirable would be shot or hanged in the town square to serve as an example.

One day Joseph was out collecting food. On his return to the house, he pulled back the heavy cabinet and opened the trapdoor to the cellar. What he discovered defied comprehension. His wife was lying face down sobbing on the makeshift mattress, and the two other women were comforting her. Their two husbands sat on another mattress, motionless, their heads in their hands. There was silence, but for the sound of birds outside. On the floor on a blanket, Joseph's baby girl lay dead.

The Nazis had been given a lead that Joseph was shopping in the square for more than himself and his wife. They turned the house upside down, but found nothing. As the Gestapo stomped on the floor above the cellar, searching for a hollow sound to give away a hiding place, the families beneath sat still as stone. Then the baby began to grow restless, making small, impatient sounds. She needed feeding, and in the soundless cellar, these barely perceptible noises were amplified unbearably.

Joseph's wife attempted to muffle the baby's noises in the swaddling, trying to get her to latch on to a breast to feed, whilst the others looked at each other nervously.

It was of no use. The baby opened her mouth as if to begin screaming, and as she did, the two men pulled the baby from her mother, putting her on the floor and placing a pillow over her head. As the other women held the mother back, the two men suffocated the baby. The whole thing happened in total silence.

When Joseph returned, he stood rigid in the cellar.

He looked down at his arms and legs, as if they were detached from his body. Joseph and the other motionless figures in the cellar were like characters in a medieval painting; each frozen permanently till the end of time. He knew one thing for sure. They were all dead. In that room, every one of them had ceased living, regardless of whether they survived the war or not. They had stopped existing in the moment they killed his baby, but would carry on breathing perhaps for decades to come.

'What did you do next?' Olga asked, as Alina and Stefan remained silent.

Joseph told the families that because they had murdered his baby daughter, he would no longer help them survive. No more food, no more shelter, they were on their own. Joseph left the cellar and began walking. He had no thought other than to put one leg in front of the other, and for this motion to continue until he died too. His eyes registered people pulling carts and conversing in the street. The villagers stared at him as he stared right through them. None of this life has a right to carry on, he told himself.

Joseph found himself in a forest. In the silence of the trees, he contemplated suicide. Then he thought of going back and murdering everyone in the cellar, including his wife. Finally, Joseph decided to do nothing at all, and he stayed in the forest till nightfall.

Whilst he was away, the Nazi soldiers went back to the house and discovered the cellar. When Joseph returned from the forest, he found the heavy cupboard that concealed the trapdoor removed and the trapdoor open.

Someone had seen Joseph leave the house, walking away in a high state of agitation. They had alerted the Gestapo, who decided to look again. They found the cellar and shot everyone down there – one bullet to the temple, another to the neck. The Gestapo deliberately left the bodies on the floor, so whoever was helping them would find the scene as they had left it.

As Joseph told his story, the carriage was quiet but for the sound of the train passing melodically over the railway tracks. Joseph said that when he was in the forest for all those hours, thinking over and over what had happened, the truth of the situation suddenly dawned on him. He realised he had been worse than the two men who killed his baby girl. They had killed out of fear for their lives, he had acted out of revenge. They did what any animal would from instinct, but he acted out of selfishness and ego. Joseph decided to return to the house and tell them they were forgiven.

But instead, when he got there, everyone was dead, and because they were dead, he had been proved right. He was responsible, and worse than them. It was a test from God, Joseph said, and he had failed.

'*Im yirtse hashem,*' he said in Yiddish. ('If God wants.')

## December 1941, London

Michael spent his days winding his way from his accommodation in King's Cross through the blitzed streets of the city to meetings with his AK comrades.

He had given up on Olga and Alina. Michael had no way of knowing if his wife and daughter had even left Siberia. The only hope he clung to was based on something that was said by the human trafficker he met in a café in Bloomsbury over a year ago: it would take time. Since then, however, he had heard nothing.

Michael met secretly with groups of serious-looking men each week in different rooms around London. With Russia now an ally, the Polish government-in-exile worked night and day to free Poland from the Nazis. The AK would become by far the biggest resistance force in Europe, with 300,000 women and men recruited to fight the Germans. In 1941, it was still being turned into a guerrilla army.

Recruits known as the *Cichiociemni*, the 'silent and unseen', were sent to Scotland for tough SAS-style training. They learnt how to jump from planes and parachute onto Ringway airfield, now Manchester airport. They were sent to Audley End, a stately home in Essex (known as 'Station 43'), to learn close hand-to-hand combat, how to build and conceal bomb factories and assassinate the SS.

By the time the women and men of the AK were parachuted behind enemy lines, culminating in the Warsaw uprising of 1944, they were the fiercest and best-drilled underground force of the Second World War. The Nazis had no idea what was about to hit them.

Because Michael was trained as an architect and engineer, with expertise in railway stations and bridges, he was vital in the planning of AK attacks on the *Deutsche Reichsbahn*, the German railway system. The very bridges and viaducts he had helped to build before the Nazis came to power, he now determined how best to blow up. He studied drawings and targeted weak spots, calculating the most damaging trajectories of demolition. If a bridge was destroyed the right way, it could never be rebuilt. Railway lines covered by half a mountainside, or buried at the bottom of a valley, could take months to be repaired, if ever.

The disruption of the *Deutsche Reichsbahn* was a key objective of the AK, because the European railway system was at the heart of the plan taking shape within the upper echelon of the Nazi party.

Following the fall of France in 1940, Adolf Eichmann had first proposed the 'Madagascar Plan', to move the Jewish population of Europe en masse to the French colonial island just under 2,000 kilometres off the coast of Africa. Siberia and Palestine were also briefly examined, then dropped.

The removal of all Jews from Europe had been a rhetorical goal of the Nazis since the mid-1920s, but in 1941, 'relocation' was abandoned and an alternative idea developed by Heinrich Himmler: death by *Einsatzgruppen*. SS killing squads carrying out mass killings by firing squad.

In addition to the entire Jewish population of Europe, any group of civilians in Nazi-occupied territory deemed 'degenerate' were to be shot: priests; members of the Polish intelligentsia and resistance fighters; criminals; the disabled; those with mental illness; and anyone gay, artistic or promoting 'deviant' values. High on the Nazi list were *dungervolke*, but the priority was the Jews. The *Einsatzgruppen* was the new 'solution' to murdering these myriad groups marked for death.

By mid-1941, Himmler identified a problem. The sheer scale of killing so many people with rifles and machine guns had, he said, created an 'adverse effect' on the morale of Wehrmacht soldiers. In August, Himmler personally attended a mass shooting of Jews in Minsk, after which he vomited. Killing with guns, he said, should be replaced by gassing in specially customised vans. Himmler had got the idea from Lavrentiy Beria, the chief of the Soviet secret police, the NKVD.

Gas, not bullets, was now the 'solution'. During the Soviet purges of the late 1930s, an NKVD subordinate of Beria's called Isaj Berg adapted an airtight van for gassing 'enemies' of the Soviet regime. Vans were equipped with valves through which gas was pumped to the back. Prisoners were stripped naked, gagged and thrown into the van, where they were asphyxiated. The NKVD had a nickname for these vans: *dushegbka* or 'soul killers'.

Himmler devised his own gassing van: lorries disguised as removal trucks with *Kaiser's Kaffee Gescaft* written on the side. The 'Kaiser's Coffee Shop' vans were tested out by an enthusiastic Nazi commander called Arthur Nebe, chief of the *Reichskriminalpolizeiamt*, the central criminal investigation department. Nebe recorded the amount of time it took to die and how much gas was required.

After a month of 'testing', however, Nebe told Himmler that the van gassings did not work. They were too distressing for his soldiers, he said. It took up to twenty minutes to kill the people in the back and the driver could hear the victims screaming. Another 'solution' was required.

# 6

## *Sweden*

A month after leaving Siberia, and over a year after Michael paid money in a Bloomsbury café for them to escape, Alina, Olga and the smuggler Stefan reached Tallinn, the beautiful capital of Estonia.

On Christmas Eve 1941, Olga and Alina arrived to a city on its knees. Six months earlier, the Nazis had been bombing Tallinn. Now the Germans were in control of the city and it was the Allies who pummelled the city with their new allies, the Soviets. Tallinn was a key strategic prize for both sides, so the Nazis had mined the harbour to make sure no one could get in or out.

Tallinn was bedlam. On 22 June 1941, six months earlier, the Nazis had begun Operation Barbarossa, Hitler's long-planned invasion of Russia, tearing up the Nazi-Soviet pact. Overnight, Russia and Germany locked horns, and a 1,600-kilometre front opened up, the longest military advance in history. Three million soldiers were in active combat. The scale of war between Germany against Russia was mind-blowing: for every Allied soldier killed on the western front, eighty Russians were killed in the east.

Barbarossa was step one of Hitler's *Generalplan Ost* (Operation East) to turn Russia into a huge labour camp of slaves for the Third Reich. In 1940, Hitler broke his plan down into the *Kleine Planung* (Small Plan) and a *Große Planung* (Big Plan).

The Small Plan was to win the war first. Crush the enemy in a swift campaign, Hitler told high command, with a *Blitzkrieg* such as the one that proved so successful in Poland. His Big Plan was then to annihilate and ethnically cleanse all Russians and Slavs from a 6.6 million-square-mile area, creating *lebensraum* (living room) for Aryans. Whoever was left alive would be enslaved. It was unprecedented in human history.

The Holocaust, the 'final solution' for the Jewish people of Europe and apex of the Nazis' realised evil, was initially conceived as a trial run for this Big Plan. When my mum and Olga rolled into Tallinn, they had no idea that the Russians were now fighting the Nazis. At the time they were sent to Siberia, the two snakes of Russia and Germany were allies; two years on, they were mortal enemies.

In August, the siege of Tallinn threatened to make the harbour unusable for smuggling. One hundred and ninety Soviet ships were scuppered in the harbour or sunk, leaving a half-submerged graveyard of sunken destroyers filled with explosives, and mines bobbing in the wreckage. One trade in Tallinn was still thriving – human trafficking – but escape through the port was now extremely risky. What might once have been a secure exit point was now a sunken minefield.

Stefan wove through the blacked-out streets with what Olga hoped was a clear destination in mind. 'Where are we going?' she whispered.

'Quiet,' Stefan replied. A bomb exploded, making his need for quiet redundant.

Alina asked Olga if they could go back to Siberia and the comparative safety of their hapless Russian camp.

'I'm afraid not,' Olga replied, smiling.

Under Nazi control, the Jewish community of Tallinn, who had been integral to the culture of the city since the fourteenth century, were either ghettoised or executed. For centuries,

Tallinn had been a thriving cosmopolitan hub – the Constantinople of the North – melding Russian, Scandinavian, Estonian and German cultures, and with an easy-going, live-and-let-live culture. Jews, Protestants, Russian and Greek Orthodox lived side by side, the city's Jews largely avoiding the anti-Semitic pogroms of neighbouring states.

When Alina and Olga arrived in Tallinn, they entered a huge terminus for thousands of people in exodus to neutral Sweden. All sought forged or stolen papers, exchanged at an extortionate price in an alleyway or in a café, and all under the watchful eye of the Gestapo and their spies.

The streets at night were under curfew and empty, but behind drawn curtains and in steamed-up restaurants, Tallinn was a hive of activity. Deals were being struck with families desperate to escape: the more frantic you were, the more expensive the smuggler made it. Tallinn was the Casablanca of the Baltic.

Stefan said he wanted to try and find someone trustworthy to get them to Sweden. Olga imagined he would have sorted this already. They spent fruitless hours traipsing the curfewed streets, Nazi ground-to-air gunfire lighting up the sky as it strafed Allied bombers.

Stefan told Olga he could not trust anyone near the port; they were either charging too much, or were Nazi spies. But Olga was obstinate; she said the streets were dangerous. They needed to go to the first house of smugglers he had an address for and do a deal.

'Do that,' warned Stefan, 'and the first thing they'll do is call the Gestapo. The Nazis are giving a reward for fugitives and it's easy money.'

Eventually they found a house that both were happy with. The name had been given to Stefan by a smuggler he trusted. It made no sense to Olga, but that's what they did. Alina got a good feeling from the house; it was cosy. Candles dotted around the tiny fishing cottage gave a comforting glow, and there was a smell of home cooking. The family didn't look like smugglers. They had a daughter about the same age as Alina.

A woman in an apron, with hairpins all over her head, sat on a weak wooden chair discussing the money deal with Stefan. She said it was going to cost a lot. Her husband would take them across. His peacetime job as a fisherman now earned him nothing, and smuggling fugitives to and from Sweden was what he did now. But because the harbour was mined, she said, the risks of crossing to Sweden had escalated dramatically.

Prices had gone up.

Olga was furious. 'Shame on you,' she said, 'charging innocent people to escape the Nazis.'

Stefan grimaced, knowing this was no strategy for negotiation. The woman waited for Olga to stop, then continued talking to Stefan.

'Roubles are best,' she said. Her husband knew the best channels and where the Nazis looked. 'You will not be caught.' Fishermen had the best cover as smugglers, she explained, they had to go to sea, so were less likely to be stopped. They were to leave in two hours, in the night, if they could afford the fee. She left a tin on the table for the money to be put in and resumed cooking.

In fact, fishermen were more likely to be stopped than anyone else. They hid their human cargo beneath nets and fish. The Gestapo boarded boats and machine-gunned the fish to make sure no one underneath was alive. The most successful human traffickers were the Gestapo themselves, taking back-handers. Corrupt Nazis were often part of a complex network of profiteers that included border guards on the other side.

Olga agreed to the extortionate price. She told the woman that Alina had a stomach upset and needed the bathroom. As they looked for the door, Olga pointed at a side table telling

Alina to steal a needle and thread. In the bathroom, Olga cut open the lining of her coat with scissors, then she ripped out the thick padding and plunged her hand into the hole. Olga never took off her big Russian fur coat and Alina was about to find out why.

Olga took out a wad of roubles, handing it to her daughter. From the hidden seam that ran round the bottom of her coat, she pulled out gold coins and a handful of loose jewels she had concealed two years earlier, before the Russians came to the house. There was yet more money and jewellery pushed into the lining under her armpits.

'This,' Olga explained to her daughter, holding up the roubles like a talisman, 'is our ticket to Sweden.' Her whole life, Alina thought her mother was an idiot. In this moment, she realised she was a genius. *This*, Alina thought, *is going to save us*.

Olga knew that if she magically appeared from the bathroom with the money, the smugglers would steal it from her, or worse. So she instructed Alina to leave the bathroom and secretly give the money to Stefan, who would pay the woman. When Alina was gone, Olga set about customising her daughter's coat, cutting the seams open and transferring half the gold and jewellery into the lining of Alina's coat.

Each of them was now carrying half the money. Mother and daughter were spread-betting the risk of losing everything. What Olga didn't tell Alina was her real reason: that if either of them was killed, the other could carry on.

The fishing boat left Tallinn at 2 a.m. From the sea, my mum watched the cathedral lit up by sudden flashes of Allied bombs exploding in the old quarter. They illuminated every detail of the decimated outline, slowly fading to leave a murky afterglow; a deep red stain hanging in the sky.

Their boat wove in and out of sunken destroyers. The water was littered with frightening metal orbs, bobbing around the hull of their fishing boat, the legacy of Russian and Nazi mining. Each time they narrowly missed one, Stefan grinned and pointed it out to Alina like an excited child, miming a 'Boom!' explosion with his hands and laughing. He rarely smiled and Alina had never seen him so happy.

The fisherman stood at the wheel saying nothing, eyes fixed on the icy water. He wove effortlessly between the hulls of upturned ships, the jagged metal carcasses of the Soviet fleet destroyed in the siege. He was so calm, it induced a false sense of security in his passengers. The truth was that every night he sailed these waters, he was as terrified as the night before.

Within a couple of hours, they were free of German waters and officially in Swedish jurisdiction. The boat slowed to a walking pace and began to amble on big swells, the engine stuttering like a small moped. Out of the early-morning mist, a boat appeared. Olga immediately assumed it was a Nazi patrol ship, but no one else was panicking. The two captains nodded briefly. The boats came alongside and Olga, Alina and Stefan clambered across without a word.

There was little ceremony between the captain of the Tallinn fishing boat and the captain of this new boat: a small, bad-tempered Swedish man with appalling halitosis. He made no greeting, only gestured to the three to get in the wheelhouse quickly.

Alina was reassured by the efficiency. They were so nonchalant, it felt like two bus drivers swapping shifts. Olga, who rarely showed emotion, clapped her hands excitedly together and hugged her daughter. 'We have made it!' she said. They were in Sweden.

Olga clutched Alina's arm tight and pointed at the shoreline. Her grip was so tight Alina could feel her mother's fingernails through her coat. Olga looked at her daughter and smiled broadly. Alina never forgot that smile.

There was a problem. The man with halitosis wanted more money, and at this Stefan became angry, cursing and gesticulating at the Swede from the other end of the boat. In the early-morning sky, the silhouette of two dark shapes shouting at each other looked like a mad puppet show.

When they landed, they were taken by car to the Red Cross camp near Boo, just outside Stockholm. Halfway there, Stefan had the car stop and he got out. He pinched Alina's cheek, but said nothing to Olga. In a second he was gone. They never saw him again.

*'What was it like?' I ask my mum. 'The camp?'*

*We have gone to Cartons coffee shop on Stanmore Broadway. My mum likes coming here, because the Polish waitresses make a fuss of her and tell her she reminds them of their mothers back home. As they clean the tables around us, I'm convinced they are trying to listen in, perhaps suspicious of what this man is up to with their beloved Alina.*

*'Oh, it was wonderful! It was like a hotel! There were all these private rooms, there was a huge, clean toilet right in the centre of an even bigger washing room. It was spotless, all this gleaming porcelain and tiles. They had a canteen with amazing food, and this was all thanks to the Red Cross. Jewish families were coming here from Germany, there were French families and even some Poles. I met these little girls in the grounds and we played for hours. It was fantastic.'*

*'What about your father, Michael? Was he there?'*

*'This was the first thing I asked my mother when we arrived. Is my father here? She just said "no". There was no explanation, she didn't even look at me. She just said no and walked away. I ran down every corridor looking for him, shouting his name. I couldn't believe it. He had arranged for our escape. He was my hero. And he was supposed to be there when we arrived, and I was supposed to hug him, and he was nowhere to be seen.'*

'This was when Olga reverted back to her old self. Alina asked her, "Where is he? Why isn't he here? What's happened to him?" Olga's expression changed. It was like a light going off, my mum says. Olga told her daughter to shut up. She raised her hand to Alina, exactly as she had in Warsaw, and slapped her daughter across the face.

'I believe she would have hit me again if she had the energy, but after the first slap she just seemed exhausted. All the energy had gone out of her. She told me to leave her alone in the room.'

The waitresses have stopped pretending to clean up and formed a semi-circle around our table.

'I blamed Olga,' my mum continued. 'I knew it was her fault. She never expected my father to be there. I'm sure it was a trick. I went out into the garden and played by myself. Then I carved her initials into a tree with a penknife and I stabbed it.'

## January 1942, Red Cross Hospital, Southern Sweden

Before the war, the Red Cross hospital where Olga and Alina were staying had been a hotel. Built to accommodate the well-to-do Stockholm elite weekending away from the city, the corridors were lined with fine paintings and the stuffed heads of moose and bears. It was bizarre that no one had bothered to remove these objects before turning the hotel into a hospital.

The whole place had a surreal, well-ordered feel. Doctors and nurses funded by Red Cross donations carried stethoscopes and wore crisp cotton uniforms as they patrolled largely empty wards. Less than fifty miles away, across the water in Estonia, civilians were being butchered by the Nazis and left to die. In the pristine Red Cross hospital, everyone had immaculate uniforms and was ready to treat patients. There was just no one to treat.

Alina could not get over the fact that her father wasn't there. She blamed her mother and began to think that Olga had arranged it somehow, lying to her from the start. When Olga sensed her daughter's renewed hostility, she was secretly relieved. It meant they could go back to the familiar old ground of hating one another.

They stayed out of each other's way. Olga sat in a high-ceilinged communal room with huge windows. It was empty from morning till night. She turned her tarot cards, missing the audience she'd had in the Siberian camp. Alina filled her time playing in the long corridors with children who had made it over to Sweden from all over Europe. One afternoon, she sat in the garden with a little girl who had come from Poland. Alina asked how they had got to Sweden.

'We paid a man money,' the girl said.

'So did we!' Alina replied, her eyes brightening.

One morning, a small, dark-haired woman with a quick, mischievous smile approached Olga as she was sitting staring blankly out of a window. The woman was called Avital and she became Olga's friend. Avital's family came from Belarus, less than fifty miles from her own house in the forest. When the Nazis came, Avital and her family were transported halfway across the country to the Jewish ghetto in Lodz.

Avital and Olga were kindred spirits. They both believed in fate and tarot cards, recognising one another's disdain for the real world. They spent hours huddled together in the big communal room, rapt in conversation. They had both come from the same part of Poland, both escaped death (twice) and both believed their husbands to be stupid.

Avital explained bitterly how her wealthy relatives had emigrated in 1938 to America.

'Why didn't I go with them?' she cried. 'Why? I ask myself that question a hundred times a day.'

The reason they stayed in Poland, she said, was because her husband maintained a steadfast belief in humanity, and in the Pilsudski regime protecting Polish Jews. As the anti-Semitic atrocities ramped up, her husband continued to place his trust in the common decency of Polish people. He was blinded by his utopianism.

'More fool him,' Avital told Olga.

'More fool you,' Olga responded, 'for marrying him to start with!'

The women laughed.

Avital said her husband had been incredulous that their neighbours could be so cruel. Jews were informed on to the Gestapo by friends they had shared meals with days before. The Jews were forced to dig their own graves and then shot.

'How far will this barbarism go?' Olga asked Avital.

'It's personal,' Avital said matter of factly. 'We are Jews.'

Alina snuck into the room and sat listening to Avital speak, enthralled by her vivid depiction of the cruel world and its manifold injustices. She remembers Avital describing the sifting of human beings in the Lodz ghetto in biblical terms: the wheat and the chaff.

*'What did she mean?' I ask my mum, as we walk down to the bank to pay in a cheque. Telephone banking, let alone online payments, are not real to Alina, only a physical representation of value.*

*'She said that Jews were the wheat because they were the families who had been chosen to be sent to the ghettoes. It stuck with me. She put it like this. Jews were the chosen people of God and yet they were also the chosen people of the Nazis. Chosen to die.'*

*'This was her understanding of what it meant to be chosen people? That Jews had been singled out for atrocity?'*

*'It was a paradox, Avital said. I remember thinking that maybe it was best to be chaff in this world. To be nothing special, after all.'*

The Swedish hospital was one of the happiest times in Alina's life. Playing with other children and seeing her mother make a friend in Avital. Perhaps the first true friend she'd ever had.

Alina was allowed to do the things a child should be allowed to do: play hide and seek, build dens and explore, free of danger. It was a respite from what was happening beyond the walls of the hospital garden, but it did not last long.

One morning Olga woke bolt upright.

'We're leaving,' she told her daughter. 'Pack your clothes.'

*'Did she give any reason?'*

*'She never gave reasons for anything. She didn't think she needed to. I just assumed it must be to punish me. Because here we were in safety. My father had arranged it, so she must be against it. I could only assume it was to hurt me.'*

*We have gone to Cartons for a coffee again and the Polish waitresses are definitely listening in, pretending to clear up dishes.*

*'How did you feel about leaving the Red Cross hospital?' I ask.*

*'What do you think I felt? I was angry. Why do you ask me, what did you feel? I felt betrayed. Remember, please, my mother took me back to the forest and away from my family weeks before war started. My brothers and sister stayed in Warsaw. Why? Why do that?'*

*'Because she made a mistake?' I say, sensing I need to tread carefully.*

*'She said it was because I was nasty and strange and different from the others, and couldn't get on with them. Why didn't they come back with us like any normal person would decide to do? Ask my mother. Oh, you can't.'*

*Alina looks down at her cake, untouched for once.*

*'We had safety for the first time in Sweden and I was happy. So she decided to leave and go to fucking Warsaw where the Nazis were. Why? Because she felt guilty about leaving my brothers and sister behind? Well, what about me?'*

*The waitresses look shocked. Alina stares up imploringly at them, at all of us.*

*'What about me?'*

          ★     ★     ★

I don't want to be disloyal to my mum, but it is my duty here to see it also from Olga's perspective. Olga had no idea what had happened to her children. Warsaw was under Nazi control and for all she knew, they were dead. She had to find out if they were alive, whatever the danger to herself and my mum.

Olga was quick to make preparations. She asked around the hospital, seeing if anyone knew a way to be smuggled back into Nazi-occupied Poland.

'Why do you want to go back there?' Avital asked her, angry with her new friend.

'Don't ask, and don't tell anyone,' Olga said. 'Just make enquiries for me, please.'

There were dozens of smugglers to choose from, and these were not like Stefan, the stinking bear of a man covered in animal skins, who had got them out of Siberia. Against all the odds, Stefan had been trustworthy.

Olga never understood why he had not robbed and killed them. Stefan had done his job: taken them to Sweden and then disappeared into the early-morning mist. The fact he had known all the time that Olga had a small fortune hidden in her coat and not murdered them both when they were sleeping, was nothing short of a miracle.

Olga's choice now was brutal: stay safe in Sweden, or risk both their lives to find Kazhik, Juta and Pavel with no guarantee they were alive. They could all be dead at the end of such an endeavour. Such a decision is the intricately detailed work of the devil. For Olga, there was only one option. They were doing this.

Olga had no trouble finding a smuggler. She cut the lining of her fur coat open for the umpteenth time and dispensed some more Russian roubles into a stranger's hand. Funds were depleting. His name was 'Orhan', although Olga had no idea if that was his real name. He looked young, in his early twenties.

He said he came from Turkey and was a very successful smuggler.

Orhan had been trafficking Jewish families into Sweden for three years. It was highly lucrative and this job would be money for old rope. It would be a lot easier, he said, getting into Poland than coming out.

'Why?' Olga asked.

'Because no one wants to go back *into* Poland,' Orhan said. 'It's crazy. Absolutely insane. I like it.'

They left when the sun went down; it was the best time to cross. There was only one problem, Orhan said. The sea had frozen over and they would need dogs to pull them across. Some areas were thick with ice and safe to traverse, but others were too thin for a sled; they could fall straight through and drown. They would only find out, he said cheerily, once they started.

The plan was to go from Sandhammaren in Southern Sweden and cross to the Danish island of Bornholm, where they would get a chance to warm up, be handed over to another guide and get fresh dogs.

On a map, the journey is fifty miles. A pack of dogs can cover twenty miles in an hour. Crossing a frozen sea with dogs, Orhan explained, was less risky than by boat on open sea. The dogs would be faster, so they would spend less time exposed to Nazi spotter planes.

The most dangerous point would be as they approached land again near Kolobrzeg, in Poland. The Germans patrolled with planes, and huge searchlights scanned the ice from the shore. The only good thing was that they were looking for refugees going the other way. Nevertheless, a dot on the ice was still a dot that could be seen.

At this point in the journey, they would need to start walking. Dogs barking would draw too much attention. They would be cut free. Orhan didn't explain how they would avoid being spotted or machine-gunned to pieces. He said he had a plan for that.

They left on schedule as soon as it got dark. In winter that is three in the afternoon. All things going well, he told them optimistically, they would be in Poland before midnight. That presupposed all things would go well.

Orhan packed the sled so high, there was barely room for Alina or Olga to clamber on board. As well as trafficking his human cargo, Orhan did a roaring trade in black-market food, morphine, visas, furs, coffee and anything else someone was willing to pay the right price for. War turned every racketeer into a one-man Switzerland, trading with anyone who would pay, preferably with gold. Some customers were Poles, others Jews and Nazis. It made no difference to Orhan.

They made good progress across the ice. The wind roared in their ears and it was viciously cold. In late January 1942, between Sandhammaren and Kolobrzeg, the night-time temperature was between minus 20° and minus 30°.

At such a temperature, the lungs fill with tiny crystal shards. The eyes secrete tears that turn to ice, and eyeballs are coated with a thin sheen of frost. No wonder Orhan thought it necessary to stop on Bornholm to defrost his passengers. If they arrived dead, he didn't get paid.

The first half of the journey was uneventful. Even though Orhan suggested they smear themselves in lard, Olga refused. The intense cold, exacerbated by the wind-chill, forced Alina and Olga to burrow beneath several layers of Orhan's smuggled furs. How Orhan managed to stand at the front of the sled, running the dogs without turning to stone himself was a mystery. A flask of brandy must have helped.

At Bornholm, everything changed.

# 7

## *The Frozen Sea*

The sled approached the island, where lights flickered in distant windows. For some reason, Bornholm had not bothered to black out from Allied bombers. That should have been a warning to Olga. Searchlights sashayed dramatically across the frozen sea in random sweeps, like the start of a Broadway show.

Bornholm was not the deserted stop-off point that Orhan had led Olga to believe. It was a heavily fortified Nazi stronghold; a key strategic panopticon in the middle of the Baltic. From Bornholm, the entire sea was controlled by the Nazis. They could watch the Baltic from every direction.

Bornholm's commander, Kampz, was legendary in the German army for his lunacy. He later became famous for refusing to surrender to the Russians, even when completely surrounded by gunships. Kampz demanded reinforcements be sent from Berlin to defend his rock. They should fight to the death, Kampz bellowed to his soldiers, and if Hitler's bunker fell, Bornholm would be the last outpost of the Third Reich. Kampz later changed his mind and said he would surrender, but only to a lone British officer. Never a Russian.

Olga became increasingly anxious as their sled approached Bornholm. Searchlights criss-crossed the ice. He told Olga to remain calm. Orhan had arranged to meet their 'contact' – the next sled that would take them on to Poland – at a deserted inlet on the north side of the island.

But Orhan had miscalculated. They were on the south side of the island, nowhere near their meeting point. He had directed them near the Luftwaffe runway instead, the most heavily defended part of Bornholm. It was a massive cock-up.

*'What did you do?'*

*Even the waitresses at Cartons are all ears. My mum is munching her way through an apple strudel.*

*'What?' she finally says, through a mouthful of pastry.*

*'What did you do?'*

*'Oh, we walked.'*

The sled came to a juddering halt a couple of thousand yards off shore.

'What do we do now?' Olga asked.

'You take these,' Orhan said, pulling a white bed sheet out of a rucksack.

They began tracking by foot across the ice, one step in front of the other. It was so cold, Alina could no longer feel any of her limbs. The cold was burning a fire deep inside each of them, powering them across the ice.

Suddenly the wind dropped and there was silence. The only noise my mum could hear was a deep, methodical thumping; it was her heart beating. They walked in single file. Then they heard the plane.

It was a distant, tinny sound at first, but as it approached, its engine grew relentlessly louder. On its wing, close to the cockpit, was a searchlight that pierced the dark. It shone directly onto the ice, which acted like a mirror; the single light becoming a thousand searchlights, each refracting off the undulations and indents of the gnarled surface. The plane's searchlight turned night into day.

It was the most terrifying moment of Alina's life. They had been lucky so far escaping death, but this cancelled everything. The plane was a Luftwaffe reconnaissance light aircraft, out on a scout. As it approached the three crouching figures on the ice, the searchlight on its wing became impossible to hide from; without realising, my mum urinated in her pants.

Luck plays a huge part in whether you live or die in war, Alina says, and maybe it is the only thing that matters. The pilot had an apparently infinite plain of ice before him. The procedure for Luftwaffe reconnaissance on Bornholm laid down by Commander Kampz was that they were to pepper the search area with machine-gun fire at regular intervals, to smoke out any movement. If they saw people running for their lives, they must double-back and finish the job.

Orhan knew that Olga and Alina would panic as the plane approached. It was not a weakness, it was what everyone did; he had seen it many times. In a single balletic flourish, he threw the white sheet over all three of them.

He was so calm, he looked like a waiter in a French bistro. It was so fast, my mum didn't know it had even happened. One moment they were standing exposed on the ice waiting to be shot at, the next lying flat on the ground with a bed sheet over them.

The reconnaissance plane was firing uncreatively in regular ten-second bursts, hoping to scare any fugitives into scurrying away. It flew fast and low, and as it approached, my mum lay still under the bedsheet. Orhan stared intently at his boots, as if he had only just noticed their fascinating stitching for the first time.

It was down to Olga to pray to God. She jabbered a half-remembered religious incantation to herself, crossing herself in complicated ways and weeping quietly beneath the sheet. Alina could smell her breath. She heard nothing but a rushing sound in her head, like a huge wave building high above them, before crashing down to destroy them all.

The plane shrieked as it passed over, low enough to lift the sheet clean off the three bodies on the ice. The group were exposed like plucked chickens. At the moment they were revealed, the pilot climbed steeply away, content that there was no one below.

Orhan's incompetence had saved them. Had he gone on course, they'd have been on a known smuggler route and the pilot would have paid more attention. He had not anticipated finding refugees less than a quarter of a mile from the Luftwaffe runway on Bornholm; least of all, travelling towards Nazi-occupied Poland. It was too stupid to be attempted. The plane's engine receded, and Orhan instructed Olga and Alina to wait on the ice.

'What? After all that?'

'He told us to wait on the ice.' *My mum launches into a scone with her knife.* 'He said he'd go ahead and find a safe house. Then come back and get me and my mother. He never came back.'

'What?'

'He left us there.'

*One of the waitresses, Ursula, cannot contain herself.*

'He never came back? Why not?'

*Alina looks pityingly at her audience.* 'Why would he? If you were a smuggler, would you come back? No.'

Orhan knew the Nazi guards on Bornholm; he traded in everything with them – goods, people, and best of all, information. Orhan calculated that if he was not going to make it safely across with these mad Poles (who wanted to go *back* to Poland), he could sell them out to the Gestapo the moment he stepped on to Bornholm. That is why he left my mum and grandmother on the ice; his best market option at that point was to check out of the game.

Alina and Olga wandered back to a trunk filled with their clothes, which had been abandoned on the ice, and sat down in the middle of the frozen Baltic Sea.

'Where are the dogs?' Alina asked Olga.

'He must have cut them loose before he pulled the sheet,' Olga said dispiritedly. They didn't even have the means to pull the sled. It was not looking good. Then something happened that might make you believe in God, or perhaps in the good fortune that follows the lucky wherever they go.

A sled came.

It trundled across the ice from the direction of Poland and was heading for Bornholm. Whoever was riding it was incredibly stupid, because they had a lantern swinging from side to side. They may as well have put up a giant flare, my mum thought, spelling out the letters: COME AND KILL ME.

Olga had a decision to make. She didn't trust the smuggler to return, but why trust the people on this sled either? She and her daughter were now so close to hypothermia, she needed to do something, and fast. Without thinking, Olga lit her own lantern and began swinging it crazily.

Believing this to be the signal from the people they were supposed to be meeting, the other sled diverted course sharply and began approaching Olga and my mum. When Olga saw them coming, she began waving her arms like a castaway on a tropical island. It was a risky gambit, for it was quite possible that the Gestapo would see the two lantern lights and send another plane out to machine-gun the whole lot of them. No one on either sled was aware of the huge risk they were taking.

The lantern got closer until eventually the sound, smell and heat of dogs was upon them, and a train of huskies stopped in a great cloud of steam. The whole charabanc emitted a strong smell of hot stew, which my mum remembers as the most heavenly thing she had ever smelt.

There were six people on the sled and it had taken them a couple of hours to get to Bornholm. They had hurtled across the ice from Poland and the dogs were in another league from the ones that pulled my mum and Olga to Bornholm. These were Siberian huskies: the apex ice traveller. They had run flat out for two hours and were still jumping off the ground, hungry for more running; their wolf eyes glinting in the lantern light.

'They were Ashkenazi.'

'Who?'

'The family. They were Ashkenazi Jews.'

'And what did you do?'

'We lied. We said we were their contact. What were we supposed to do?'

'You had no sled, no dogs, you must have looked a bit suspicious sitting there on a trunk in the middle of the ice.'

'We told them that we had been double-crossed by our guide, which was true. The man, he wasn't concerned by that. He just said, "What the hell are you doing?" My mother explained that we were going from Sweden to Warsaw to look for my brothers and sister.'

The man was a solemn-looking doctor from Munich, who had left Germany in 1934 with his family, only to see his new home of Poland go the way of Nazi Germany and begin persecuting Jews again.

'They are dead,' the doctor told Olga. 'Your children are bound to be dead. Have you any idea what you are doing? You don't, so I will tell you. You are going to die. What kind of mother takes her daughter from safety into hell?'

Olga was indignant but said nothing, because she knew he was right.

'You are an irresponsible woman,' the doctor continued. 'Go if you must to Warsaw but leave the little girl with us. We will take her back to Sweden, and you go on. But do not take her.'

The doctor's wife had ladled stew into a bowl for my mum, kept warm by a stove held tight in the slats of the sled. She put Alina under blankets and spoke Yiddish to Olga. Alina understood only a few words, but she knew for sure they were talking about her, and it was about her future.

'For the love of God,' the wife told her. 'If not you, her.' The same phrase was repeated over and over by the woman. 'If not you, her.'

It was a plea from one mother to another. It sounded to my mum like a lullaby, sung gently to put her to sleep. Alina was overwhelmed by tiredness and began to doze in the woman's arms. As she drifted off, she could hear the woman imploring Olga: 'Madam, please. Save the girl. Save the girl. Save the girl.'

*'What did you want to do?' I ask my mum, eighty years later.*

*'What do you think? I wanted to go! Christ, these people wanted to save me! They could see what danger we were going into. They had just escaped and here we were, my stupid mother, taking us straight into it.'*

*My mum takes a sip of tea.*

*'You know what I thought?'*

*'No.'*

*'I thought, God forgive me. This woman, this woman, should be my mother.'*

Alina's actual mother, Olga, was having none of it. She ate their stew, warmed herself by the stove and declined the doctor's kind offer to save her daughter's life.

In the meantime, the German family's intended contact spotted the group on the ice and diverted course to join them. The doctor and his family quickly departed for Sweden, but without Alina. Sensing a business opportunity, the family's original guide told Olga he could take them back on his sled to Poland, for a price. It was an easy decision. She tore open the lining of her coat and pulled out more roubles. They sped across the ice south, the Siberian huskies driving them back to Poland.

Alina wanted more than anything for her mother to be proved wrong. She loved her brothers and sister, but also hoped secretly that a big bomb had fallen on their heads. Then she could finally have her mother all to herself. If they were dead, Olga would see the error of her ways, repent to Alina and be forced to do the right thing for the first time in her life. Love her daughter.

## *January/February 1942, Kolobrzeg to Warsaw*

Olga and Alina crossed a country they scarcely recognised. The Nazis had poured kerosene over Poland and set light to it. Every town they passed through was a burnt husk – a collection of charred objects arranged on the blackened ground, some of which had once been alive. My mum had seen mutilated bodies in Siberia, but not on this scale.

They lay piled against the side of the road mixed in with the black, oily snow; hung from trees in stilted poses, or stood against crucifixes in fields like melting scarecrows. Murdered by the Gestapo for collaborating with the resistance, or the other way round, traitors murdered by the Polish Home Army.

The dead were less disturbing than the living: young women sitting naked outside their homes covered in scratches and mud, laughing at nothing in particular, or people going about their daily business as if everything before their eyes was a mirage. A well-dressed man was meticulously cutting the neat hedge outside his house, even though his home was now a smoking ruin.

On a bright February morning in 1942, Olga and Alina arrived in Warsaw. It had taken them nearly four weeks to get from Kolobrzeg on the Polish Baltic to the capital, a distance of almost 500 kilometres.

*'I think you aren't describing it properly.'*

'What do you mean?'

*My mum has been unhappy for some time with the way I've described these sections.*

'Well, this journey. You should have said that the journey is normally quick. The Nazis had the trains running well. It was because I was really sick, and we had to stay in Kolobrzeg for nearly three weeks for me to recover. That's why it took nearly a month. You've made out that it's because of all the destruction that it took so long.'

'But there was all this destruction. You described it to me.'

'Some villages were destroyed, others were fine. Why do you keep having to make it all sound so terrible?'

'Wasn't it terrible?'

'I keep telling you. It was a war. Terrible things happened, but I was with my mother, we were doing these things together and that made me happy. That's the truth. I enjoyed the fact we were together.'

'And when you got to Warsaw?'

'It all changed.'

'What happened?'

'It was early morning, 6 a.m. when we arrived. The city was quiet. We went straight to the flat.'

'What were you thinking you'd find?'

'My mother was terrified. She was always silent when she was fearful. She had been up all night reading her bloody tarot cards. They didn't tell her what she wanted, so she kept turning them.'

'What did she want them to say?'

'What kind of stupid question is that? She wanted to know she'd find her children alive.'

*February 1942, Warsaw*

Alina had not seen her brothers and sister for three years. They pushed open the heavy door to the street and climbed the stairs. The building was exactly as my mum had remembered it; unopened post sat in small metal trays, with some letters dating back to 1939. The apartment block had not been destroyed, as Michael was told by the AK. It was very much standing.

'What if they're not here?' Alina whispered nervously to Olga as they climbed the stairs.

'They are,' Olga said.

Olga had embarked on the seemingly suicidal journey from Sweden to Warsaw because she knew her children were alive. The cards had foretold it. They may have wobbled at the last moment, but generally the cards augured well. In that big, empty room in the Red Cross hospital, three cards, pulled at random from the deck, told her all she needed to know.

The first was a fool, representing the past. It was – in tarot terms – a major arcana: a life-changing card.

*'The fool card does not mean you are fool,' my mum explains. 'The fool is wise, in that he is always guided by the knowledge that he really knows nothing. It's only people who think themselves wise who are real fools.'*

*'So what does the fool card mean?'*

*'Are you asking me what Olga took from it? I have some cards – I'll show you.'*

*My mum took a pack of tarot cards from a dressing table.*

*'What do you see?' she asks, showing me the fool card.*

*'A young man, on the edge of a cliff, gazing upwards.'*

*'And beside him?'*

*'A small white dog.'*

'The fool is about to embark on a long and dangerous journey. He is stepping off the cliff, but he is fearless, because he has no sense of the danger he is putting himself in. The fool card represents courage, and a new beginning. It's a very positive arcana.'

'And the dog?'

'That's me,' Alina said, laughing. 'The loyal companion, following the fool wherever he goes.'

The second card was another major arcana: the chariot, guided by six stars burning in the celestial firmament. Black and white sphinxes pull the chariot. The divination of the chariot is obvious to anyone: you are embarking on a long journey, both physical and metaphorical. The two sphinxes will pull in opposite directions, suggesting unbearable choices that will have to be faced.

The third card Olga drew was more troubling. It was a two of swords: a woman, dressed in a white robe, holds two long blades, crossed. She is blindfolded, meaning that she cannot see the way forward in life. The swords represent the duality of heart and mind, and being torn between them. In the distance are rocks (sure-fire trouble ahead) and a crescent moon – a sign that you will need to trust your emotions in these perilous moments.

'What was her problem with the two of swords?' I ask my mum.

'It can be a positive card, but Olga was obsessed with the fact she had failed to pull the four of swords instead.'

'Meaning?'

'The four of swords is peace of mind. Olga had drawn the four of swords so many times in her readings, she'd come to believe in the swords as literally representing her four children.'

'So if there were only two swords?'

'She thought it meant two of her children could be lost.'

★    ★    ★

Olga leant on the circular ivory doorbell of their second-floor apartment: the end of a journey of thousands of miles to be reunited with her children. The buzzer had barely any life in it, and the shrill noise dwindled pathetically to a faint dying whine the longer she pressed it. Olga looked anxiously at Alina, who looked at nothing.

Kazhik woke from a bad dream. He had been sitting in the kitchen alone, stirring his milky soup breakfast with a spoon. Initially, he thought the broken bell might be a neighbour. He didn't want to open the door in case it was a Nazi raid (he would find out soon enough if it was). Kazhik ignored the noise, but it kept on buzzing. Eventually, annoyed, he stood up and went over to the door. Kazhik stood perfectly still, straining to hear any whispering.

'*Klo to jest?* (Who is it?),' he said, with feigned courage.

'*Matka* (Mother),' Olga replied.

They stood in the kitchen and embraced.

'*What was it like, seeing them?' I ask my mum.*

'*It was amazing. My brother Kazhik was like a grown man. Tall. He was twelve. When I last saw him he'd only been nine. And he was now the man of the house.*'

'*Did you not feel anxious? The last time you'd seen them, they'd bullied you.*'

'*That was before. This was like the new life, reunited. My mother just sat on the chair, weeping. Pavel put his arm around her. Kazhik told me a joke and pinched my cheek. I remember finding it an odd thing to do, but he was a twelve-year-old boy. What was he supposed to do? I think he couldn't believe we were there. None of us could.*'

'*What about Juta?*'

'*She just stood there with her arms folded.*'

\*     \*     \*

There was no turning the clock back to 1939. No one wanted to go back anyway, because life in the family had been terrible. There were plentiful elephants in the room that day they reunited: Alina biting Kazhik; the sugarbowl incident that caused Olga and Alina to go back to the country; and whether they still believed Alina was adopted.

Kazhik had not forgiven Olga for abandoning them in Warsaw to fend for themselves. Their father was nowhere to be seen, and never mentioned. Was he dead? The children wanted to know. Kazhik, Pavel and Juta had formed a unit in their mother's absence, and Kazhik believed they had survived very well, thank you. They went to school, avoiding the *lapanka* death squads; they had fed, clothed and educated themselves. In truth, Hela had done all three.

Kazhik was the new master of the house. Following Alina and Olga's return, he made this clear by making a point of not listening to what his mother had to say about anything. Olga made suggestions about what to eat and he would laugh and walk out. Pavel, his elder lieutenant, followed Kazhik obediently.

Pavel and Kazhik spent hours in their bedroom and built a barricade of broomsticks and broken chairs preventing entry. They stole more boxes of ammunition from the school and hid them beneath the floorboards. No one knew what they were doing and they planned to keep it that way.

The school head, Madame Graminski, told Juta she was one of the most gifted pianists the school had ever seen and whatever the outcome of the war, she should go to the Paris Conservatoire de Musique. Juta beamed: she was shaping her own destiny. But now her mother had turned up and ruined everything. Juta was determined that she was going to get what she wanted.

Life coalesced into the three children versus two strangers. Kazhik, Juta and Pavel against Olga and Alina. The children continued to go to school and be taught how to become model

New Aryans. Olga and Alina stayed at home, unsure what to do. No one knew how to behave anymore and so an uneasy truce developed, with everyone keeping out of each other's way.

For Alina's part, she was just happy they were back together. She didn't think she would be, but she was; she forgave the others for calling her adopted and bullying her. Kazhik started to include her in their trips to the park, and began using Juta's nickname for Alina: *Alencu* or 'little sister'.

Juta gave Alina piano lessons: scales and endless *Für Elise*. In return, Alina told her about the Russian and Nazi soldiers that came to their country house at the beginning of the war, about the smuggler with the animal skins, the Swedish hospital and the sled across the ice. One day, Juta showed Alina her wardrobe full of beautiful clothes and asked her if she wanted to touch her dresses. It was like an Aladdin's cave to Alina.

'Where did you get all these clothes?' Alina asked her.

'A man at the school bought them for me.'

It was the SS officer with the greying temples. Alina said nothing and never mentioned it to Olga. She suspected Olga already knew.

Meanwhile, Hela busied herself with the practical necessities that no one else cared about: shopping, cleaning and making sure that this family who cared nothing for practical things had food on the table and clean beds to sleep in. Hela didn't have the luxury of self-reflection; she was too busy keeping the Basiaks, and therefore her own family, alive.

*April 1942, Warsaw*

Alina was sent to the *komplety* school with her brothers and sister. Olga was invited to meet Madame Graminski, who told her what an inspiration Juta and Kazhik had been to her other pupils.

Olga laughed. 'What? Them?'

The old Bavarian soldier got up from the corner of the room and hobbled over to Olga, and then clasped her hand with his own shaking hands.

'*Diene shone, frau, sind meine shone.*' ('Your sons, madam, are my sons.')

Alina hated her time in the school and could not believe what her brothers and sister had become. She sat in German lessons and refused to say a word, whilst Juta parroted back her German vocabulary with perfect diction.

As they took their lessons, the AK resistance that Michael was helping to train in London were being parachuted into Poland. They laid explosives and destroyed bridges, power lines and railways. In Warsaw, AK agents assassinated a number of high-profile SS commanders and blew up death-squad lorries.

The Gestapo began sweeps of residential properties, looking for AK safe houses. If one was found, the family harbouring the partisans were shot or hanged in the street, then every resident in the same street would be herded into the road and machine-gunned as an example to others.

One night, a number of AK safe houses were uncovered across Wola, where Hela and her family lived. Hela spent three nights a week in the Basiak apartment, and did not know what was happening to the district where her family lived. Death squads moved in with machine guns mounted on the back of trucks and shot hundreds of Wola's residents, before lighting the bodies with kerosene. Women were raped and children burnt alive on the pyre of dead. It was a taste of what was to come for everyone in Warsaw.

The Gestapo carried out a city-wide sweep for partisans. The first Olga and her family knew about it was the furious banging of rifle butts on the door. Hela opened the latch and was thrown to the ground, punched in the face with a gun as the Gestapo pushed through the door.

They passed through the apartment like a whirlwind, as if terror was the point, rather than finding anything. Olga was also hit in the face, when she tried to ask one of the guards what was happening. Juta and the other children stood motionless in the dining room as the Gestapo swirled around them, smashing the last ornaments they owned and ripping open the beds and armchairs with knives.

When they had gone, Pavel and Kazhik rushed to their bedroom and lifted the floorboards. Their armoury of bullets remained undiscovered. Alina was standing in the doorway watching them.

'What are you doing?' she asked.

'What do you think we're doing?' Kazhik replied.

'I have no idea.'

'You'll find out soon enough,' Pavel said, and clasped arms with his brother.

The following day, Olga and Alina walked down to the red wall separating Aryan Warsaw from the Jewish ghetto. Everyone on the Aryan side knew what was happening to the Jews. Hela told them that local people had been smuggling food and throwing bread over the wall, but the increase in *lapanka* death squads now made helping the Jews too dangerous.

On that walk, Alina heard screams and gunfire from the Jewish ghetto. Rumours started that disease was rife – typhus and cholera – and this would soon spread to the rest of the city. A Polish man on the Aryan side was shot for trying to get clean water in to the Jews through a plastic pipe run along the sewer floor.

The Poles who had first seen blood oozing from the small drainage openings at the bottom of the wall now saw tiny children being squeezed through the same drains to scavenge for food and medicine on the Aryan side. Day by day, life was being choked out of the million Jews crammed into the ghetto. Their desperation to survive created a business opportunity for Poles and even some enterprising Nazis, who began selling food, medicine and escape over the wall, or through the sewers.

The ever-worsening situation in the ghetto made the offer of 'relocation' on trains to the east by the German administration too good to be true. People wanted to believe in salvation, so they did. The name for this place of salvation was never given, but some had heard a word being uttered in the ghetto for the first time: 'Auschwitz'.

# 8

## The Jewish Ghetto

*July 1942, Warsaw*

Juta had a secret.

She was meeting someone twice a week on the riverbank beneath Poniatowski bridge. Not the SS officer with the greying temples, but a boy her own age called Kacper, whom she had met when she was buying oranges in a shop in Mokotow. Kacper was sixteen, like Juta, and was a tall, gentle soul. He had a wave of long hair fringed across his face and spoke quietly and falteringly.

They had been meeting secretly for months. They would rendezvous at the same bench along the river each Wednesday and Saturday morning, hold hands and talk about how much they were in love and would go and live in Paris after the war. Juta said she was going to attend the Conservatoire de Musique and Kacper would become a writer.

My mum says Juta was very much in love and scared for Kacper, because the school had been receiving packages from the SS guard who had spoken to her so strangely at the concert. In the first was a pretty dress and a note.

'*Fur deinen nachsten konzert.*' ('For your next performance.')

More dresses had followed, and then more, each with a new note. Madame Graminski called Juta into her office one morning.

'Juta, you understand what this man wants?' she said.

'He is infatuated with me,' Juta replied, casually.

'You understand what will happen to my school if the SS go against me? They could close me down and end your piano career. God knows what they could do to your brothers.'

Juta stood before Madame Graminski listening patiently. Her eyes scanned the school head up and down. Madame Graminski's expensive woollen suit, the one she had bought from Chanel before the war, was looking frayed and stained around the hems and cuffs, as if tired itself of the strain of keeping up appearances.

Juta was aware for the first time in her life that she possessed power. A high-ranking Nazi was obsessed with her, Madame Graminski's livelihood was dangling by a thread and the future of her school was dependent on what Juta decided to do. All this power, and she had no clue what should happen.

'I understand,' Juta replied slowly, but she didn't.

Madame Graminski looked straight at Juta.

'I will protect you, Juta, no matter what happens. The Nazis are animals and will stop at nothing to get what they want. When this war is over and Poland and the allies have defeated them, I want you to go out into the world and become the greatest concert pianist that has ever lived.'

Juta ran over and hugged Madame Graminski for the first and last time. They never spoke of the SS officer again. When he called unannounced at the school to see Juta, Madame Graminski told him that Juta had been horribly disfigured in an Allied bombing raid and would not be returning to the school. The SS officer never called again or sent another dress.

*19 April 1943, Warsaw*

Alina and her sister sat side by side at the piano, the drawing room flooded with light. Alina was having a lesson and it was going badly. Each time she played a note wrong, Juta put her hand across Alina's and stopped her: '*Jeszcze raz* (Again)'. From the window they could see the park, yellow with a carpet of daffodils. It was a perfect spring day and the windows were open.

The first thing they smelt were the flames; the burning of wood and oil drums. Juta and Alina got up from the piano and looked out. The Jewish ghetto was on fire. Juta touched Alina's hand and gestured her back to the piano.

'Again,' she said.

Alina sat back obediently and looked at the page. The notes were a blur. Juta pointed at a piece on the next page, a polka.

'Play.'

'Are you serious? You want me to play a merry dance and this is happening?'

Juta looked at her sister and repeated herself. 'Play.'

Through the open windows of the city, everyone heard the screams and cries of Jews being murdered. Alina knew exactly what the flames meant, and so did Juta.

As Alina played the jaunty polka, the sky turned redder, the air thick with acrid smoke. Twelve-year-old Alina was numb. She assumed that Juta was trying to distract her from the horror by playing this happy tune, but she felt complicit, providing musical accompaniment to the death of thousands of people.

Alina continued to hammer out the notes more heavily and crudely, turning the dance into a grotesque parody. It was her only way of protesting to Juta. She was disgusted that her sister had continued the piano lesson, but didn't say anything.

The fire in the ghetto began on the eve of Passover, fourteen months after my mum and Olga returned to Warsaw from Sweden. Two thousand Wehrmacht soldiers marched behind the wall of flames into the ghetto to complete *Grossaktion Warshau*. The erasing of Warsaw's Jewish population.

The burning of the ghetto was the culmination of 'the plan'. Nine months before it started, the SS began deporting the population of the ghetto to a mystery destination. Between 22 July and 21 September 1942, more than 310,000 people were rounded up in the Jewish ghetto and ordered to report to Umschlagplatz, the main square renamed in German, where they boarded trains. In total, a million Jews were deported from Warsaw without a clue where they were going.

They were told they were being taken out of the ghetto for their own safety, consistent with SS Gruppenführer Heydrich's theory of compliance. Jews needed to be tricked into thinking they were being 'resettled', he said, thus becoming unwitting cogs in the conveyor belt of death.

In January 1942, as my mum and Olga were travelling across Poland to Warsaw, Heydrich prepared to address the Wannsee Conference, a specially convened meeting of the party's senior officials and scientists in a mansion house in the suburbs of Berlin. At Wannsee, Heydrich told them how the 'final solution' to the 'Jewish problem' would be realised.

Heydrich was the Nazis' Nazi. More Aryan-looking than the rat-like Hitler or short-sighted weasel Goebbels. Colder and more cunning than Eichmann, yet also more *Total-Verrukt* (psychopathic or 'super crazy') than Himmler. There were no boundaries to Heydrich's insanity or calculating intelligence. His cool determination to erase every Jew off the face of the earth created awe even in Hitler. Rumours circulated in high-up Nazi circles that Heydrich had a secret and this was the reason he was such an anti-Semitic zealot. It was said that he was secretly Jewish himself and had been bullied at school for it.

When Himmler asked Hitler if the rumours were true, Hitler replied, 'Are you going to ask him?' Heydrich was not Jewish. But anti-Semitism, a thousand years in the making in middle Europe, had shamed the schoolboy Heydrich too. The only way he could show his taunting classmates that he wasn't Jewish was to wipe out every last one.

In 1941, Hermann Goering wrote a memo to Heydrich. The practicalities of relocating Europe's Jews to Madagascar or Palestine were impossible, he said. Mass shootings were inefficient, as were the gas wagons. What was required was a system of mass murder that minimised emotional distress to the German soldiers. Heydrich was tasked with organising it.

'I ... charge you', Goering said, 'with submitting to me promptly an overall plan of the preliminary organisational, practical and financial measures for the execution of the intended final solution of the *Endlosung der Judenfrage* (Jewish Problem).'

The Wannsee Conference was Heydrich's chance to go down in history as the 'architect' of the Holocaust, but he was less vain than his superiors imagined. He lacked even this human weakness, because there was nothing human within him. Heydrich was like the Greek myth of the Hydra, whose name he subliminally conjured, the serpent with many poisonous heads. Chop one off and another simply grew back, more vicious and powerful than before. He was the ultimate monster.

The Holocaust was a collaboration between the inner sanctum of the Nazi party. The outcome of group-think. But they all knew – from the top down – that Heydrich would be the one to make it happen. The first thing Heydrich said was that Warsaw was to be the fulcrum around which the 'final solution' would pivot.

As my mother and Olga were crossing the frozen Baltic Sea, Heydrich put the finishing touches of his address together. The extermination camps – Belsen, Treblinka, Dachau, Auschwitz – would be merely the beginning of an extermination programme for all non-Aryan peoples. First the Jews, next the Russians, then a world holocaust of all 'degenerate' races. The planet, Heydrich believed, would be purified by fire so it could begin again.

As the flames from the Warsaw ghetto began to consume the old town, people began going up to Krasinski Square, close to the ghetto, to see what was happening. Juta, Kazhik and Alina didn't go.

*'Why?' I ask my mum. 'Why didn't you go?'*

*'Because the burning of the ghetto was a tragedy. Not an entertainment, or a spectacle.'*

What Poles believed to be the beginning of the end of the ghetto was, in fact, the start of the Jewish uprising, the most extraordinary fight back in human history. When the Wehrmacht marched on the ghetto, the Jewish resistance were waiting. German soldiers were greeted not by defeated people broken by starvation, but a rain of Molotov cocktails, home-made grenades and metal pipes, thrown from sewers, alleyways and windows.

The SS commander in charge of the burning of the ghetto, Von Sammern-Frankenegg, was forced to retreat, leaving behind fifty-nine German casualties and two burnt-out armoured cars. When news reached Berlin, Himmler was incandescent with rage. Sammern-Frankenegg was relieved of his post and replaced by SS Brigadeführer Jurgen Stroop, chosen for his brutality on the eastern front.

Stroop's first decision, at Himmler's prompting, was the immediate 'liquidation' of the ghetto. The Wehrmacht were to put down the uprising by systematically destroying anyone living; every building was to be obliterated one by one, street by street.

The uprising by the Jews of the ghetto was not a spontaneous act of desperation. It had been a long time in the planning. The two main underground resistance groups in the ghetto, the ZZW (Jewish Military Union) and ZOB (Jewish Fighting Organisation) were trained and armed for three years by the government-in-exile in London, the AK.

When it began, my grandfather Michael sat with the rest of the AK by the telephone waiting for news. Those fighting in the ghetto knew the result from the start. Marek Edelman, a ZOB commander, told recruits they were rising up not to win a military victory, but to reclaim their humanity before inevitable execution. 'To pick', he said, 'the time and place of our deaths.'

They were prompted to fight by the realisation that 'resettlement' was a lie, and their real destination was the death camps. When Adam Czerniakow of the Jewish Council realised he had been duped into helping send fellow Jews to their death by cooperating with the SS 'resettlement', he committed suicide.

Rumours had circulated in the ghetto of the death camps ever since Witold Pilecki, one of the AK's founders, volunteered to infiltrate the newly opened Auschwitz in 1941. Pilecki smuggled himself in as a prisoner and then organised a resistance group within the camp, sending messages to the government-in-exile detailing the atrocities unfolding. These were relayed to the French, English and American governments, who all did nothing.

*April 1943, London*

In London, Michael met a woman called Marta. She was an AK agent and one of the government-in-exile's most respected fighters. Marta had trained with the famous Major Zofia Franio and her second-in-command Antonina Mijal, code name 'Tosia'.

These formidable women led an AK all-female sapper unit, one of the most feared fighting machines in Poland. They ran a dozen explosive factories dotted around Warsaw and created insurgent cells across the country. They were responsible for planting hundreds of bombs on German train lines and attacking arms depots.

Marta was sent into Nazi-occupied Poland three times to train partisan cells against the Germans, returning to England through the underground network of safe houses. When she met Michael, she was working with Major Sikorski to persuade the British government to bomb the train lines to the concentration camps directly.

The Allies had known about the camps since 1941, when Pilecki first infiltrated Auschwitz. In spite of mounting knowledge of the Holocaust over the next two years, nothing continued to be done.

In 1941, my dad was a schoolboy in Edgware, north London. He remembers being given a leaflet by a friend whose father was a bomber pilot. It was one of thousands being dropped on Germany as part of an Allied propaganda drive. The leaflet showed a picture of prisoners in pyjamas with chimneys belching smoke and a promise that if Germany surrendered, 'this killing can be stopped'. Clearly people knew, either what was happening, or what was about to.

By 1942, following Heydrich's 'final solution' address at Wannsee, the Allies already had documented proof that two million Jews had been murdered, and a further five million were at imminent risk of extermination. But it did not suit their political plans to get involved.

The British Foreign Secretary, Anthony Eden, spoke before Parliament in December 1942, stating what was by then common knowledge within the inner circles of Westminster: 'The German authorities, not content with denying ... the Jewish race elementary human rights ... are now carrying into effect Hitler's oft-repeated intention to exterminate the Jewish people.'

But in March 1943, only four months later, Viscount Cranbourne, a minister in Churchill's war cabinet, told his fellow ministers that Jews should not be considered a 'special case'. The British empire, he said, was already 'too full of refugees to offer a safe haven'. The British priority was holding on to what was left of its empire and not opening up British-controlled Palestine to a mass influx of Jews, jeopardising British strategic interests in the area. By liberating the concentration camps, he said, they would create a migrant crisis.

So nothing was done, and it was not only the British who were reluctant to stop the Holocaust. US President Franklin D. Roosevelt's envoy to the United Nations War Crimes Commission, Herbert Pell, tried to bring the mass genocide of Jews, Poles and Romany gypsies before the UN and was blocked by the State Department.

Pell later said the State Department were concerned with maintaining good relations with Germany after the war to thwart Soviet ambitions across Europe. If the Nazis were forced to surrender, proceedings against war criminals could compromise post-war relations with Germany. The State Department did not want to take the risk.

Anti-Semitism was also in play. It wasn't just the State Department that prevented action (Roosevelt was twice talked out of bombing the railway line to Auschwitz by officials in the State Department). The *New York Times*, a Jewish-owned paper, was pressurised by Capitol Hill to under-report or bury stories about Auschwitz and Treblinka.

Whether it was anti-Semitism or strategic considerations or both that drove the Allied agenda, it amounted to the same thing.

Nothing was done.


*May 1943, London*

Marta and Michael began an affair. They met at his cramped King's Cross flat, with the curtains covered in railway soot from the station, and the sound of the steam trains chugging out ten an hour, night and day, transporting supplies the length of

Britain. They slept in his single bed, smoked cigarettes and drank *Kawa Plujka*, Polish coffee made with grounds and hot water.

Michael told Marta that he had once had a family. They lived in the forest, and now they were dead. Three of his children, he believed, were blown up in Warsaw. His wife and youngest daughter were in Siberia. He had organised their escape to Sweden, and although they had reached there, they had since disappeared and were presumed dead too.

Marta listened intently. She was tall and serious, with shoulder-length dark hair and strong, dramatic features. She had Iranian blood, she told Michael, though no idea how many generations ago. He laughed at that, which he didn't do very often.

Marta came from Katowice in Silesia, not far from the Czechoslovak border. She had trained as a draughtswoman in a small engineering firm. When war broke out, she told her family she was joining the army to fight for Poland. Three days after signing up, her family were killed by friendly fire during the Nazi advance. A Polish mortar accidentally hit their apartment block, killing her parents and two sisters.

Marta joined the AK and began as a courier, relaying messages between spies and insurgents in Katowice. In 1940, AK colonel Stefan Rowecki said that women should be fighting shoulder to shoulder with men, not sending messages. The Women's Military Service was created as part of the AK and Marta received training in hand-to-hand combat.

Marta knew many legendary women of the resistance. Couriers like Anna Zakrzewska, known as 'White Hannah', and Stefania Grzeszczak, code name 'Swist', who traversed the ghetto delivering orders from one battalion to another.

Michael talked a lot about fighting, but Marta had actually killed Nazis. The resistance in the ghetto had one big advantage over the Nazis, she told him. They knew the ghetto inside out

– every rooftop vantage point for a sniper, every cut-through, alleyway, attic, basement or tunnel (and where it led).

Marta was right. As the Nazis blundered into the ghetto to 'liquidate' the Jewish uprising, the resistance retreated, absorbed into the old town. ZOB fighters holed themselves up in bunkers, cellars and hiding places under the rubble. When they were discovered by sniffer dogs, the Nazis threw in smoke bombs, and then incinerated the occupants with flame-throwers as they stumbled out coughing.

Each day, news reached Michael and Marta in London that the ghetto uprising was slowly but surely being crushed. The government-in-exile had long debated the timing of an uprising against the Nazis, but the Jews of the ghetto had decided for them. The time was now.

## 8 May 1943, Warsaw

In spite of being outnumbered 150 to one, the Jewish uprising held out against the Wehrmacht for three weeks. On 8 May 1943, the Germans discovered a large dug-out at Mila 18 Street. It was the ZOB's last hiding place. SS commander Stroop was tempted to capture resistance leader Mordechaj Anielewicz alive, in order to hang him and display his body to the rest of Warsaw as a warning.

Anielewicz refused to be captured. He didn't want to be tortured and give up names of comrades, so he swallowed a cyanide capsule and was found by German dogs. Two boys climbed onto the roof of the main building in the old town square and raised two flags: the red and white Polish flag, and the blue and white banner of the Jewish resistance group, the ZZW. It was a signal to the whole of Warsaw. The flags were visible from the Aryan side so every Pole could see them, and they flew side by side for four days.

Olga and the children saw the flags like everyone else. People gathered in Krasinski Square and sang the Polish national anthem in defiance of the Gestapo, who watched them.

*I ask my mum what it was like standing there, watching the ghetto burn.*

'We knew. Everyone knew what this meant now. They were finishing the Jews and they refused to die. This was bravery. True bravery. The Jews had been crushed, and yet they were fighting back. They would inspire the whole city to rise up. This was their gift to humanity, to the world. To fight.

'We on our side of Warsaw had not suffered a tenth, a hundredth of what they had suffered – and yet still they were rising up. They had nothing. Absolutely nothing. And yet still they had the guts to do this.

'What did I think? That's what you ask? Shame on the Nazis, and shame on us for not fighting before now. The Jews changed everything. They inspired everyone. Now, we will fight.'

The elite AK *Kedyw* unit attacked the German sentry posts guarding the ghetto wall, planting explosives to breach it at six different points from the Aryan side. Jews and gentiles – men, women and children – now fought either side of the wall to destroy the coffin of the ghetto.

SS commander Stroop, aware that the resistance movement was gaining strength across Warsaw, offered the uprising leaders the opportunity to surrender themselves. Their reply was a round of AK gunfire and a handful of dead Germans. The SS now knew they faced a city-wide rebellion against their authority. They turned for the first time on 'Aryan Poles' and began shooting anyone seen to be part of a 'collaboration' with the Jewish uprising.

At the *komplety* school, Pavel and Kazhik broke into the ammunition room to grab whatever was left, but the old Bavarian monitor was waiting for them with a gun.

'You!' he shouted at the boys. '*Mein jungs!*' ('My boys!')

He knelt on the floor and cried. Pavel and Kazhik stood before the crippled German, unsure what to do. Then Madame Graminski appeared and put her arm around the old soldier to comfort him; the veteran was sobbing uncontrollably. She gestured for Pavel and Kazhik to go, so the boys quickly took their ammunition and left. The old Bavarian was too heartbroken even to report the boys to the Nazis.

The Wehrmacht and Gestapo were not so charitable. They began a policy of 'dissuasion': shooting and torturing whole streets of families on the 'Aryan' side of the city where resistance fighters were found, in order to extinguish any chance of the Jewish ghetto uprising inspiring a wider revolt across Warsaw.

Far from a defeat, the Jewish ghetto uprising was one of the greatest victories of the war, perhaps all wars. They had known from the start that there was no chance of winning, yet still they fought. With no hope, they lit a touch paper that would ignite across the city.

Three days after the ZOB HQ at Mila 18 Street was captured, a man clambered out of a manhole cover on the Aryan side of Warsaw. It was Marek Edelman, the last remaining commander of the Jewish insurgents. Edelman and a handful of survivors had used their knowledge of the sewer system to navigate an escape through the sluices and tunnels of subterranean Warsaw.

After the war, Edelman went back to college and studied to become a cardiologist. He went on to invent a life-saving surgical procedure that bore his name, treating thousands of patients over a forty-year career. In Warsaw, there is a mural of Marek Edelman at 9b Nowolipki Street, where he emerged from the sewer. On it are transcribed his words on escaping: 'The most important is life, and when there is life, the most important is freedom. And then we give our life for freedom.'

When Olga heard the Jewish uprising was crushed, she had the family sit down in the kitchen. She told them that they were now to stick together. No more separation. Whatever happened from now on, they were to agree on a plan of action together.

Alina had never heard Olga speak like this before. She believed it was because her mother was scared of what would happen next; she knew Kazhik and Pavel were going off each night and she had no control over her sons. The speech was an attempt to be taken seriously, but it sounded to the boys like a desperate plea.

Kazhik laughed at his mother.

'Are you joking?' he replied, scoffing at her. Kazhik was the leader now; when he spoke, he knew it was for all of them and his siblings would back him. 'Have you looked out of the window in the last month? The *Judischer Ordnungsdienst* are here now.'

In the ghetto, the feared recruits of this sadistic death squad had thrown people from balconies. They made Jews fight one another in the street for their entertainment and sing the German national anthem before being killed. Now they were doing the same across the whole of Warsaw. The family needed to prepare, Kazhik said, for what was to come.

The *lapanka* death squads would only get worse, he continued, rounding up and shooting anyone at will. Warsaw's inhabitants were no longer 'Aryan' Poles in the eyes of the Nazis; the reprogramming project had failed. They were just Poles, the *dungervolke* again. The people who came from shit, were made of shit and would return to the shit when they were pulverised. What the Nazis had done to Warsaw's Jews, Kazhik said, they would now do to us.

The twenty-year-old Pavel stood behind his younger brother, nodding his head sombrely in agreement with everything Kazhik said. When he mentioned Poles who had been 'fooled' by the Nazis, Kazhik looked pointedly at Juta, who stared impassively through him.

Olga had lost all authority. Alina could see it and felt sorry for her mother. She caught Pavel staring judgmentally at Juta.

'What are you looking at?' Alina said.

'Mind your own business,' Pavel replied, contemptuously.

Alina was undeterred. 'What do you know about Juta? You're the ones who had medals pinned on you by an old German soldier. You're the Nazis here, not us.'

'What do *you* know about Juta?' Kazhik cut back, sharp as a knife. 'You haven't been here for three years. Sitting in your Swedish hotel. What do you know about the war?'

The family sat staring at each other, battle lines drawn. Olga opened her mouth to intervene, but Kazhik could not be stopped.

'You know about Juta, do you Alina?' he continued sarcastically. 'Did you know that she received all those dresses from an SS commander? I bet you didn't know that! That your sister is a *kurwa*, a whore for the Nazis.'

Juta stepped over to Kazhik and slapped him hard across the face. He smiled and winced simultaneously. She then punched him in the stomach for good measure and he fell to the floor. Juta stood over Kazhik and pushed him with her shoe, so she could stare him properly in the face.

'Little boy,' she said. 'You don't understand anything. My boyfriend is called Kacper and he is a commander of *Kedyw*. You know what that means?'

Kazhik gulped and looked up at his big sister.

'It means that very soon, your life will be in his hands as *your* commanding officer. So I suggest you be a bit nicer to me.'

# 9

## Warsaw Uprising

*16 May 1943, Warsaw*

SS Commander Stroop celebrated the crushing of the Jewish ghetto by personally blowing up the Jewish synagogue on Tlomackie Street.

'What a wonderful sight!' he recalled in his diary. 'I called out "Heil Hitler!" and pressed the button. A terrific explosion brought flames right up to the clouds. The colours were unbelievable. An unforgettable allegory of the triumph over Jewry.' Thirteen thousand Jewish resistance fighters died in the uprising. The Germans lost little more than a dozen men.

Before the ghetto, Warsaw's Poles were treated very differently from their Jewish neighbours. Hitler had a dream that once 'Nazified', 130,000 hand-picked 'Germanised' residents would live in a new Warsaw rebuilt to look like a Bavarian fairytale village; whilst 80,000 Polish slaves (*Untermenschen*) would keep Warsaw functioning, living on the west bank of the Vistula in a shanty town. Polish children with the requisite Aryan features of blond hair and blue eyes would be taken from their families and given to childless Aryan couples.

Before the ghetto uprising, Poles were seen as convertible to Nazi ideology. After the ghetto, they were a lost cause to be destroyed; there was no longer a distinction between 'Aryan' and 'ethnic' Poles. Warsaw's residents had shown their true colours, Hitler said, by fighting alongside their Jewish neighbours. He now had a simple order for Stroop, kill them all.

Life was about to change dramatically for my family.

*June 1943, London*

In London, Marta and Michael behaved like a newly married couple. They strolled hand-in-hand through Hyde Park and along the Thames Embankment, with barrage balloons making dark shapes on the water, like the shadows of whales.

They would also walk from his King's Cross flat to dozens of meetings hastily convened by the AK. There were many factions and splinter factions who had long argued about when best to strike; but following the uprising in the Jewish ghetto, they were in agreement. The time was coming.

When Marta spoke at meetings, the room went quiet. She had fought behind enemy lines, blown up Nazis, and killed them with her own hands. She told the men in the room that Edelman, the leader of the Jewish ZOB resistance, had been right when he said the ghetto uprising was not a defeat, but a victory. It showed the world that the mighty Third Reich was not invincible.

The Nazis were not a colossal army of supermen, Marta told them; they were weak. Confronted by starving people in the ghetto with metal pipes and home-made bombs, Berlin had panicked. Imagine, Marta said, if Warsaw rose up as a whole.

*June 1943, Warsaw*

As she spoke, Hans Frank, the Nazi governor-general of Poland, dramatically increased the shootings and round-ups in the hope of smoking out AK resistance fighters. Olga was terrified for her children. Kazhik and Pavel were now out all night, turning the key slowly in the lock as dawn broke so as not to wake her. No one knew where they had been. Juta would meet at night with her boyfriend, Kacper, part of the *Kedyw*, the AK's elite insurgent corps.

Alina saw her mother through the crack in the kitchen door,

turning tarot cards without conviction on the table, scared witless that any of her children leaving the flat would never come back.

One day it was Olga who went to buy food and didn't come back. Alina was first to notice something was wrong. She ran to find Juta, who called the boys into the kitchen.

'When did you see her last?' Juta asked.

'About two o'clock,' answered Alina.

'And it's now nine?' There was only one conclusion.

'She's dead,' Kazhik said.

'Shut up!' Juta replied quickly, cutting off her brother mid-sentence.

They could hear the *lapanka* death squads shooting in the street outside. Plaintive rounds of machine-gun fire and commands to shoot more. There was silence in the flat. Juta took control and told them that they must prepare the evening meal, and carry on with what they were doing.

Each child tried separately to come to terms with the fact their mother was dead. They were now adults, alone together in the world. There was to be no mourning or crying, Juta declared, but in the corner, a quiet snivelling could be heard.

It was Pavel, now twenty years old. No one ever asked Pavel what he thought or felt about anything. He was the only actual man of the house, but to his brother and sisters, he was still a baby. Alina tried to put her arm round this giant and console him, but she couldn't reach across his shoulders.

At midnight, Olga let herself quietly back into the apartment. The children always wondered where she went that night, but no one ever asked her.

*My mum begins phoning me six times a day to ask me the same question.*

*'What have you done with my credit card?'*

*I know this is not who she really is, but the dementia talking. It is wrong to make her feel bad about behaviour that is not her fault. I answer the same every time.*

'Yes, I have it. No, I'm not using it.'

'What day is it?' she asks for the tenth time in an hour.

'Tuesday,' just like it was five minutes ago.

*At about midnight, she phones again.*

'Christ, what now?' I blurt out in exasperation. 'And no, I'm not using your credit card . . .'

'I was just phoning to say I remembered something you were asking about today. Olga rummaging through the house one night. I found her looking inside cupboards and turning over drawers, inside jars and jewellery boxes.'

'What was she doing?'

'She said she was looking for gold. She'd hidden it in the flat before we went back to the country. It was a lot. She forgot to tell the children or Hela, who I don't think she trusted.'

'So they sold everything in the flat to stay alive and all the time they had a small fortune hidden away?'

'That's right.'

'Why was she looking for it now? You were back in Warsaw and I'm supposing she didn't have any further plans to leave?'

'The tarot cards.'

'Of course.'

'They told her something terrible was about to happen.'

## Christmas Day 1943, Warsaw

Olga's fears were premature. After the crushing of the Jewish ghetto, even the Nazis expected the citizens of Warsaw would soon rise up against them. Their intelligence from London suggested the AK government-in-exile was priming the city for an insurrection, but for some reason, it didn't happen.

The desire of the citizens of Warsaw to expel the Nazis from their capital was immense, but as Christmas approached and after nearly four grinding years of war, so was the desire of ordinary Poles for some normality in their lives; even as the *lapanka* death squads continued to shoot women and children in the streets.

Olga was determined to give her family a Christmas they would remember, because lurking at the back of her mind was the fear that this could be their last: the imminent doom foretold by her wretched cards.

She asked Hela if she could buy the family a carp on the black market for *Wigilia*, the feast of twelve dishes traditionally held on Christmas Eve.

'Are you joking?' Hela said, incredulously. There were families catching and roasting rats to stay alive, and here was this ridiculous woman demanding a carp.

Before the war, the Basiak family celebrated Christmas Eve in their country house surrounded by dozens of candles, the floor scattered with hay, as was customary, gorging themselves on dumplings, sauerkraut, mushroom soup and *golabki* (cabbage rolls). There would be party games, and songs around the piano. They would then eat poppy-seed cake and *piernik* (gingerbread) before making the freezing journey to church for midnight mass.

In Warsaw, Olga and her three children sat around a bare Christmas table with a tin of sardines and some bread and lard that Hela had managed to procure from a black marketeer. There was a single candle in the middle of the table and a spare chair, as was also traditional, for an unexpected visitor. Alina prayed that her father would walk magically through the door and whisk them away from war forever.

They sat in silence, the sound of chewing as the only interruption. Olga asked her children if they could remember their beautiful home in the country, and the Christmases they had spent there. Silence.

'What about the Christmas of 1938? Surely you remember what happened then?'

Kazhik shrugged his shoulders, but Alina perked up.

'I remember it,' she said. In truth, they all did.

Every winter, snow would cut their forest off from the outside world. In these snowbound winter months, wolves would come near the house because they could smell the horses in the stable. Hungry wolves were known to dig under the fence and take down a horse, pulling it from the neck and devouring chunks of the steaming meat before the alarm went up. It was an occupational hazard of living in the depths of a forest.

On this Christmas Eve of 1938, bellies full from their twelve-course feast, the Basiaks strode out into the sub-zero night and clambered onto their sled for the long journey to midnight mass, held in the Russian Orthodox church, some six miles away. The sled was piled high with thick blankets to keep them warm, the driver holding a flaming torch to ward off wolves. By his side was a rifle, in case the flame was not enough to scare them away.

As the sled rushed through the forest, the stars erupted across the clear sky. Trees cracked loudly from the cold, with bark splintering off and pinging like shrapnel. The steaming breath of the galloping horses turned to ice crystals the instant their breath hit the air. Then the wolves came from nowhere. There was no warning, no howls, only their blazing eyes rushing out from the darkness.

The horses reared up, the sled jack-knifing. A wolf lunged, but the old man who drove the sled was faster, the flint of his firing rifle illuminating the forest like a party sparkler. The wolf was killed in an instant, the rest scattering back into the gloom, whimpering.

When, some half an hour later, my mother spotted the gleaming onion spire of the Russian Orthodox church through the trees, she had never been happier. They were alive, and what's more, the enemy had been vanquished.

'Yes, mother,' Alina said, as they sat together around their bare table in Warsaw. 'I remember that Christmas well.'

'To kill a wolf,' Kazhik said, between mouthfuls of bread, 'you need a gun.'

'And bullets,' Pavel added.

The children nodded in agreement as they munched their sardines. They said nothing more.

## 6 June 1944, London

By June 1944, the people of Warsaw were growing in confidence against the Nazis. They had listened on their radios to the fall of Stalingrad in 1943. Now, on 6 June, they heard live coverage of the D-Day landings at Normandy. The Allies were coming from the west, the Russians from the east, and nothing would halt either. The Germans were losing the war.

The London government-in-exile accelerated their plans for the long-anticipated city-wide AK uprising of Warsaw. They were now in a race with another government-in-exile, the Soviet puppet regime in Lublin, and the AK needed to be first to plant their flag in liberated Warsaw.

Stalin was planning to swoop on Poland to make it the jewel of his post-war Soviet empire. 'Perhaps,' he told his generals, 'we should encourage the AK to rise up. A failed Warsaw uprising by the AK could play beautifully into our hands.' If the AK was crushed by the Nazis, the Soviet army would simply waltz in and take full control of Poland.

The AK in London knew of Stalin's intentions, so a new plan was put into action: 'Operation Tempest'. As the Russians advanced into Poland, the resistance in every major Polish town and city would come out of hiding and attempt to take control of the civil administration before the Russians did.

Marta was summoned without warning to a meeting with the AK commander-in-chief in London, Tadeusz Komorowski; a former army officer and Olympic showjumper, who led a double life as the underground movement leader known as 'General Bor', after his code name *Bór*, meaning 'Forest'.

Komorowski ordered Marta to return immediately to her home town of Katowice and join the coordination of Operation Tempest there with the underground resistance.

She met Michael at his cramped King's Cross flat one last time and Michael gave Marta a ring that he had worn on his finger since he was fifteen, an heirloom of the Sobanski family given to him by his mother. It was a symbol of love and loyalty to the end. They kissed and said goodbye. After losing his family, he was now losing the only person still alive that mattered to him.

*My mum and I are heading out to buy a pint of milk. She nods to a couple of friends she sees, but doesn't stop to chat, because we are deep in conversation about Warsaw. What was it like there, I ask, knowing that war was coming to its end game, and change was on its way?*

*'We had a strong sense that the Russians were coming and they would save us,' says my mum. 'I remember really clearly these new shows of strength by the Nazis after the ghetto was crushed. They would march in full uniform down the main boulevard. Hundreds of Wehrmacht soldiers in full battle dress, and the SS driving in cars behind them.*

*'We stood on the pavement and watched. It was like a big show, and we were expected to be terrified, but instead we just mocked them. People jeered. My brothers laughed, and I remember Kazhik saying that they were finished. This was like their last hurrah.'*

## 10 July 1944, Warsaw

People could sense the moment to strike was nearing. Girls and boys belonging to dozens of special resistance groups in the city attacked German soldiers on patrol in the street. It was called *rozbroneie* ('taking arms'). They spotted a soldier alone and beat him to the ground with clubs, stole his gun and bullets, but left him breathing. Killing him would have resulted in reprisals on civilians.

My mum joined the crowds lining Jerusalem Avenue to watch bedraggled Wehrmacht soldiers retreating from the western front. They were exhausted and seemed half-dead; the life was gone from them. It was the first time Poles had seen Germans looking defeated and it only strengthened their resolve for the coming fight.

One morning, Olga went into her bedroom and saw Hela the housekeeper on the floor behind the wardrobe, crouching on all fours and ripping up her clothes.

'What are you doing?'

Hela looked up sharply and held the small knife she was using in front of her. She spoke rapidly and without stopping to draw breath.

'Don't stop me, *Pane* Basiak. I know you have money here. I only need a small amount. The Russians are coming. Tell me where the money is or I will tell the Gestapo about your fortune and about your husband.'

Olga smiled at Hela.

'Go ahead, Hela. Tell them. I'm sure they'd be very interested in your husband too, who sold food and water to starving Jews in the ghetto at extortionate prices. No one cares, Hela. Not about you, nor me, not your husband, nor mine anymore. The Germans are abandoning the city and soon they will kill all of us.'

'Please, madam,' Hela continued. 'Some money. Mercy.'

Olga took one of her dresses from the wardrobe and tore it open in a single ripping motion. Dollars fell from the sleeve and she gave them to Hela.

'Go home to your family and use the money to get out of Warsaw. Good luck, Hela. Thank you for keeping my children safe when I wasn't here. I will never forget it.'

Hela grabbed the money and got to her feet, running out of the apartment without looking up.

Olga had never had to do anything for herself before, because she'd always had servants. First in St Petersburg as a child, then in the big country house, where the suspicious Polish peasants she employed called her a stuck-up, aristocratic bitch behind her back. In Warsaw, there had been Hela, and now she was gone. There was almost no food left, but Olga found some dried fruit and a tin of soup, and she prepared a dinner for her children for the first time in her life.

From her bedroom window, Alina heard drunken German soldiers falling about wildly outside, banging metal dustbin lids with pipes and singing crude songs about Hitler – that he had syphilis and no penis, and that he was a Jew and wore a dress for Eva Braun in the bedroom.

Minutes later, a death squad passed, Gestapo guards with a machine gun mounted on the back of a truck. The Nazis appeared now to be a schizophrenic mess – one minute drunk, the next shooting anyone they came across in the street. But Alina remembered what Kazhik had told her when they were back in the forest as children: 'A snake is always most dangerous when it is cornered.'

The German bureaucrats were the first to leave the city. Governor Ludwig Fischer and Mayor Ludwig Leist abandoned Warsaw on 23 July 1944, leaving in cars piled high with valuables. The administration was in meltdown, and trains used to send Jews to Auschwitz were now commandeered for the Nazi great escape.

It gave a big morale boost to the resistance, who were awaiting their moment. In London, missives were sent to the AK underground in Warsaw coordinating the precise plan for the coming attack. Resistance leaders posted boy and girl scouts to follow Nazi patrols and watch machine-gun posts for the precise times the guards were changed. Preparations were becoming precise.

Polish residents became openly defiant. At Okapowa Street, a string of white eagles, the symbol of Poland, was hung from tram cables, and the Nazis did nothing. Warehouses were broken into and flour taken; clothes were torn up and sewn back together to produce the AK's red and white arm-bands. Everyone assumed the Nazis would be gone or defeated in days, but they were not beaten. Quite the opposite.

Hitler had not forgotten Stalingrad.

A year before Warsaw planned its uprising, the mighty Sixth Army of Germany were ground slowly to death in Stalingrad by a Russian counteroffensive unlike any seen in history. For six months, both sides dug into the ice and rubble, and Stalingrad became the most epic siege since Carthage.

The Wehrmacht soldiers, abandoned by Berlin, scavenged the streets like dogs desperate to survive; they lopped off their own frostbitten hands and feet to keep the blood flowing, and ate the corpses of fellow soldiers. When the Nazi general Friedrich Paulus was found by Russians lying bearded and drunk on a bed surrounded by his own excrement, he was told to clean himself up before surrendering. Hitler branded Paulus and the Sixth Army 'pathetic cowardly traitors'. They had betrayed the Third Reich.

Hitler vowed that Germany was never going to be shamed again. In Warsaw, the German army would take the stand they failed to take in Stalingrad; the Poles and Russians would be given a taste of what the Third Reich was truly capable of. The Ninth Army were instructed to march through the main streets of Warsaw in full uniform as a sign they weren't beaten, and Hitler diverted resources from the eastern front in preparation for the uprising. This time, Hitler declared, Germany would fight to the last man.

Kazhik and Pavel listened nightly to Soviet radio broadcasts in Polish, urging the AK to rise up and kill the Nazis. They laughed, fully aware that the Soviets were setting a trap for them.

## July 1944, London

In London, their father, Michael, told the AK the same thing. In fierce meetings involving the rival AK factions, Michael warned his superiors that the Warsaw uprising was a trap set by the Soviets.

'We're playing into Stalin's hands,' he said. 'He will do nothing to help us. The ferocity of the uprising will only grind down the Nazi defences, leaving the door open for the Soviet army.'

The voices against an AK uprising grew in strength. Wladislaw Anders, the Polish Spartacus who had led the famous 'Anders Army' – a renegade band of Polish fighters – halfway round the world to fight the Third Reich, was doing everything in his power to warn the AK in London against a premature attack.

Anders had been tortured by the Russians at the beginning of the war and only released so long as he promised to lead a motley crew of warriors to fight under Soviet leadership. Most of this thousand-strong army had also been tortured and imprisoned themselves in the Russian gulags. Under Anders' command, the Anders Army marched thousands of miles, crossing Iran and Syria before returning to Poland. The Russians had cynically created this renegade force as cannon fodder, yet they had triumphed. By 1944, they had won dozens of epic battles against laughable odds.

Anders told the AK leadership in London that the Warsaw uprising would end in catastrophe. They didn't listen. Michael and his compatriots were barred by their superiors from meeting the Polish resistance leader; General Bor did not want his 'enemies' ganging up on him. Michael told friends that he had always thought the Nazis and Russians were the enemy, not fellow Poles.

Things came to a head at a crisis meeting in a room loaned to the AK by Churchill's government near South Kensington. Stanislaw Mikolajczyk, the AK's political leader, listened with increasing anger as one voice after another warned him that if the uprising was crushed, the government-in-exile would have their credibility with the Polish people destroyed. The Russians would then step in as saviours of the day and take power.

Mikolajczyk stood up slowly and addressed his detractors; Michael sat with his arms folded at the back.

'You are endangering the future of Poland,' Mikolajczyk said. 'You think we are stupid? You think we don't know that the uprising won't end in defeat? In the massacre of our families? The people of Warsaw have no choice but to fight.'

If there was no uprising, Mikolajczyk continued, the Soviets would take power in a matter of days anyway. Poland's enemies had always been the twin monsters of Germany and Russia. Nothing had changed.

After the meeting, Michael was taken to a Lyons Corner House and told over a lukewarm cup of tea that his services towards the Polish people were no longer required. A quiet man called Adam, whom Michael had known for four years in London only as 'A', was tasked with breaking the news to him.

'They are making a mistake,' my grandfather said despondently.

'You are naive, Michael. The uprising is not the point,' said Adam. 'Everyone knows it will fail. Warsaw is finished. This is about the politics of who will govern Poland next. Go home to Warsaw and fight, Michael, if that is what you really think matters.'

In that moment, Michael realised what he had failed to understand since arriving in London. He was no politician, he was an idealist, and now he had been frozen out of Polish politics for good. Adam had facetiously told Michael to go back to Warsaw, but perhaps he was right. He should return and fight, because for him, that *was* what mattered.

If Michael didn't hurry, there would be no Warsaw to fight for. Hitler was planning a Biblical decimation of the city. If the Second World War was lost, the obliteration of Warsaw would be Hitler's legacy: the destruction of a beautiful European city with a thousand years of multi-faith culture turned into a pile of dust. It was the only thing that now mattered to Hitler. He diverted battalions from Berlin's defence to make it happen and had a simple instruction for his generals.

Kill anything that moves.

*1 August 1944, Warsaw*

Michael heard the news on the BBC Home Service. The Warsaw uprising had begun, three hours ahead of the designated AK start time of 5 p.m.

In the Zoliborz district, teenagers wearing bulky coats to hide their weapons opened fire unexpectedly on Nazis smoking cigarettes in the street. A fierce firestorm ensued, with the SS drafted in to quell what they believed was merely a one-off incident.

Kazhik sat poised on the edge of his bed, his rifle by his side. He was waiting for Pavel, who burst through the door. Pavel was beaming.

'It's begun, brother!'

Kazhik nodded, and they hugged one another.

They knelt on the creaking floor and pulled up the loose wooden boards. Over the months of their break-ins at the school, they had amassed hundreds of live rounds, which they had hidden under blankets and piles of newspaper.

The boys scrambled desperately in the dusty cavities and looked bewildered at one another. The bullets had gone. There was not a single box left. Kazhik leapt up from the floor and ran like a man possessed through the apartment.

Olga was sitting quietly by a window, peering out at the scene of chaos in the street below. People were starting to build barricades and attach AK flags to lamp posts. She had arranged a number of pebbles and stones in a pattern on a tray to ward death away from her family.

'Where the fuck is our ammunition?' Kazhik shouted at his mother.

Olga looked up, as if genuinely surprised by this interruption to her afternoon.

'It wasn't her, you stupid little boy.' Juta was standing in the doorway. 'It was me.'

Kazhik leapt at his sister, his eyes shot through with rage. He launched at Juta's face, his gun held like a club, but Juta gripped his arm and twisted it round. Kazhik yelped in pain.

'Or more accurately,' Juta continued calmly, 'it was Kacper.'

Her brother sat deflated on a chair.

'This is not a game, Kazhik. You're not at school now, or shooting birds in the forest. This is war, and no one wants you hurt. You are my brother, and I will do whatever it takes to keep you alive. So no bullets for you, I'm afraid.'

Kazhik was unsure what to do; whether to hug his sister or hit her. He wanted to cry and he wanted to kill someone. Kazhik was fourteen and he had felt the full weight of responsibility for looking after his family since the day war broke out. He was the man of the house, so he kept telling himself. Now he felt humiliated and he burst into tears.

'I want . . .' he sobbed, as Juta held him in her arms. 'I want my father.'

Hitler referred from the outset to the Warsaw insurgents as 'bandits'. If they were classed as 'soldiers', they had rights under the Hague Convention. If captured, they had to be taken prisoner rather than killed.

The AK referred to themselves as soldiers, but were really just children. They were led by 'Monter', a veteran colonel of the Austro-Hungarian Empire whose real name was Antoni Chruściel. After the First World War, Monter had joined the Polish army, and the AK resistance appointed him overall commander because he looked like he knew what he was doing.

Monter's immediate objective was to capture a huge, heavily fortified German prison in Mokotow, not far from my family's flat, where Jewish and Polish prisoners were held.

Kazhik went to his room and prepared to fight. He and Pavel had spent months in secret training with *Baszta,* a unit of the AK. But at the last minute, they had been selected for different missions when the fighting started. Kazhik attached the bayonet to his rifle, and took out the metal helmet with the red and white AK insignia painted on its side. Juta came into the room and stood over him, her hand on his shoulder.

'Don't go. Stay here and protect your family.'

'Where's your boyfriend?' Kazhik replied, sarcastically.

'He's not here, Kazhik. You are.'

Kazhik wanted to stay. He didn't want to go into the street and be killed the moment he went out, but his pride was telling him that he had no choice.

'Poland needs me,' he said pompously, without looking at his sister.

The AK attack on Mokotow prison was a surprise success. Boys aged fourteen and fifteen with little more than clubs, pipes and dustbin lids breeched the walls and released 300 inmates. They raised red and white flags in the prison and surrounding streets to signify liberation. The AK leadership were taken aback by the lack of Nazi resistance; there had been no more than a handful of soldiers defending the prison, easily overpowered.

Three hours later, the AK insurgents heard a strange sound, the low rumble of five Panzer tanks powering over barricades towards the prison. As an AK scout scrambled down from the roof to warn his comrades, the turrets of the tanks swivelled and fired.

The walls of the prison splintered into thousands of stone shards, pinging like arrowheads on the inmates. Within forty-five minutes, the AK surrendered and the prison was recaptured. The SS walked in and found 1,794 freed prisoners who had refused to leave their prison cells, terrified of the unfolding chaos in the streets outside. The SS executed them all.

From the apartment windows, Olga, Juta and Alina could hear the prison being blown up by tanks. Kazhik and Pavel were long gone. Olga had stood in the hallway as the boys pushed past, her outstretched arm little more than a token gesture of defiance. She knew she couldn't stop them, and did not dare ask the tarot cards what would happen to her sons.

The SS began smashing down the doors of the flats and houses by the prison. Olga watched fearfully from the window as they drew closer. Five SS men, supported by around thirty Gestapo, marched into a nearby building, pulled out the families and shot them. It was fast and there was no ceremony; a retribution for the prison.

They moved quickly on to my mother's apartment block. Olga seemed frozen to her spot by the window, as she watched figures in jet black uniforms arrange a firing squad in the street, then start smashing the door on the ground floor with an axe. She could hear the wood splintering.

Juta was the one to act. She knew the flat below had been lived in by a Jewish family, who had been removed to the ghetto. Their furniture and belongings had been looted, but the flat was empty and the door unlocked.

Juta pushed Alina and Olga down the single flight of stairs. They heard the heavy door to the street cave in and the SS clattering noisily through the hall. There was a distant commotion in the flat on the ground floor. A bad-tempered old woman lived alone there, and the SS guard shot her through the glass panel of her door before she even opened it. The officer leapt up the stairs, hungry for more killing.

Alina and Olga rushed through the empty flat to the kitchenette at the back, where they crammed themselves into a tiny larder and pulled the door shut with the tips of their fingers. Juta was last, careful to leave the door of the flat ajar, so as not to raise suspicion. Juta pushed her body into a dark corner behind an oil heating drum. She didn't dare breathe.

The SS guard moved like a spider through the flat, assessing each space in an instant by sensing the fear in the air. He stood imperiously in the centre of the room listening for breathing or whimpering, the usual giveaways.

Nothing.

He sighed. This was a waste of his time. He could smell boiled food in a flat on the next floor and left, his gun cocked. In the space of an hour, the SS killed 500 women and children in the flats and houses immediately adjacent to the prison. Alina, Olga and Juta survived, staying in the kitchenette in the empty flat till nightfall, when it was safe to come out again.

# IO

## *The Wola Massacre*

The AK's commander, Monter, had set the insurgents a list of highly ambitious objectives to be captured within the first few hours of the uprising. They nearly all ended in disaster. The first were the two main bridges over the Vistula – the Kierbedz and the Poniatowski. Kazhik and Pavel were attached to rival AK resistance groups; Kazhik's group were tasked with recapturing part of the ghetto, and Pavel's were to storm the first of the bridges.

Kierbedz and Poniatowski bridges were key to controlling the city. Rival bandit groups – some aligned to the communists, others anarchist and some conservative or even monarchist – put aside their political differences to coordinate an attack on the Kierbedz. It connected Warsaw to the major capitals of Europe, and the entire 500-metre span of the railway bridge was enclosed by intricate steel mesh walls and a roof. Once entered, it was impossible to escape, and the Nazis had nicknamed it the 'Rat Trap'. The 2nd Panzer tank battalion pointed their guns down the length of the trap and waited.

Pavel was one of the first child soliders on the scene. He was joined by others with antique rifles and home-made explosives. They were instructed by Monter to be an example to the Warsaw uprising; to show the people of their city how brave they were by charging at the Nazis without fear.

Down the long mesh corridor of the bridge, it was impossible for the bandits to make out the precise gun emplacements of the Germans. Sandbags were piled high with slits for the machine guns, and behind them was the 2nd Panzer tank battalion. An attack would be obliterated with a single barrage. It was obvious to anyone.

No one was in charge of the rebels. They had been given instructions to capture the bridge, but none of the group was sure how, or who would give the command to attack. The commanding officer they expected was rumoured to have been killed by a mortar yards from his house, moments after leaving it. Whatever had happened to him, he wasn't at the bridge.

Gentle Pavel had always had his brother and sister to guide him; even though they were younger, they had always known what to do.

There was nothing for it. Pavel loaded his gun.

*'When did you find out your brother was dead?' I ask my mum.*

*'After the war. I found out he'd been part of the attack on Kierbedz. That's what they said.'*

*'Where were you when they attacked the bridge?'*

*'Who cares where we were?' she says, suddenly angry. 'Why do you ask me that?'*

*I realise for the first time that I'm treating my mum not as my mother, but as an interviewee to be pressed for more information: the details of her brother's death. My own uncle.*

*'I'm sorry,' I say.*

*'Sorry for what? It wasn't your fault.'*

*There's an awkward silence.*

*'For questioning you like that.'*

*'There was no one there to protect Pavel,' my mum says, eventually. 'That was the tragedy.'*

★      ★      ★

Witnesses saw the first AK wave mown down by a machine gun seconds after beginning its charge across the bridge. The bravery of the bandits was mentioned in numerous accounts of the assault on Kierbedz, but not one of the dozens of girls and boys massacred – for they were just girls and boys – was ever named.

They were the unknown soldiers.

In death, as in life, there was a hole where it came to Pavel. My mother was later told he died on that bridge, like a huge tree falling in a silent forest. No one from his family even saw it happen.

*'We didn't know Pavel was dead. We had gone back to the flat. Juta said it was safe, because the SS wouldn't look twice in the same place. The boys had been gone for hours and we suspected they were both dead. I got really angry with my mother.*

*'"The streets are on fire," I said to her. "Your sons are fighting, and you are sitting here looking at your tarot cards for what to do. Staring at little symbols on some pieces of paper. What kind of mother are you?"*

*'She didn't reply, she just kept turning those cards as always.'*

*August 1944, Warsaw*

The lead taken by Pavel's group on Kierbedz was followed across the city. Monter recommended to his boy and girl soldiers that they showed how much they love Poland by charging at the Germans shouting, *'Niech Zyje Polska!'* ('Long live Poland!'). Like Pavel and his comrades, most carried little more than metal pipes and clubs, and were mown down in seconds.

Monter soon realised the terrible equation that had been created by the uprising. For every small gain – a street or building captured – there would be huge casualties and massive Nazi reprisals against civilians.

The city quickly became a bewildering chessboard. In some areas, the Wehrmacht found themselves cut off, surrounded by hundreds of AK 'bandits'. In others, like Zoliborz, Ochota and Powisle, it was the other way round. The audacity of the bandits was undermined by their incredible tactical naivety. Nazi commander Stroop marvelled at the level of AK disarray; there appeared to be no plan, he told his officers, and they walked into every trap we set.

Pavel and Kazhik's commanding officers aided and abetted the massacre. The bandits had no military experience, and were learning hand-to-hand combat for the first time when they charged with kitchen knives and broken guns at Nazi barricades. It was a long way from pretending to use a broom as a bayonet in the school back garden.

The Wehrmacht, by contrast, were men with weathered faces ravaged by years of gruelling campaigns on the eastern and western fronts. Many had survived long, draining sieges such as Odessa. They knew how to dig in for the kind of siege that Warsaw was fast turning into.

*'Did you stay in the flat?' I ask my mum.*

*'Christ, no. There was a block of flats opposite. This man came over to us from there after a few hours. We knew his wife, she would get food for us sometimes, and he'd been told to see if we were still alive after the SS sweep. He said it was a miracle we'd survived, but Olga said, "Thank Juta".*

*'The man said it wasn't safe to stay where we were. The Nazis would come again and kill everyone left behind. So we went with him. The street outside looked like a bomb had gone off. There were already the barricades being set up by the AK at the end of the road in preparation for a new assault on the Germans.'*

*'So your district was controlled by the AK?'*

*'At first, yes. Some areas the AK controlled, some the Germans*

*controlled, and it would change every five minutes. The Nazis would lose control of a street, or we would in a firestorm, and then capture it back. It was a very fluid situation and hard to work out who was winning. We thought the AK were, but we didn't know if they really were.'*

*'Where did he take you, this man?'*

*'There was a cellar in their building. It was huge, and everyone from their flats had gone down to it. There were all these families down there, babies crying and children wailing. It was bloody awful and I can remember thinking this was a very bad idea. There was no way out. I had a very bad feeling that this was not a safe place to be.'*

The Germans were initially caught unawares by the Warsaw uprising, but were now reasserting their control over the city by utilising their best weapon: terror. Stuka dive bombers dropped screaming from the sky, obliterating each district one by one. As a Stuka fell vertically down, its pilot's face would turn ghostly and concave from the G-forces he was pulling. The wings had sirens attached, which wailed as the plane plummeted. The noise was deafening on the ground, as the Stuka dropped like a hawk on a mouse.

*'We sat in this cellar listening for the screaming of these planes. There was this extraordinary moment just before the bomb dropped. The screaming from the plane would suddenly stop, and there was this silence, which was when we knew the Stuka had pulled out of the dive and released its bomb.*

*'You could count "one", "two" and by "three", the bomb would explode. The whole building would judder. Plaster would fall around you, but you would see that you were still alive.'*

*'Was this just you, your mother and sister at this point? Had you any word from Kazhik?'*

*'No. I only found this out after the war, but for the first couple of*

*weeks of the uprising, Kazhik came back one or two times to the flat to get food. We had gone, so he assumed we'd been shot by the SS.'*

### 3 August 1944, Warsaw

Kazhik stumbled and fell his way around the city. This was not war as he had envisaged it. He had no idea what to do or where to go. Kazhik was terrified, and he spent the first two days of the uprising hiding in a doorway, bombs falling all around.

In the sweltering August heat, he went back to the ransacked family flat, but no one was there. He slept for a few hours sweating in a heavy coat in his old bunk bed, unaware that his mother and two sisters were hiding in a cellar less than a hundred metres away.

Kazhik was one of thousands of boy and girl soldiers cast adrift in Warsaw. They had been waiting for years to rise up against their Nazi oppressors. but now it had happened, they were clueless, and so were their leaders.

Hitler issued his umpteenth Order for Warsaw: 'Every citizen of Warsaw is to be killed, including men, women and children. Warsaw has to be levelled to the ground in order to set a terrifying example to the rest of Europe,' he said.

The SS commander Stroop, was deemed to have failed in the job, so SS General Heinz Reinefarth was dispatched to make it happen. Reinefarth was suave, ambitious and unstintingly loyal. Something he had already proved to Hitler. On 20 July, eleven days before the Warsaw uprising started, a group of Nazi generals led by General Claus von Stauffenberg, convinced that killing Hitler was the only way to bring an end to the war, attempted to blow him up in his beloved 'Wolf's Lair'. The plot was a tragic farce worthy of its own movie, of which there are several.

At a meeting of the high command, Stauffenberg managed

to place a briefcase containing a bomb under Hitler's chair, but by a complete fluke, Colonel Heinz Brandt, who sat next to Hitler, moved the briefcase with his foot under a conference table leg. The bomb went off, but because of its new position, the blast deflected away from Hitler. Instead, Brandt lost his leg and was killed, and twenty others were seriously injured. Hitler got away with a singed trouser leg.

SS Commander Reinefarth, ever the opportunist, pledged to the Führer that he would root out the traitors and shoot them himself. The plotters were found and summarily executed, and Reinefarth used the failed coup as a way of cementing his relationship with Hitler; with fatal consequences for the people of Warsaw.

Reinefarth was like a Hollywood parody of a cold, murderous SS officer. He was charming and ruthless, with a deep duelling scar across his left cheek. After the failed bomb plot, Hitler said he could not trust anyone except Reinefarth, and he ordered him to do what every previous commander had so far failed to achieve in Warsaw: exterminate its million surviving Polish inhabitants without mercy.

Reinefarth arrived eager to get the job done. On the way from the station to his residence, he was furious to see the route of his car blocked by thousands of people in the streets.

'Why aren't these people being shot?' Reinefarth demanded.

They are, he was told. The crowds were being rounded up by Wehrmacht soldiers and taken either to designated walls to face a firing squad, or marched to the station to be sent to a concentration camp. But not fast enough for Reinefarth's liking.

*I have been meeting my mum at Cartons coffee house on Stanmore Broadway, and enjoying spending our time together. But halfway through writing the book – where you are now – the Covid-19 global pandemic started.*

*What started as a race against time to record my mum's memories before her dementia took full grip was now a welcome distraction from a pandemic that threatened to kill us all.*

*The parallels between war and pandemic were not lost on my mum.*

*My parents, holed up in their house in Stanmore, refused initially to follow orders. At ninety-two and eighty-nine respectively, they saw little reason to be told what to do. My mum had survived Auschwitz. Why was she going to listen to this?*

*The invisible enemy of a virus bringing death as whimsically as the Germans did was hard for her to take seriously, no matter how true it was.*

*'If only washing your hands could have stopped the Gestapo,' my mum said.*

## 5 August 1944, Warsaw

'*Raus, raus! Schnell los!*'

The Wehrmacht came at dawn to each of the five districts simultaneously to begin the final annihilation. They barked orders but gave no one time to follow them, lobbing bags of white incendiary powder through open windows, into doorways and cellars where they knew families were hiding, followed by grenades.

The powder coated anyone inside with a fine dusting and the grenade ignited a spontaneous chain of combustion setting every human inside alight. The Nazis watched as people ran out of buildings screaming, their bodies and hair a ball of flame. In some cellars, the Wehrmacht chose instead to go in and rape mothers in front of their children. They would then insert a grenade in the woman's vagina to kill everyone inside.

This was real, existing Nazism. Between 1933, when they first took power in Germany, and their demise in 1945, Hitler and Himmler cultivated an image of deeply held ideological conviction, but this was not who the Nazis were. Down in those cellars in Warsaw was who they really were.

Wola, a working-class district to the west of the city, had always resisted Aryanisation, and long been hated by Berlin. It was where much of the AK resistance were concealed, and Hela and her family lived. Reinefarth decided to use Wola to test a new kind of genocide: mass immolation, or death by fire. In the dictionary, 'immolate' means to sprinkle with sacrificial meal as an offering to the gods. The people of Wola were to be sacrificed as an example to Warsaw.

Reinefarth said it was not enough simply to kill Wola's inhabitants. To stop the uprising, a sadistic orgy of torture needed to be enacted, the like of which had never been seen before.

There was only one man, Reinefarth said, capable of making this happen on the ground. SS Oberführer Oskar Dirlewanger, a swirling orb of darkness nicknamed 'Gandhi', on account of his painfully thin frame and misleadingly benign manner. Back in 1940, Hitler and Himmler had the idea of creating an elite military unit from convicted criminals; men in prison with feral, survivalist skills in hunting and poaching wild animals.

Hitler was romantically taken with the idea of loners, who operated outside the parameters of civilisation, and could kill with their bare hands. Men who manifested, he said, the 'pure Nietzschean primitive of the German'.

Oskar Dirlewanger was a party official who had been convicted of kidnapping and raping a fourteen-year-old girl. Small, thin and intensely odd, Dirlewanger had a huge bald head and a habit of coughing uncontrollably when nervous. People who knew him said he masked his self-disgust with a bashful smile, often a prelude to unleashing uncontrollable violence against his powerless victims.

With his criminal record, Hitler said, Dirlewanger was a

'living Nazi'. He was not one of the effete, opera-loving intellectuals of the Nazi hierarchy in Berlin, or connected to the treacherous upper-class generals who had plotted and betrayed him.

'I want you to create', Hitler told Dirlewanger, 'the most feared and terrifying military unit in history.' Dirlewanger hand-picked men with 'potential' – serial murderers, thieves and fellow rapists – and he interviewed psychopaths who had been certified by doctors as criminally insane. He then selected seventy of the maddest, shaved their heads and began training them for combat.

Even by SS standards of boundless brutality, the 36th Waffen Grenadier Division was notorious within the elite corps. They were known to the people of Warsaw as 'The Black Hunters'. Within the SS, they were called simply by their leader's name: *Dirlewanger*.

Having an entire division named after the commander was a personality cult usually frowned upon by Hitler. An exception was made for 'Gandhi', the freaky little man that even Hitler found hard to fathom. Mere mention of Dirlewanger's name, one Nazi general said, was like a cloud passing in front of the sun.

On 5 August 1944, the 36th were sent into Wola to do what they will. In churches, they were said to have anally raped priests using altar crosses, before hanging them from the pulpit. Pensioners were skinned alive and fed to dogs. At the hospital, they pulled drips from patients and sat with their feet up, watching them bleed to death. Women were forced at gunpoint to cut their own children's throats. If they refused, they were raped. If they complied, they were raped anyway.

The Wola massacre was an inversion of justice. Murderers and paedophiles presided as judge and executioner over 50,000 law-abiding people. The crime of Wola's inhabitants was that they were not yet dead. Hela and her family were found guilty, like everyone else.

'Warsaw is on fire,' the Nazi governor Fischer declared proudly. Dirlewanger personally lit buildings to watch people jump from balconies; those who survived the jump from the inferno were shot. The streets had new barricades made of corpses, piled metres high. One was made of small children, who had been asked to raise their hands before being executed, their heads then crushed with rifle butts.

This was not a plan, but a lust for murder. Blood flowed like a thick stream down the ancient stone gullies, as it had a year earlier in the Jewish ghetto.

In the neighbouring district of Czerniakow, residents were so scared of being tortured by the *Dirlewanger*, they fled to the riverbank of the Vistula; the opposite side, only a hundred metres away, appeared to offer salvation. Crowded on the shoreline, hundreds crashed into the river, thanking God for their escape, but the Wehrmacht rained down machine-gun fire on them; whilst Messerschmitt fighters flew the length of the packed beach, strafing thousands of escapees.

Those who swam out hoping to reach the other side were caught by the current and dragged under. Some made it to a half-sunken pleasure boat called the *Bajka* (*Fairytale*), its hull upturned in the dark water. As they clambered on, fighters circled back and opened fire, their bodies sliding slowly back into the deep.

The massacre was watched from the far shore by the Soviet army, Poland's ostensible ally. Two weeks before the uprising, the Russians reached the northern shore of the Vistula. They now peered through binoculars as the Nazis completed the obliteration of the people the Soviets had come to protect.

*My mum recalled it vividly.*

'We knew the Russians were in the city. Everyone was excited that they would save us. Then news came that they had parked their tanks on the other side of the river and were sitting there waiting for the Nazis to kill us all. It was Stalin's plan. Everyone knew it. He wanted the AK destroyed, so when the Soviets finally came in to wipe out the Nazis, they could set up their puppet government.'

Days before the uprising began, the Polish Prime Minister of the government-in-exile, Stanislaw Mikolajczyk, flew to Moscow to implore Stalin to advance his tanks and save the people of Warsaw. After Mikolajczyk made his impassioned plea, Stalin had only one thing to say.

'Have you finished?'

## 28 August 1944, London

When news reached Michael in London of the Wola and Vistula massacres, he was in a café in King's Cross. Life in London was returning to a semblance of normality. People commuted to work, buses ran a regular timetable and cinemas and theatres were packed with people celebrating their new-found optimism. The Germans were on the run in Europe and the British were waiting for the inevitable day that Hitler would surrender.

Michael had no family, no political career (laughable as that may ever have seemed) and the woman he loved was gone. The news from Warsaw was no surprise – it was what everyone knew would happen, even the AK generals who ordered the uprising.

The Soviets were going to get away with being accessories to mass murder and end up rulers of the Polish nation. If they had watched the Nazis killing Poles from the other side of the River Vistula, what would they do when they governed? It was too much for him. Michael vowed to return to Poland and fight the enemy who had always been the enemy: the Russians.

He had nothing to live for, so this would be his reason to live.

## 28 August 1944, Warsaw

Kazhik was lucky. Cut off from his AK comrades, he was alone, which meant he could stay one step ahead of the *Dirlewanger* or Wehrmacht. He foraged for food in empty flats, put his mouth over broken taps to drink water that wasn't there and turned out the empty drawers of strangers in the hope of finding clean clothes.

The Nazis had one final task: to destroy the last remnants of AK resistance holed up in what had once been the Jewish ghetto. Reinefarth ordered the old town to be encircled. He wanted to crush the uprising for good.

Kazhik, disconnected from his old unit, wandered through the city. There was an odd calm in the wreckage of Warsaw. He stopped to look at shops he had visited with his parents, now burnt out or blown to smithereens, and squinted at the remnants, trying to remember what they had once looked like with happy shoppers inside.

Sitting crouched behind a half-wall to smoke a cigarette, Kazhik saw a Wehrmacht soldier joking to his comrades as he held a baby above his head, before throwing her into a bonfire.

A block on, he saw an old man walk his cow down the street; bullets flew past, but neither he nor the cow got a scratch. A woman played an accordion beneath a fountain. Kazhik remembered her busking at the same spot before the war, and he saw some amused Nazi soldiers toss a few coins in her cap, laughing.

As the Nazis marched on the old town, Kazhik was swept up by an AK unit rushing past. A girl no older than him wearing a dead Wehrmacht soldier's helmet was in charge. She had dark ringlets of hair, which gave her a Spanish appearance, and piercing hazel eyes. Kazhik could marry this girl, he thought, have a family and live with her forever, but there was not even a chance to begin a conversation.

She pointed at the sewer and shouted, 'Go!'

Kazhik and another boy were to patrol a kilometre of the underground tunnel system leading to the old town. Warsaw was no longer a functioning city, so the sewers became a subterranean lifeline for transporting supplies of food and ammunition to the trapped AK.

On 2 September, a month and a day after the start of the uprising, Reinefarth ordered the Wehrmacht to enter the old town to finish off what was left of the resistance. More than 3,500 tons of shells had been dropped in a two-kilometre-square area in under a month. When the war was over, 95 per cent of Warsaw had been destroyed. More of Hiroshima stood after the atomic bomb than was left of the Polish capital; it was bombed more heavily than either Dresden or Aleppo.

The scene that greeted the advancing Nazis was unearthly: the air was thick with dust and rotting flesh. The living and dead were barely distinguishable from one another, lying mutilated and dazed in a moonscape of craters and ravines. There were no buildings as such, only the ghosts of structures on mountains of debris. A single stained-glass window had miraculously survived and it stood alone like a solitary tooth. The glass in the window depicted Christ on the cross; the church that once encased it reduced to fine dust.

German soldiers faced no resistance, just the low, guttural moan of bodies still breathing, their stomachs blown away. Rats ruled the old town now, moving like a rolling black wave across the human debris, squealing with delight.

Reinefarth was disappointed by the lack of opposition. The remnants of the AK he had hoped to burn alive had gone. Hours before the Wehrmacht made their move, the AK had escaped through the sewers to freedom, just as the Jews had done a year before.

Kazhik never saw the girl with ringlets again.

# II

# The Firing Squad

## 3 September 1944, Warsaw

After leaving the sewer, Kazhik was seconded to a resistance group in Srodmiescie, just beyond the ruined walls of the old town.

Kazhik was given a functioning gun and told to man a barricade in the centre of the road. He was unhappy with the situation; the Nazis were regaining control of the city and any AK would soon be cut off. More pressingly, he was exposed from the back. The old Bavarian soldier at the school told him always to have his spine to a wall, or he would lose the top of his head.

There were four boy and two girl comrades lined up at regular intervals along the barricade. They each chose a different sniper spot. They were told by a commander to lie low and fire only if they were fired upon first, otherwise, 'save bullets'. If the Wehrmacht sent a lorry or tank laden with explosives, they were to abandon the barricade and run for it.

Kazhik had had a growth spurt in the summer months of 1944 and was now a tall, gangly fourteen-year-old. I asked him years later, on holiday in the pretty town of Kazimierz, if he ever thought he would make it to fifteen.

'Fuck, no!'

Anyone still alive in Warsaw in 1944 had no future and no past. Their family was deceased or lost: it was too unbearable to remember the happy times, so memories were deliberately erased. They had only the present, which they barely held onto with their fingertips.

Kazhik waited for the fighting to start.

From his vantage point behind the barricade, he could see the flames of the old town as the Wehrmacht burnt the last survivors. It was quiet where he knelt. He was aware that the boy kneeling three feet from him was talking; he could see the boy's mouth moving, but couldn't hear a word coming out.

The next thing he knew, a bullet flew past his left ear. It was the single most shocking moment of Kazhik's life. A small piece of pointed metal moving at 2,000 feet per second – 1,700 miles per hour – travelling three times faster than the speed of sound and moving so fast that its human target only heard the bullet after being hit.

It pinged comically off a mudguard of the upturned lorry that Kazhik was crouching under, an inch from his head. The bullet was not supposed to hit anyone; it was an exploratory probe designed to smoke out any movement from behind the AK line. The single bullet gave away little of what was to follow it.

A 7.92mm Mauser MG 42 – 'Hitler's zipper' – began pummelling the belly of the lorry. It was like a hammer inside Kazhik's head, thumping a dozen times a second. The heavy machine gun was fed by a huge anaconda-like ammunition belt, positioned inside a newsagent's kiosk at the far end of the street. The Mauser was the backbone of the Wehrmacht. The speed and force of its cylindrical firing mechanism mounted on a tripod were enough to push a dead horse across the ground, or so boasted its designer, Louis Stang.

The firing didn't last long. An AK scout, a boy of maybe no more than eleven or twelve, jogged up and nonchalantly lobbed a grenade through the slit where the Mauser was peeping out. The newsagent's kiosk blew straight up in the air like a tent taken out by a storm. The kiosk landed almost entirely intact, metres from where it had started. The Germans inside were destroyed, but the kiosk had survived.

The boys around Kazhik were firing spasmodically at nothing in particular. The kid who had been chatting before the firestorm was laughing, though Kazhik thought it more of an odd grimace. A nervous embarrassment, perhaps, at the idea of shooting hopelessly into a cloud of dust and knowing he would imminently be hit himself.

One Wehrmacht soldier hidden from view at the other end of the street had spotted Kazhik's position. He fired repeatedly at the mudguard above Kazhik's head, methodically perforating it to create a pretty doily pattern. Kazhik had no option but to sink to the ground, trapped. He sat in a ball praying to an unspecific God for the shooting to stop and, beyond that, for the war to end. He remembered the crippled Bavarian soldier at school and cursed his useless advice about stabbing with a broomstick, wishing he had been taught something more useful about surviving a fire-storm.

Kazhik's prayers were answered. The shooting stopped as quickly as it had started. He peeked cautiously through the doily holes of the mudguard; there was no movement at either barricade. He peered down his line of comrades. The boy next to him was dead, keeled over, but still with a smile on his face. A boy next to him was wiping the barrel of his gun, oblivious to anything, focused on his cleaning job.

The silence was broken by a deafening rocket exploding in the old town. Kazhik poked his head above the mudguard, but there was still no movement from the Nazi side. He stared intently at the German barricade, a makeshift structure constructed from bicycles, wooden crates and random elements of Warsaw's old life – a beautiful pram, a dead woman, an iron bed and a mattress. The war had reclaimed all matter living and dead – animal, vegetable and mineral – mashed together as putty remoulded for the fight.

From behind a metal panel, Kazhik saw slight movement. It was hard to work out what it was, even if it was human. Dogs and rats moved freely through the city, VIPs with a free pass to roam and scavenge at will; they were first on the scene of a firestorm, chewing on the half-dead. The movement was probably an animal, Kazhik thought. But it was methodical and repeating itself now. It was definitely human. About forty feet from where he knelt, Kazhik began watching what looked like a flat fisherman's cap passing between two panels.

Soldiers would sometimes put a hat on a stick and march it like a Punch and Judy above a parapet to draw enemy fire. Kazhik began counting the seconds the fisherman's cap took to travel between the first and second panel. It didn't move like a hat on a stick; it moved like a man. Kazhik counted the time it took in his head. Concealed by left panel: two seconds. Out in the open: two seconds. Concealed by right panel: two seconds. Then back the other way.

The more Kazhik watched, the more the repeated movement seemed to hypnotise him. Left to right; right to left; left to right; right to left. It was sending him to sleep like a baby's lullaby. Something about the regularity was suspicious. It felt like a trap.

Kazhik lifted his rifle and leant it gently against the wafer-thin rim of the mudguard. He peered down the broken sight and focused on the sliver of open ground between the two panels. His window of opportunity. The fisherman's cap was still moving two seconds concealed, two in the open. This nonsense went on for another three minutes. It was as if Kazhik had become so mesmerised by the ritual, he was now part of it.

A silence enveloped the two main players: the German soldier and Kazhik. They were now bound together in a piece of performance art that could carry on forever. Perhaps they would both grow old in Warsaw. The owner of the fisherman's cap traversing back and forth; Kazhik watching with his gun cocked, waiting for Godot.

For no reason Kazhik fired, as much to break the spell as anything else. The gun made a comical popping sound like a plastic cork; it seemed instantly ridiculous to him. The moment the bullet left his gun, Kazhik fell to the ground to protect himself from return fire. He didn't see the fisherman's cap flop to the floor, lifeless. Kazhik looked up. There was no more movement.

For all his playing at war as a child in the forest, bayoneting with a broomstick and dreaming of becoming a soldier, it was the first and only time in Kazhik's life that he fired a gun at a living person, and the only time he killed someone.

Kazhik waited for an hour. He couldn't move. He was overcome with tiredness and a desire to sleep forever. There was further activity behind the enemy barricade, but this time he was sure it was dogs. He could hear them gnawing on flesh and fighting between themselves.

Kazhik later told Alina – in the mid-1960s when they talked about it properly for the first time in Paris – that he was fixated on the clouds after he fired the gun. It was a beautiful late summer's day, and billowing cumulus nimbus drifted across the sky. Over twenty years later, he could recall the exact detail of every shaded indent and curve of the clouds that day.

Impulsively, he jumped to his feet and began walking towards the enemy barricade. The ground underfoot was thick with the washed-up detritus of war – broken crockery mixed with machine-gun cartridges, gramophone records and splintered furniture.

Srodmiescie had been an extraordinary district before the war. It was on Freta Street that Marie Curie was born. The area was a melting pot of bohemianism: artists, musicians and writers, with the Jewish and Polish intelligentsia living side by side. Kazhik crunched his way through the broken artefacts of this long-gone, pre-war world, walking slowly and determinedly towards the Nazi barricade.

When he got there, he faced a slope of grease, earth, wood and blood. He began climbing. Over the other side was a mirror image of what he had left behind at the AK barricade. There were a number of unmoving bodies in threadbare Wehrmacht uniforms, and behind the panel he'd fired at, the corpse of a boy lying flat. He was the same age as Kazhik, with his fisherman's cap obediently next to him. The bullet had punctured his neck.

Kazhik knelt down and opened the boy's jacket. He found a packet of cigarettes, a lighter and a small leather wallet containing five or six photos. There was a picture of a couple whom Kazhik imagined to be the boy's mother and father. Another photo had the same people in it, but this time with the boy he had shot, much younger than he was now, maybe eight or nine. They were standing together in a garden with a big tree in the foreground.

There was a picture of a much older woman, probably his grandmother. She was in a deckchair on a beach. It was clearly cold – maybe on the Baltic or North Sea. She was wrapped in a big coat and had one hand holding down her hat, which the wind was blowing furiously.

In the second pouch of the boy's wallet were his identity documents: his *Wehrpass* and *Soldbuch*. These were given to every German soldier. The first contained details of his enlistment date, illnesses and injuries; if a soldier was killed, the *Wehrpass* was sent to the next of kin. The *Soldbuch* detailed paygrade, hospitalisations and family details: address, education and religion.

Kazhik looked through the boy's *Soldbuch*. The boy he had killed was called Jonas Peter Becker. He was fourteen like

Kazhik, but his *Soldbuch* lied, saying he was sixteen, so he could be conscripted to the front. *Jungvolk* as young as ten were being sent to fight the Russians and Poles as the German army collapsed. Wehrmacht soldiers were deserting in their thousands, so they were replaced by boys.

The most famous of these boy soldiers was twelve-year-old Alfred Czech, who was awarded the Iron Cross by Hitler in the final days of the war. By then, Hitler was unable to control the Parkinson's disease in his left arm, so he hid the violently shaking limb from view for the photo taken with Czech.

After the publicity shoot, Czech and a handful of other decorated *Jungvolk* were ordered to join Hitler in his bunker for a glass of champagne. As the Allied bombs fell, Hitler's secretary recalled the Führer uncontrollable with excitement at having the boys there; his face was purple, and he was transported momentarily in rhapsodic pleasure. The Führer and the boys danced hand-in-hand together to a popular gramophone record of the time: 'Blood Red Roses Tell You of Happiness'.

Kazhik put Jonas Peter Becker's wallet in his pocket and moved on.

*As the Covid pandemic takes hold and lockdown empties the motorways, mine is the sole vehicle on the road, driving up to the house to leave food on the doorstep. My mum and dad are living through another conflict now, and coping well.*

*They are very wartime about the whole thing. My dad wants pre-1945 provisions, like Carnation milk and tins of sardines. My mum is keener on bottles of wine. Because of her growing dementia, she seems blithely unaware of the dangers of going out, telling me she could always go to the shops if they ran out of food. My dad has to parent her.*

*'But you can't go to the shops,' he'll say. 'They're all closed.'*

*'Why?'*

'Because of the virus.'

'Oh,' she replies, shrugging her shoulders.

*Alina sits in the garden with a glass of wine. Seeing her there, contentedly in her deckchair, I think to myself that this isn't such a bad place to end up after everything she has been through. Rescuing a life from what happened in the war.*

'What did you do next?' *I ask her.*

'What do you mean?'

'In Warsaw. What happened next?'

'When? In the seventies?'

'No, the war. For the book.'

'What are you talking about? What book?'

'The book I'm writing about you.'

'Why would you want to do that?'

*The following day, I'm in the kitchen and the phone rings. It's Alina.*

'Did you want to speak about Warsaw in 1944?'

'Well, yes. If that's OK?'

'Do you have your tape recorder ready, because I'm ready.'

'Give me a second.'

*I fiddle around, sort out my phone and begin recording. Yesterday's Alina is gone and the war is back, and she can't be stopped.*

## 12 September 1944, Warsaw

Olga, Alina and Juta were hiding in a basement. The only plan was to stay one street ahead of the killing squads, so they moved every few hours. The cellars they found were tiny and cramped, already filled with families crammed on top of one another in the infernal heat. Olga and her two daughters had run out of food and were too fearful to go outside, so they drank hot water to keep their stomachs full, but more often than not, had to beg other families to give them any water at all.

At 5 a.m., a man crashed down the stairs into the darkness of a basement where they had been hiding for three days. The man was so scared, he couldn't speak. Eventually he got his words out.

'Leave now. Out! Out!'

The Wehrmacht were in the next street, moving block by block with flame-throwers incinerating anyone that moved. They were led by Romanian SS officers drafted in specifically for the 'clean-up operation', chosen for their ferocity, and because there were so few Germans left in the city.

For Olga, the fear was too much to bear. She began weeping silently and turned her face to the concrete wall. The other families began gathering their belongings to move to the next hiding place. Olga couldn't do it, she said, and told her daughters they were all going to die. Juta stroked her mother's face and assured her calmly that they were getting out alive.

Before they could reach the stairs, a strange kerosene mist descended the steps. Three elderly women laden with bags on their way up the stairs peered hopefully into the light above, and were engulfed in a second by a huge plume of fire.

Alina and Juta stood transfixed. There was nothing left of the women but a black oily lake on the steps. They had no time to compute what happened. The paws of German guard dogs skated on the flagstones above, desperately scratching to come down the steps. Then there was a familiar shout.

'*Raus! Raus!*' ('Out! Out!')

In the fresh air, it was cooler than it had been for a month. A blissful breeze wafted across Alina and Juta's faces as they emerged blinking from the kerosene-stinking cellar. They filed one by one onto the street. It was strangely quiet; no gunfire, no planes, nothing.

Alina would never forget the SS officer. He was shabby and heavily stubbled, with a strong smell of tobacco and months of stale sweat. He was nothing like the confident Nazis that came to their house in 1939, Alina thought; he was young, but seemed very old. There was a weariness to his barked orders – an utter absence of conviction about what he was doing. Olga shook herself out of her desolation and sniffed the air, as if it would give her a clue how to get out of this.

'Are they *Dirlewanger*?' Alina whispered to Juta.

'No, just Gestapo.'

There was a calm about the three women, as if they were sizing up their enemy. If this was to be the end of their lives, so be it. There was no screaming or shouting. Olga, Alina and Juta watched the Nazis coolly; six female eyes on a group of beaten men, waiting for their first move.

The SS officer was directing the captured. Male prisoners to the left; women and children to the right. He looked straight through each face as they passed, and to Alina, that look of boredom was almost worse than anything else she had seen. The sheer tedium of having to massacre all these people.

Before the prisoners from the cellar had been sorted, the men were shot. Alina didn't even see it; she was walking away with her back to them, when she heard a flurry of gunfire. She turned and saw a scattering of bodies on the floor.

Alina now knew she would die. Her mother's weepy prediction in the cellar was right. Alina felt oddly detached from her own fate; she thought instead about the logistics of the task facing the SS officer. It must be better to kill the men first, she calculated, as they would fight when they saw their families massacred. It made sense and was logical.

There was an aimless lethargy to the killing. The soldiers seemed unbothered whether they carried out their orders or not. The SS officer seemed distracted from the task at hand, as if he had better things to do, or places to go. He stopped one young woman filing past, her whole body shaking uncontrollably, to compliment her on her hair. It was as if he was meeting a pretty stranger on a bus and none of this was happening.

A heavily armed Romanian soldier, ammunition belts crisscrossing his chest, told the women to sort themselves into two groups, left and right. He didn't care who went where. The ambiguity of his order caused confusion and the women began shuffling around in circles like a game in a playground.

This strange dance went on for some minutes, as the Romanian watched without intervening. He was squat and had thick coal dust and black grease smeared across his face; his cap was pulled tight, and he wore a thick overcoat. Next to him was a flame-thrower, still hot from incinerating the women on the steps.

Olga had had enough. She stepped out of the stupid chaos of the sorting dance and pulled her two daughters with her. Olga stood with her arms folded in front of the Romanian guard, who seemed faintly amused that she had defied him. The three women stood together, staring obstinately at the Romanian.

Alina bent down to tie her shoelace, and as she did, another soldier began firing at the women. They lay motionless in a circular shape, a couple of the bodies still moving slightly. The Romanian powered up his flame-thrower and incinerated them.

The SS officer came back over and looked annoyed. He stared at the Romanian, then at Alina, Juta and Olga. Was he annoyed that these three were still alive, or that the group of women had been killed without his say-so? He gestured with his hand to Olga.

'*Prosze.*' ('Please.')

He was almost polite, directing them to stand against a wall. Olga, Alina and Juta moved over and arranged themselves in a line, as if posing for a photograph. Then the SS officer walked off.

Thirty feet away, another group of men were shot – the last men from the basement. They fell in an orderly fashion to the ground, as though they knew how to arrange themselves even in death: massacre had its own etiquette. Two of them shouted, 'Long live . . .' but never made it to 'Poland'. It was quiet again, but for the cool breeze rustling in the trees.

A discussion between the SS officer and his Gestapo subordinate began. Alina picked up that it wasn't about them. The two Nazis were pointing at one another and seemed to be in some disagreement. It was as if Olga, Juta and Alina had been lined up to be shot, but now something more important had come up.

Alina studied the rendered wall they stood against. It had been untouched by fighting, surviving five years of war without so much as a crack. She stared at the contours of the cement as if it was an aerial photograph of a great prairie. She imagined herself high up in the sky, gazing down on a vast and incredible landscape.

The SS officer returned. He seemed relieved, as if he had resolved his problem. Wehrmacht soldiers herded a new group of women from a neighbouring cellar to stand with Olga and her daughters against the wall. The soldiers reloaded, and Olga told Alina to shut her eyes.

Some of the women were praying, but Alina was annoyed. She wanted total silence. Olga was cradling Juta's face in her cardigan. *Why isn't she holding me?* Alina thought.

Then she saw a bird, maybe a finch. It was small, with blue and yellow on its chest. Alina wondered how long it had been there. That was the curious thing; you would often see flocks of birds in Warsaw during the uprising, even in the middle of the fiercest fighting. They would wheel around the sky, hundreds of them, without a care in the world.

The bird was sitting there on a wall and Alina looked inquisitively at it. Tomorrow morning, she said to herself, I will be dead, and this little bird will still be flying around Warsaw; flitting from tree to tree, picking spiders and aphids from the bark, or perhaps sitting on a wall, watching another massacre being carried out. This bird would be alive and she would be dead. Alina thought about the bird, not in a sad way, more as if she was observing it neutrally and was already dead.

The Nazis fired, and a portion of women directly in front of Alina fell to the ground. Olga pulled her daughters hard down onto the ground with them, lying in the dirt with the corpses. A woman in her early sixties lay motionless with her back to my mum, not more than six inches away. The corpse had translucent hair, as if it had just been blow-dried.

*My mum sips her tea in the garden and shuts her eyes.*

'*I remember thinking how beautiful her hair was. It was if she had just come from the hairdresser. It was the strangest thing about the whole situation. How could she have her hair so beautifully prepared in the middle of this?*

'*It was so stupid what we had done. Lie down and pretend to be dead. It was like that child's game, sleeping lions. My mother had told us to do this stupid thing, and I imagined the Germans were either laughing at us or didn't care.*

*There were dead bodies all around and there were living bodies in amongst them, there were people standing who were about to be shot, and somehow there was no difference between any of us. We would all be killed in a second anyway.*

'*But you didn't die,' I remind my mum. 'And Olga saved you.'*

'*Yes, I suppose she did,' my mum replies slowly, her eyes opening. She stares at me brightly, as if this thought had never occurred to her before.*

'*We were lying there waiting for a lifetime and the order to fire again didn't come. The way I'm telling you now, you must think I was scared. I wasn't. You're not frightened to die, and you're not really surprised you've lived. You take it all.'*

'Why didn't they fire?'

'Every day I used to ask myself that question. I thought that maybe the pretty girl the SS man liked was in the group still alive. I don't speculate, not anymore. Someone decided not to kill us.'

In the end, concluded Alina, what did it matter why she, her sister and mother were spared? Nothing had changed. It only meant that they would die tomorrow.

Or maybe be lucky again tomorrow.

# 12

## *Pruszków*

*15 September 1944, Warsaw*

There was a good reason why Olga and Alina were spared. Twenty-four hours before the Nazis discovered their cellar, Reinefarth began issuing orders contradicting Hitler. The conversation between the SS officer and his Gestapo man in front of my mum at the wall presumably reflected a confusion about whether it was still policy to massacre civilians.

Like much of the Nazi high command, Reinefarth feared that, in defeat, he would be put on trial for war crimes. Surrendered combatants and civilians could not simply be shot anymore, they had to be taken prisoner under the Geneva Convention.

When my mother, aunt and grandmother were lined up, German soldiers on the ground no longer knew what to do. Some units continued to kill 'anything moving' in accordance with Hitler's orders; other SS officers were preparing to avoid execution by the Allies and told their soldiers to spare civilians.

The women, men and children shot were killed because their murderers had not got the new memo from Reinefarth. My mum, grandmother and aunt were put up against a wall at the very moment the new orders were being debated in front of them by the SS officer and his second-in-command.

On 11 September, Himmler's directive to kill every man, woman and child in Warsaw was formally rescinded, and the ambiguity ended. A new memo arrived in Warsaw. The Reich was now stretched to breaking point, it said, and due to an alarming depletion of slave labour in the east, it would now be necessary to send Warsaw's surviving inhabitants to Pruszków, a sorting camp just outside the city.

There they would be 'processed': either to the east, or to the extermination camps that required new labour to dismantle the killing factories; helping to destroy all evidence of the Holocaust.

### 23 September 1944, Pruszków Camp, Central Poland

Alina, Juta and Olga were crammed in total darkness. They had been standing for three days, ever since they left Warsaw. Every inch of the train wagon was filled with human bodies; several people had died from thirst and exhaustion, but remained upright, held in position by the living.

For the first two days in the train, they sat in sidings not moving. Through tiny gaps in the slats, Alina saw other trains passing extremely slowly, and Wehrmacht guards walked past, smoking cigarettes and chatting. There was silence in their wagon, except for the low moaning of one old woman and the crying of a baby that Alina never saw.

On the third day the train lumbered into motion, travelling at a snail's pace through the outskirts of Warsaw and out on a flat plain. Alina observed the buildings disappear entirely and farmland open out, then day turned to night, and the train stopped. They heard the noise before they saw anything. Shouting and dogs barking. Piercing white light poured through the cracks in the wood, illuminating exhausted faces in the wagon. Suddenly, the heavy doors were pulled open and they heard a refrain they knew well by now.

'*Raus! Raus!*'

Alina had no idea where they were. Floodlights surrounded a marching square, like a football ground. There were dogs and machine-gun posts, and people stood between chalked lines with hastily assembled belongings – prams, typewriters and birdcages – on the ground beside them. People had been told before boarding the train to leave their belongings behind, but many had ignored the order. Many were dressed in their best Sunday clothes, told by the Nazis they were being 'relocated'. Gestapo officers barked orders, kicking and punching people in the queue. Ukrainian soldiers shouted in Polish, whilst Polish police officers stood back watching. Some were playing cards on a wooden box and laughing, others looked pensive. The place felt edgy.

Alina, Juta and Olga got off the train and plunged their heads into a cow trough filled with water. It was the best water my mum had ever tasted – her first drink in seventy-two hours. They were prodded with a long stick by a Ukrainian guard, who didn't utter a word. He was prompting them to stand in one particular queue together. Across the ground, Gestapo officers were shouting out a mechanical metronome: '*Links! Richtig! Links! Richtig!*' ('Left! Right! Left! Right!')

Men were told to go left, women and children to go right. To the back of the area, in shadow, a low-slung Citroën Traction was parked. Two SS officers sat on the bonnet, their faces in darkness, watching impassively.

They were in Pruszków, a sorting camp for Auschwitz. It was here that it was decided whether they would go to Auschwitz Birkenau II and the gas chambers, or the hard labour camp at Auschwitz I; there was also a chance they could walk free. The three women stood patiently, awaiting their fate. Olga believed all fate was pre-ordained, including everything that happened in the war. Fate, however, could sometimes be encouraged in a certain direction by a little human intervention.

As she stood waiting to be questioned by the SS, Olga held in her left palm a small pebble that she rubbed between forefinger and thumb; maybe if she rubbed it hard enough, the stone would deliver her and her two girls from evil. In five years of war, Olga was sure that her powers had guaranteed their survival, and her fingers had worn a tiny indent into the stone's middle.

Pruszków was a place of formalised terror. One Ukrainian guard was seen lurching into the mass of people and biting a woman with a headscarf in the middle of the face. There was no reason for the attack. The guard sunk his teeth into her forehead, then as quickly as he'd lunged, he retreated back to his starting position in the gloom, like an eel retreating to a crevice. Alina had seen many things in the war, but not this.

Blood poured into the woman's nose and eyes, but she stood resolutely straight. She knew that if she fell to the ground, she would be killed. The Ukrainian soldier had moved further down the queue, looking to repeat his trick. Two frantic dogs on the end of chains tied to a thin, bent post jumped in frenzied circles of excitement, smelling blood.

In the centre of the large, floodlit gravel area was a desk with two chairs. It was an oddly cosy set-up, like a doctor's surgery. A German SS officer sat primly behind the desk with a short Polish police officer – a translator – hunched next to him.

Olga stood waiting to be called, and looked about her. Dogs gnawed bodies on the ground, whilst women sat on the ground breastfeeding their babies as rats scuttled between their legs. There were children wailing on separation from their parents: they would plead with the guards to be together, only to be silenced with a bullet or a boot. Olga pulled her daughters closer to her chest.

In spite of everything she had been through, Alina sensed the quality of evil here was different. The entire light-drenched arena had the air of an antechamber to something primal and unprecedented.

Olga was called forward, her two daughters trailing obediently behind her. They looked mismatched and suspicious as a family:

Olga was short and dark-haired; Juta, now aged eighteen, was tall and pretty, with straw-blonde hair; and thirteen-year-old Alina was short, dark-haired and plump, like her mother.

A Polish family with four children went before them in front of the SS officer. The father was asked a question through the translator and the SS officer waited patiently for his reply.

'What's he saying?' Alina whispered to Juta.

'I can't hear.'

After the father spoke, the SS officer consulted with the translator and then, without warning, gestured casually to the exit gate. The family picked up their suitcases and walked to what appeared to be freedom.

'My God,' Alina whispered to Juta. 'We could get out of here if we play our cards right.'

'Shut up,' Juta replied, without looking at her sister. 'You've no idea where they're going.'

The SS officer gestured delicately with his hand for Olga and her daughters to come forward. He had a big book, and was looking down at it as he spoke. The translator repeated the Nazi's question in Polish.

'Where is the children's father?'

'He's in London.'

The Nazi looked up, and studied Olga in more detail.

'What is he doing there?' he said.

'He's involved with the Polish government.'

Juta and Alina exchanged nervous glances. What the hell was Olga doing?

The SS officer began scribbling in his book.

'He's dead,' Olga blurted, suddenly changing tack. The truth was she had no idea where Michael was, or if he was alive.

The Nazi said nothing, and carried on scribbling. Eventually he spoke again.

'Other children?'

'I have two boys, back in Warsaw. They're good boys, all grown up now, I have no idea what they're doing there. Kazhik has a medal, for courage at school . . .'

Olga began to mumble and contradict herself, filling the silence with inane, irrelevant words. If she carried on speaking at speed, she thought, perhaps this whole terrible situation would magically disappear. The SS officer said nothing.

The truth was that the last time Olga had seen her sons, they had mocked their mother for pleading with them to stay in the flat. On the streets, the Warsaw uprising was starting. They had ignored her, clattering out of the door with two faulty rifles. She had no idea if her sons were alive.

The SS guard pointed at Olga's two remaining children: her daughters, trembling in skimpy summer dresses in the cold autumn night.

'Do they speak German?'

Olga was back at him before he'd even finished the question. 'My oldest, Juta, yes sir. She speaks fluent German . . . and French.'

Juta stood stiffly to attention. The SS officer looked her up and down, then turned back to his book.

'Age?'

'*Osiemnascie*,' Olga said. 'She's eighteen.'

'Over there,' the SS commander said to the translator, scribbling again in his book.

'What?' Alina whispered to her sister.

'Over there,' Juta replied, looking confused. Neither knew what this could possibly mean.

The translator ordered Juta to join a group of women standing apart from everyone else. Juta hesitated, and then the translator barked without warning. '*Tam! Schnell!*' ('Over there! Quick!') Juta looked imploringly at her mother, and then shuffled uncertainly towards the women.

'Where are they going?' Alina asked.

'She speaks German,' Olga replied dismissively. 'She'll be fine.' Olga had no idea if Juta would be fine or where she was going.

'Perhaps I shouldn't have said that,' Olga whispered, as much to herself as to Alina.

The women chosen were cordoned off, guarded by three Wehrmacht soldiers with a machine gun on a tripod. The crowds beyond the cordon were beginning to mill in a more anxious way, their panic rising. Some people were shouting and wailing that they would be shot. The crowd surged forward and then as quickly ebbed, the crescendo of fear rising and falling with each new volley of barked commands from the Germans.

The SS officer sat at his trestle table in the middle, an oasis of calm. His interview with Olga was about to end. The Nazi had said nothing for what seemed an age.

Alina gazed through the crowd of bodies, looking for her sister.

'They're pretty girls,' Alina whispered to Olga, gesturing to the group of women Juta had now joined. It had all happened so quickly. One moment Juta was there, the next she was gone. Olga looked pleadingly at the SS officer. She wanted her daughter back by her side, but it was too late.

'Are you fit?' the Nazi asked Olga suddenly.

'Sir?' Olga replied, unsure what he had said.

'Are. You. Fit?'

Olga nodded. He gestured with his hand for Olga and Alina to join another, far larger group. It was utterly unclear how this Nazi system of classification was working. In the chaos of Pruszków, different groups had been chosen for fates only the SS knew about, yet it was unclear if even they knew who was destined for what.

Olga and Alina went over and sat on the ground on the far side of the arena with a hundred or so people. Some were asleep, some lay motionless with their eyes wide open, staring at the sky; they looked as if they had been there for days. There was a large painted sign above them, nailed between two telegraph poles: *ARBEIT* (WORK).

Alina looked across, hoping to see her sister's group again. The women were mostly of about Juta's age, some were much younger – fourteen or fifteen – and two or three were in their forties. Some were crouched on the ground, sobbing quietly. One was applying lipstick and straightening the seams of her tights, as if preparing for a night out.

## 24 September 1944, Pruszków Camp

Juta tried to catch Alina's eye. They were ten metres apart, awaiting deportation on different trains to separate camps at Auschwitz. Juta stood with the group of chosen women.

No one in the huge floodlit arena had any idea what time, or day, it was anymore. The milky pre-dawn mist hung in drapes around what had become thousands of people lying on the ground. The *Arbeit* group had expanded hugely, whilst Juta's group of women remained no more than twenty.

A Gestapo guard, the arbitrary invisible line between the two groups, leant on his machine gun, lolling in and out of consciousness. The SS had gone, and the Ukrainian guards were drinking alcohol in a shed.

Alina could feel herself drifting off to sleep too. Olga was already lying with her face against a stranger's battered suitcase, snoring. Then Alina heard her sister's voice.

'Alencu . . . *Alencu*.'

Alencu was Juta's childhood nickname for Alina. Juta's face loomed over, her voice crossing into my mother's dream. Alina imagined herself on a rowing boat floating on a river in sunlight. Perhaps back home. She gazed up from the floor of the boat. Juta's face, bathed in light, was beautiful.

'I'm sorry,' Juta whispered. Sun was pouring through her hair.

Juta had an expression that Alina had never seen before. She struggled for a moment to work out what it might be, then alighted upon the answer. It was compassion.

'Sorry for what?' she asked.

'I should have said it was Pavel who was adopted.'

'What are you talking about?'

'When Kazhik said you were the adopted one. We all knew it was Pavel. He knows it too.'

My mother gazed at Juta, her face mottled with the shadows of the trees. She recognised the river – it was the one just a mile from their house in the country.

'I'm sorry, Alencu.'

'It's OK.'

'Do you think you can forgive me?' Juta asked.

'There's nothing to forgive.'

'Forgive me for what is going to happen, I mean.'

'I have no idea what you're talking about. How do we know what's going to happen?'

'It doesn't matter,' Juta said, her voice distant now. The sunlight shimmered off the river, making Juta invisible now. 'Go back to sleep.'

Juta was nowhere near my mother and never spoke to her in reality. The whole conversation was a dream – a goodbye that was denied to Alina, but my mother dreamed to make her last moment with her sister bearable. To make it real. She has had the same dream many times over the years, but more often than not, the boat is empty. There is no Juta.

Suddenly two SS officers arrived in a jeep at the far end of the arena and relayed orders to subordinate Gestapo officers. It was a new day in hell, just beginning. As soon as the SS were finished, the guards were upon them. They shouted at the group of women first.

'*Diesen Weg! Raus!*' ('This way! Quickly!')

One of the SS officers sauntered casually over to watch the women being herded on to the train that had been waiting all night for them. He swaggered like a movie idol. My mother saw Juta trying to push her way futilely into the *arbeit* group, but she was punched on the shoulder with a rifle to get her back in line.

'Politely,' the SS officer scolded the guard who had punched Juta. He smiled at Juta as he said it.

There was nothing Juta or my mother could do. Juta was like a bather being taken out to sea on an undertow that was impossible to fight. There was a calm resignation on the faces of the chosen women as they hitched up their skirts and clambered on board the carriage. The SS officer turned once again to the guard with the gun, and smiled again, his eyes lingering on the women.

Alina turned to her mother, as they watched from a distance. 'They're leaving.'

Olga stared hopelessly at Juta as she got on the train. Olga had tears streaming down her face, but there was a complete absence of emotion. She did nothing to wipe them.

'You did this,' Alina continued. 'You told the SS guard Juta could speak German. You could have said nothing, and Juta would be with us. But you told him.'

Olga ignored Alina. From the train, Juta appeared to spin round, looking for her mother in the crowd. She mouthed something to Olga.

*Alina sips her tea in the garden.*

*'What did she say?' I ask.*

*'My mother wanted to believe Juta said, "I love you."'*

*'What did she say if it wasn't "I love you"?'*

*'How should I know? Olga told me forever afterwards that Juta said "I love you", but I think it was just my mother's way of forgiving herself for what she'd done.'*

*My mum pauses for a moment to reflect on that awful moment, transported back to the transit camp on the outskirts of Warsaw in the early-morning light: the dream of Juta bathed in light on the river, and then waking up to find her gone.*

*'Perhaps she didn't say "I love you",' Alina says slowly. 'Maybe it was "I hate you". That's what Juta should have been saying, at least.'*

*'That's what you wanted Juta to say to your mother,' I suggest, 'because that's what you thought she deserved.'*

*'I don't speculate,' my mum says, waving her hand dismissively in front of her face, as if to brush away the whole episode. 'I didn't see Juta get on the train. I wasn't even given that moment to say goodbye, so I have no idea. I'd already said goodbye, in my own way. My mother wanted to believe Juta said "I love you", so if that's what she wanted, that is what I will believe too.'*

Olga stared desperately back at Juta as she boarded the train, trying to form a reply with her mouth, but the words wouldn't come, and it didn't matter. The doors were locked. Juta was gone. It was the last time my mother saw her sister alive.

### 24 September 1944, Central Poland

*This next section about Juta is based on information my mother received about Juta whilst still in the camp, and from what she discovered after the war.*

The chosen women from Pruszków sorting camp were transported to Auschwitz in second class *Deutsche Reichsbahn* carriages. They sat in an ordinary suburban train normally reserved for Nazi officers, not the freight trains used for Jews and Poles, made of wooden wagons with locked sliding doors. This train was made for humans, not cattle.

The women on board settled themselves in compartments. The rain streamed across the window as the darkness outside deepened. Pruszków was on the outskirts of Warsaw, but their new destination was deep in Polish farmland. Even though the women on board the train had been 'chosen', they had no idea what this meant, or where they were going.

After about an hour, the doors to their compartment slid open and a handsome, clean-shaven SS guard stood in the doorway. He looked a bit drunk, and swayed slightly as the train lurched. He was dressed in an immaculately pressed black tunic with skulls on the lapels, and removed his cap to reveal a deeply furrowed forehead, and huge, dyed bouffant hair. He smelt overpoweringly of cologne, which crashed like a wave through the compartment.

'Good evening,' he said.

The women looked blankly at him.

'May I introduce myself. I am commander of the female population of Auschwitz-Birkenau. I have pleasure in welcoming you. We shall be arriving shortly at the camp, and I look forward to getting to know you all better. *Heil Hitler.*'

Then he was gone.

If it indeed was the commander, as he claimed, the man was Franz Hössler, a bizarre veteran of Auschwitz. He had arrived four years earlier at the newly opened concentration camp in 1940 working as an auxiliary in the kitchen, but quickly rose through the ranks, volunteering to be part of the first mass murders of Jews. In 1942, he worked on construction of Solahütte, the SS holiday camp eighteen miles south of Auschwitz, where the elite guard took a break from the Holocaust, sunbathing and hiking in the woods. On his return to Auschwitz, he was promoted to run the *Sonderkommando*: Jewish prisoners forced to participate in the gassing and burning of bodies, who were in turn murdered and replaced by new Jewish recruits.

In 1943, Hössler's reward was to be appointed *Schutzhaft-lagerführer,* the head of the women's camp, where he worked with one of the most feared of all officers in the camp, the highest-ranking female SS guard in Auschwitz, Maria Mandl, known to prisoners as 'The Beast'.

Together, Mandl and Hössler were responsible for opening the 'joy divisions', the brothels at Auschwitz. SS doctor Siegfried Schwela said that efficiently run whorehouses would be good for German soldier morale, and if the brothels were in the camp, hygiene could be policed. 'Vouchers' or green tokens to the brothels were given as a reward for hard work or 'productivity'. The brothels were known as 'Dolls' Houses' and the largest was called 'Puff' in Block 24 of Auschwitz, behind the *Arbeit Macht Frei* arrival gates.

The Nazis demanded racial segregation in the brothels, as in the rest of the camp. German guards were to have sex only with German women. But by late 1944, with the Nazi war machine collapsing, German-speaking Poles like Juta could be selected.

Women in the camp were coerced into becoming prostitutes at any time, though a few were selected long before they arrived, at Pruszków. On arrival, they were examined, had disinfectant cream rubbed into their vaginas, and given special living quarters separate from the rest of the camp. They had their own rooms, food and clothing, were given lingerie confiscated from dead prisoners and had strict instructions for sexual intercourse.

Because paranoia persisted that Jewish women might unwittingly be chosen, SS officers were instructed to have sex only with women who were Aryan in appearance. They were to have sex only in the missionary position, and this would be monitored by other Nazi officers, who watched through peepholes drilled into the walls. They were given a fifteen-minute time slot.

As a reward for becoming part of the Third Reich's sex workers, women were promised their families would gain special favours: extra food, fewer beatings and maybe even avoid the gas chamber. None of these promises were true.

Juta knew none of this as she sat in the train compartment heading for Auschwitz. She did not even know where they were going. There were two fates for the women selected for that train: the *sonderbauten* 'special buildings' (the brothels) or the *Politische Abteilung* (camp administration office), where they would participate in the implementation of the Holocaust.

Which of these fates befell Juta, the SS Commander had yet to decide.

## 24 September 1944, Auschwitz, Southern Poland

Juta smelt boiled glue. She wasn't sure if it was really glue or perhaps pig fat mixed with some kind of ash. She spent some minutes mulling over what it might be and then asked the other women in the compartment if they could smell it too. No one knew what it was.

The Commander had gone, but another guard, a woman, opened the door and ordered them to get out of the compartment. She had a square, expressionless face, and wore a brown, shapeless tunic and matching skirt.

'Out,' she said, and turned.

At first, Juta thought they were back at Pruszków. There were the same floodlights, but many more people, hundreds coming from other trains onto newly constructed ramps and being herded into a bewildering number of senseless queues. The German guards appeared to have none of the energy for the sadism that Juta had witnessed in Pruszków. They looked defeated.

The first thing Juta saw when she got off the train were huge cotton sheets being used to collect the belongings of the arriving refugees. They hung from the sides of freight wagons like giant's intestines filled with suitcases. Juta was spared the sight that greeted most prisoners when they arrived: rituals the Nazis had developed over four years of the camp's operation, honed to a fine art of cruelty.

Small girls and boys would be told to walk towards a German guard with a stick; the same kind used for fairground roller-coasters to determine if a child is tall enough to ride. Those taller than the stick lived. Those smaller were shot and thrown on a pile of bodies.

Guards shaved the heads of female prisoners with electric sheep clippers, claiming that it was to prevent the spread of lice. They then pushed them to the ground, beating the machine roughly around the head in a circular motion. The women were herded onto a rickety box car and taken on a single gauge rail-way into the camp.

These women rarely lived more than an hour after arriving. The removal of hair was not about controlling lice, but prepar-ing the bodies for the crematoria. The Nazis found that corpses without hair burnt more efficiently. The shorn hair was then used to stuff pillows.

The women on Juta's train were exempt from all of this. German and Ukrainian guards watched sheepishly as the chosen women walked past. The guards' eyes travelled predatorially along the line, lingering on a blouse, a skirt or a stocking seam, but the moment they had gone past, the guards resumed their herding and beating.

A pale grey light hung in the sky over the camp's roofed arrival arch, whilst ribbons of bulbs draped on electric fencing guided Juta and the other women to their block. They passed brick outbuildings and rows of wooden huts, but marched steadily on under escort to their special quarters in Auschwitz I, the oldest part of the camp.

If women were chosen to be prostitutes, they had separate brick quarters from the rest of the prison population, and each woman had her own room with a single bed, a lamp, basic furniture and a sink. Juta was taken to the same area, though she had no idea why.

The Commander appeared again in the corridor, as if he had transported himself magically from the train. Next to him was the block *Aufseherin*, a Polish woman in identical brown hessian sack skirt and shirt to the woman on the train. Her job was to look after the accommodation block and make sure the prostitutes were kept clean, attractively dressed and free of disease.

The Commander visited each of the women in the accommodation adjacent to Block 24, one by one. It was still unclear whether they were to be prostitutes at all, or chosen for another 'special duty'.

Juta sat on her bed, hands in her lap, and awaited his inspection.

## 13

## *Auschwitz*

*27 September 1944, Auschwitz*

Juta had been in the camp for three days. She slept alone in a building to the far end of Auschwitz I, near Block 24. It was far superior to the wooden huts where the vast majority of prisoners were held, who were often forced to sleep sideways due to lack of space.

Roll call was at 4.40 a.m. She heard sirens, and then the music. The women's orchestra had been disbanded the month before, and replaced by the echo of deceased musicians, as a muffled recording that sounded like Brahms crackled over the barbed wire. Juta rose wearily to her feet from the concrete floor, already fully clothed.

A woman was standing in the corner of the room, watching Juta. She was the block's *Aufseherin,* or manager. *Aufseherin* had considerable power within the camp hierarchy. They were little more than a step up from the cruel *kapos*, the prisoners-turned-enforcers who beat and abused whomever they chose in their huts. But the *Aufseherin* were in direct contact with senior SS officers; in Block 24, they looked after the prostitutes. In her own way, this woman held life and death over Juta.

She told Juta that her name was Lydia and she had already survived two years in Auschwitz. Lydia had arrived from Wroclaw as a prisoner, but because she spoke fluent German, she had been deemed useful to the SS. Lydia was not sentimental about the other women and girls who had come through her block and been sent to the gas chambers after ceasing to be 'useful'. She never forgot that she was a prisoner too and could be murdered at any moment.

Becoming a prostitute was no guarantee of surviving the camp, although many women 'chosen' were led to believe it might be. It was, in fact, the opposite. Commander Hössler and his accomplice, Maria Mandl, 'The Beast', were the pimps of Block 24, exploiting the women they 'chose', whilst trying to gain favour from their immediate masters who visited their brothel.

Juta knew nothing of this nepotistic system, or that it would soon be coming to an end. However, she did know, as everyone knew, that Russian gunfire was rumbling in the distance and the Germans would soon lose the war. The rats were leaving the sinking ship, she was told, and new more vicious rats were coming, making the final days of the camp perilous. Maria Mandl, who effectively ran the women's camp, was being moved to Dachau and replaced by Elisabeth Volkenrath.

Volkenrath was highly ambitious and conniving. Her real name was Mühlau and she had come to the camp first as an unskilled volunteer worker – an *ungelernte hilfskraft*. Mühlau was a nobody, but she had ingratiated herself with the SS by being sadistically violent to prisoners and had risen quickly through the ranks.

Mühlau began a relationship with one of the camp's highest-ranking SS officers, Heinz Volkenrath. In 1943, they married in a bizarre ceremony at Auschwitz, where the newlyweds were given an SS guard of honour as the crematoria belched smoke behind them, confetti mixing with the ash of human remains.

If Juta was going to survive at Auschwitz until the Russians came, she would need status there. Juta needed a powerful friend, and Lydia, the *aufseherin*, offered to help her.

Juta had no idea why, but had only one question. Where were her sister and mother?

*28 September 1944, Ożarów, on the outskirts of Warsaw*

At 7 a.m. on 28 September, the surviving resistance leaders of the AK were taken by motorcade, flanked by Nazi motorcycle outriders, to a country house on the outskirts of Warsaw.

Both sides needed peace: the uprising was defeated, but so were the Germans. The AK were to negotiate with the SS's greatest master of evasion, SS Commander Von dem Bach, a man who would do anything to survive. Even though Bach had overall command of the *Dirlewanger* in Warsaw, authorising the murder of 200,000 Poles, he later testified at the Nuremberg trial against Hermann Goering and his ex-SS comrades, so saving himself.

Bach's reward was immunity from prosecution. After the war, he changed his name to Zelewski, to sound Polish, and spent years eluding Mossad and the Nazi hunters. He worked as a night-watchman, but was finally caught in 1958. Ironically, he was sentenced for his part in the murder of an SS officer in 'the Night of the Long Knives', when he had first got a taste for betrayal.

Bach could easily have ended up in Brazil or Paraguay, hiding in the jungle as other ex-Nazis did, but he used his old Polish family name to recast himself as a victim. He even meekly denounced his own crimes in an Israeli court. Bach was an obsequious and cunning survivor, as slippery as an eel.

In the country house in Ożarów, outside Warsaw, he began by flattering the AK resistance leaders. He told the commander how brave his fighters had been.

'Street fights are some of the most exhausting for soldiers,' he said. 'The abnormally difficult conditions . . . made it very difficult for the German soldier to keep his blood cold and that is why some very unpleasant things took place, things which should not take place between two cultured nations.'

The resistance leaders knew they had to do business with this eel. The uprising could not take much more; they were on the brink of collapse and the Russians had not come to save them. They also knew that the Germans would probably go back on any treaty agreed and commit a final cataclysmic massacre: they would kill everyone left in Warsaw to complete Hitler's wish.

Bach sensed the resistance leader's desperation to sign peace and laid it on with a trowel. He was happy to compromise, he said, conceding to pretty much everything the Poles wanted – respecting civilians, basic sanitation and medical support for the dying. Bach conceded, because it didn't matter.

The war was fast moving and anything agreed would be redundant in a week anyway. The Nazis knew the Russians would soon take Warsaw. The important thing for both sides was to get out of the stalemate in which they found themselves. They both knew it.

The only stumbling block was Adolf Hitler – holed up in his bunker, still clinging on as the leader of the Third Reich – and his dream of murdering the whole of Warsaw.

When Bach phoned Hitler, he was apprehensive. Hitler was by now so unhinged and quixotic, it was hard to tell whether he would congratulate Bach on a famous negotiation, or have him court-martialled and executed for contradicting his order to exterminate the *dungervolke*.

Luckily for Bach, he got through to Hitler's unctuous brother-in-law, cavalry officer Hermann Fegelein, who was married to Eva Braun's sister Gretl. This made Fegelein family. The fact he was also a serial womaniser and a drunk, who was habitually unfaithful to Gretl and often broke down weeping in front of Hitler for no reason, was charitably overlooked by the Führer.

Fegelein boasted to anyone who would listen about what a great horseman he was and how he had competed in the 1936 Berlin Olympics. In reality, he had been eliminated in the qualifiers, but Hitler didn't care.

In 1945, close to the end, Hitler would ask Fegelein to join him in a suicide pact. Fegelein would politely decline and make a run for it. Later he was found drunk in his apartment wearing civilian clothes and with a train ticket to Switzerland. In his briefcase were incriminating documents about Hitler and Himmler that he hoped to use to barter with the Allies. Hitler had him dragged back to the bunker, where he was put before a firing squad for desertion. Fegelein was so inebriated, he couldn't stand straight to face the guns, and was said to have pissed on his shoes by way of a farewell.

On 28 September 1944, however, when Bach telephoned the bunker from Warsaw and Fegelein picked up, he was still one of Hitler's few remaining confidants. Albert Speer, who could spot a phoney from a thousand yards, called Fegelein 'one of the most disgusting people in Hitler's inner circle', which is quite some achievement, given the competition.

Hitler sat moodily in his chair, watching Fegelein speak to Bach. He was seething at this final humiliation: 'A signed peace with the Poles in Warsaw!' But before he started ranting, Hitler had one question he wanted Fegelein to relay to Bach about the leader of the resistance.

'Who is this General Bor?'

'Oh, didn't you know?' Bach replied. 'His real name is Count Tadeusz Komorowski, the famous showjumper.'

'Him!' Fegelein shouted out, guffawing with laughter. 'A fantastic guy! That changes everything. Wait a minute, please.'

Fegelein told Hitler that he and Bor had competed against one another at the Berlin Olympics. Count Komorowski, Fegelein assured Hitler, was a noble and worthy opponent.

Hitler nodded approvingly and signed off on peace. Had Hermann Fegelein not been a liar and claimed to have been a friend of the showjumping legend Count Komorowski, who loathed the man, Hitler would probably have vetoed the whole thing and had Warsaw wiped off the face of the earth.

Thanks to the boastful Fegelein, my mum survived, and I am here to write her story.

*I get a phone call at 11.30 at night. It lights up on my phone: ALINA.*

   *'Hello?' I answer. 'You OK?'*

   *Silence.*

   *'Alina?'*

   *'Alina? Is it Alina?' she answers distantly. 'Am I Alina?'*

   *'Are you all right?'*

   *'I am Alina. Why have you phoned? Tell me what you want.' She puts the phone down abruptly.*

   *The following morning, I drive up and ask my mum what happened last night. We sit in the front garden, social distancing.*

   *'Are you OK?' I ask.*

   *'What are you talking about?'*

   *'The phone call. You phoned me and seemed a bit confused.'*

   *'Do you want a glass of wine? I can tell you about Warsaw.'*

   *I am realising now how this book is increasingly coming to stand in for life. My mum is happier delving deep into her war memories than dealing with the present, which is becoming ever more fractured, incomprehensible and frightening. The past is becoming a comfort for her.*

   *It is a measure of how terrifying losing her mind must be that reliving the trauma of war is preferable. Part of me is scared for her and for us all about what the journey across the battlefield of dementia will entail.*

*2 October 1944, Warsaw*

Kazhik was captured hours before the remaining AK forces surrendered. He turned a corner, only three streets away from the family flat, and was ordered to stop.

'Halt, soldier!'

Kazhik had his back to a Wehrmacht infantryman in his early twenties. He had never been called a 'soldier' by a Nazi. In years to come, he would say this moment was the closest he came to death in Warsaw. There was no reason for the German not to shoot him, it would be nothing personal; it was simply easier to kill Kazhik than drag him to the newly created pen for POWs in the old square.

Kazhik turned slowly and stared at the soldier. He lifted his arms.

'Shoot', Kazhik said, coaxing the German on.

The Wehrmacht soldier had his gun trained unsteadily at Kazhik's chest. It wobbled when Kazhik spoke. The soldier repeated his order.

'Surrender!'

Kazhik stared defiantly at the German, refusing to move. The soldier looked imploringly at Kazhik. Then he dropped his gun to his side and stood limply, signalling for Kazhik to follow him.

'Please,' the German said. 'Please come.'

The two boys walked across the rubble together, the German with his gun slung over his shoulder. Sometimes the German would lead, sometimes Kazhik would; they both knew where they were going, careful to avoid the deep holes in the debris.

*October 1944, Stalag X-B, Sandbostel, Northern Germany*

Kazhik was now a prisoner of war under the Hague Convention. He sat on dusty waste ground at Fort Bem on the outskirts of Warsaw with a thousand surrendered AK fighters in rags, just like him. The German guards who watched over them, some conscripted only days before, shared their cigarettes with the Poles.

Days later, Kazhik was transferred to Pruszków, where his

sisters and mother had been 'processed' to Auschwitz a month before. From Pruszków, Kazhik was sent to Northern Germany, to Stalag X-B near Sandbostel, in Lower Saxony.

Stalag X-B was one of the Third Reich's largest prisoner-of-war camps. It held 30,000 soldiers from numerous countries, for which there was a strict hierarchy. Top of the pile were British and American POWs, who were treated according to the Geneva Convention. They received regular packages from their families and food and medical support from the Red Cross.

Next in the pecking order were the French and Belgians; then Italian POWs, seen as traitors by both the Germans and Allied prisoners; below them were the Russians, denied all rights under the Geneva Convention. They were shot for the tiniest indiscretion, worked with barely any food and died in their thousands in Stalag X-B from malnutrition and disease. The Russians were the Nazis' true enemy: the lowest of the low.

When Kazhik arrived, the Poles were somewhere between the Italians and Russians in order of status. But as the German war collapsed, and the SS took overall control of the camp from the Wehrmacht, Stalag X-B was suddenly inundated with thousands of new inmates: refugees and AK fighters from Warsaw and ghostly, emaciated prisoners sent out of concentration camps like Auschwitz.

Kazhik was lucky to get a place on a bunk in one of the masonry stone huts. These were warmer than the wooden huts or tents, and they were watertight. As the winter closed in, he would be very thankful of it.

*The lockdown restrictions of the Covid-19 pandemic intensify. Everyone has been asked to stay at home wherever possible, and only to meet one other person outside at a social distance. Alina pretends to agree to the new rules, but later confesses that she has 'escaped' several times a day down to the shops. Nothing was open, so she stared through the windows at the goods she couldn't buy, not unlike in Warsaw during the war.*

*Our meetings at Cartons cannot continue, so instead we speak on the phone or I sit on my parents' front lawn, ten feet away, my mum sitting on the front porch step with a glass of wine. It is a good time to talk.*

*The birds tweeting seem over-amplified in the suburban street. There are no cars. No nothing. A woman in a headscarf, wearing goggles and a face mask, cycles past very slowly, taking a good fifteen seconds to pass the front of the house.*

*'Morning, Alina,' she says, her voice muffled as she creaks painfully past.*

*'Morning, Rashida, how are you?'*

*'Not so good, Alina, feeling a bit scared.'*

*'Do you want a glass of wine? Come and sit ten feet away.'*

*18 November 1944, Auschwitz*

Olga and Alina arrived two months after Juta on a freight train carrying close to a thousand people from Warsaw. Over a million people were evacuated after the collapse of the uprising and the peace between Bor and Bach. Before being sent to Auschwitz, they were shunted through a series of transit camps, staying sometimes for weeks in huts with barely any food or sanitation. Olga and Alina were in three transit sub-camps and numerous station sidings before finally being moved on to Auschwitz.

Olga continued to consult her tarot cards obsessively – sometimes twenty or thirty times a day – and was sure Juta was alive. She was also convinced that Juta's fluent German would save them all from death in Auschwitz; Olga could tell that the SS officer at Pruszków had been impressed by her daughter.

They arrived to a camp in chaos, with Russian gunfire and

rockets flashing on the horizon; the advancing Soviet army was less than twenty miles away. The camp was being broken up by the Nazis as they sought to erase all evidence of the Holocaust.

Auschwitz was unlike anything Alina had seen before. It was vast and sprawling, and there were miles of wooden huts and brick outbuildings, separated by electrified barbed wire. It had no beginning and no end.

The lingering smell the women had detected from the train now intensified in acridity: it was the smell of thousands of corpses being hastily dug up from the grounds around Auschwitz and burnt in mountainous pyres.

Even though the camp was entering its final days, it was as dangerous as ever. Alina and Olga disembarked from their train only weeks after the killing at Auschwitz had been at its most prolific. In October alone, 6,000 people a day were being gassed and burnt; the highest rate of death since the camp was built.

The tide turned against the Nazis at Auschwitz, as in the Warsaw ghetto, with an uprising. The *Sonderkommando* Jews, sensing the Germans were weakening, rose up against their tormentors, choosing Crematorium IV as their battleground. The prisoners had been secretly planning an uprising for months, and women working at the munitions factory had smuggled out small packets of gunpowder, aiming to blow up the gas chambers and crematoria.

On 7 October, they attacked the *kapos* and SS guards with knives, axes and two machine guns. The Jewish prisoners were quickly overwhelmed, but the camp commandant, Rudolf Höss, knew the spell of fear the Nazis cast over the prison population had been broken. As punishment, 200 prisoners were forced to strip and lie face down on the ground before being shot in the back of the head.

In early November, Himmler had ordered a complete halt to the gassing of prisoners and accelerated his plan to liquidate the camp. Auschwitz I and II were to be made into one giant city of refugees. Before then, new prisoners had been sorted at the arrival ramp into two groups: workers and those to be gassed. Now they were sorted into the 'unfit' and those who would work erasing any trace of genocide.

The gas chambers and crematoria were being dismantled brick by brick, as the SS rushed to cover their tracks, and the huge burial pits, where tens of thousands had been thrown after being shot, dug up and burnt. The new prisoners who did the digging were then also killed.

At least it wasn't Warsaw, Alina thought to herself. The camp offered my mum and grandmother unexpected respite from the constant terror of the uprising. In Auschwitz, there was accommodation and meagre food. Alina felt less uncertainty than she had cowering from the flame-throwers in the darkness of the cellars. She was mistaken, but that was how it felt.

The fear of death was different here. The gas chambers were finished, but now randomised shootings were the norm. Alina saw it the moment she was pulled from the train.

SS officers walked the length of the arrival ramp, dragging lost children beside them. They shouted, 'What kind of parent leaves their daughter abandoned in a place like this?' When the parents came forward, the SS shot the family. The collapse of the camp offered different dangers: now Nazi guards had licence to do what they wanted, freed from the systems that had been in place before. It was a new kind of barbarism.

Olga was happy they had arrived. It was where Juta was, and she believed they would be reunited at last. The SS had told Warsaw's prisoners that the Red Cross were on hand and they were promised proper beds and medicine. Perhaps it will be like the Swedish hospital, she thought.

Alina and Olga were taken to Auschwitz I, the oldest section of the complex. Like thousands of other new prisoners, they were there to work, dismantling evidence of the Holocaust. In truth, Auschwitz was overwhelmed with the numbers of new prisoners from Warsaw's collapse and no one knew what to do with them; shooting and burying this unwanted fresh pay-load of human livestock would only add to the logistic problem.

Thirteen-year-old Alina was old enough to count as a woman and therefore carry out hard labour. Had she been a small child or a 'girl', she would have been ineligible to dig and shot on arrival. Alina sensed the schizophrenia of the camp the moment she stepped through the gates. Half the SS seemed absorbed in frantic exodus, packing their belongings and planning escape from the advancing Russians, the other half were intent on carrying on as normal. Guards meted out shootings and beatings to maintain the violence now denied to them by the collapse of the genocide programme.

Olga and Alina were taken to their hut, run by a Ukranian *kapo*. They surveyed the bleak, flat landscape as they walked across the hard, cratered ground. Prisoners in striped pyjamas had once worn different coloured badges: red for political prisoners, pink for homosexuals, and yellow for Jewish, except there were virtually no Jews left beyond the *Sonderkommando*.

The Nazi priority now was self-preservation, not categorising new prisoners and handing out coloured badges. Prisoners were organised into small groups carrying out different tasks. Some, my mum noticed, were smashing stones and bricks with shovels for no apparent reason, others appeared to be sifting through ash looking for bones and pieces of skull, which would then be smashed with a hammer.

A group of women were wearing their old civilian clothes – moth-eaten coats and rags that had once been smart middle-class outfits. Alina saw a woman in her forties who appeared to have a tiara on her head and had fixed her hair, as if going out for a night at the theatre. She was tilling the ground with a hoe, preparing the ground for crops that would never be planted.

At their hut, they stood by the open door and looked in at their hut-mates. There was an utter absence of connection to a single person in the gloom; eyes stared through them like points of light dotted on bunk beds. A girl aged about fourteen came up to Alina and tugged her dress; she was so thin, she looked eight. Alina smiled, thinking she wanted to make friends, but the girl began crazily pulling at the sleeves, trying to rip the dress off Alina. Olga pushed her away and the girl returned nonchalantly to her bunk.

There was no space for them, so Olga found a place on some wet straw near the bucket used for defecation. The first few nights, Alina slept with Olga on the dirty straw. The other Poles in the hut did not speak to them, nor did they want to give up their valuable space on the bunk beds. When Olga tried to get shelf-space on one, she was punched square in the mouth by a Polish man crouched in a foetal position at one end. She hadn't seen him there and assumed his body was a pile of blankets.

At 5 a.m., they received watery soup in a metal cup and a stale piece of bread: their daily ration. As soon as the *kapo* left the hut, the other prisoners pounced on Olga and Alina, stealing the food.

'Why do you do this?' Olga screamed at them.

The prisoners stared impassively at her, folding themselves back on their bunks like crows returning to their perches. No one spoke to them for six days.

They were unaware that Juta was in a block less than half a mile away.

## 28 November 1944, London

Michael bumped into an old friend called Marcus. Michael was drinking a small glass of red wine by himself at the Hearth Club on Princes Gate, in South Kensington. The club was created at the outset of war as a hub for émigrés and the Polish government-in-exile. Michael despised the place ever since he was frozen out of the circle of power for the uprising.

He spent most of his time wandering parks and reading newspapers, searching for updates on the collapse of the Nazi war. The news of their demise was bittersweet. He had spent six years fighting the enemy and lost his whole family. Now Poland was about to be liberated, only to be enslaved by Stalin's Soviet empire.

It was Marcus who spotted Michael across the room. The Hearth Club was colonial in style, with waited tables and booths for conspiring in. He went over to join his old friend at the bar for a drink.

The two men had first met in Warsaw in the early 1930s. They worked together organising refugee repatriation schemes for Ukrainian and Jewish families being targeted by the Pilsudski regime. Marcus was a member of the KPP, the Polish Communist Party. In the mid-1930s, Stalin and Moscow viewed the KPP not as allies but enemies, because they refused to toe the Soviet line. The KPP were not Soviet stooges as Stalin wished, but a rag-bag assortment of radical socialists, libertarians, Trotskyites and anarchists.

In 1936, Marcus and Michael had worked together on the 'Unified Worker and Peasant Front': a loose alliance of socialists calling for a proletarian uprising against both the fascists and Stalin's Moscow. Members of the KPP and the Peasant Front were designated enemies of the Soviet Union; they were executed in Poland by Russian agents, or rounded up and sent to Russia to be tortured. Marcus and Michael considered themselves lucky to be alive in 1944, enjoying a drink together in London, a decade after Stalin tried to have them both killed.

The two men spent several hours drinking in the Hearth Club. They discussed the fate of Poland and the imbecilic leadership of the AK, the death of 'real socialism' – the kind they had pursued with the Peasant Front – and the looming ogre of Stalin, who would devour eastern Europe as the Nazis collapsed.

By the time they left at 2.30 a.m., they were very drunk. They veered dangerously through the empty streets of Kensington, crashing from one lamppost to the next. More importantly, they had a plan to save Poland.

# 14

## *Juta*

*1 December 1944, Auschwitz*

Olga and Alina had been three weeks in the camp and as the cold took a hold, it dug into every pore and crevice of the concentration camp.

Thousands of prisoners were being deported out of the death camps on trains to Germany. It was the biggest exodus from Auschwitz since it had been created. Along with starving prisoners, the trains were piled high with stolen valuables from 'Kanada', the name given to the group of warehouses where the possessions of Jewish and Polish prisoners had been kept by the Nazis, so called because Canada was reputed to be a land of untold riches.

Olga and Alina were left behind and tasked to clean the latrines. They heard the distant thunder of Russian artillery getting louder by the day. The Nazis knew it was only a matter of weeks before the Soviets would be at the gates and some began to ingratiate themselves with the prisoners, hoping that when the Russians came, they would put in a good word.

Guards tipped off prisoners about store cupboards that had been 'left open', or a lorry of potatoes that had 'overturned'. The *kapo* for their hut forbade anyone stealing food, but when he was presented with a tin of stew by one of the prisoners, he joined in the ransacking.

By December, the gas chambers and crematoria had been entirely broken up, or disguised as outbuildings and air-raid shelters. The chimneys were smashed and the trenches filled with bodies were cleared and burnt; the hollows packed down with ashes and bones dug out and filled with turf. The bone-crushing machines were broken and even the holes through which the Zyklon B that poisoned a million people had been poured were filled with concrete.

Behind the scenes, the SS knew the game was up. They stopped tattooing numbers on prisoners. Officers who had once pledged undying allegiance to the Führer and the 'Final Solution' began destroying incriminating documents, planning their exit strategy and covering their tracks.

Many had no intention of fighting to the end. They began burning their uniforms, scratching out their own SS tattoo, or turning it into a botched version of an Auschwitz serial number to look like a prisoner. The SS sought to dissolve into the civilian population and join the massed crowds of refugees wandering across Europe, and many of them succeeded.

Key to the SS plan for surviving after Auschwitz was to kill anyone in the camps – like the Jews of the *Sonderkommando* – who could identify them in a future court of law. It made my aunt Juta's situation very perilous.

The 'Protective Custody Camp Commander' – a title Hössler had given himself – prowled the women's camp, the clattering of his crab-like limbs and gun holster announcing his presence. His job was to protect prisoners from harm – a most extraordinary title to have at Auschwitz.

It gave him unique access to women he could exploit. Lydia told Juta that Hössler had chosen women from Juta's block for his own purposes, even though this was against Nazi protocol.

Lydia had no reason to help Juta. Most *aufseherin* were *gauleiters* (officers) concerned only with their own survival; they were merciless to the girls in their block, because it furthered their careers in the camp. The crueller they were, the faster they rose through the system. But some *aufseherin* secretly helped prisoners whilst appearing to work for the Germans.

The reason Lydia helped Juta was most probably because she herself had been spared the Dolls' House brothel by the *aufseherin* who looked after her own block when she had first arrived at Auschwitz. Lydia would have been chosen for the brothel in Block 24. She might well have thought that by becoming a prostitute, it would save her life. In truth, prostitutes were soon discarded by the SS and shot or gassed, often after contracting syphilis from the officers they had sex with. Instead, she got Lydia a job as a block toilet supervisor. Because the *aufseherin* saved Lydia, she now tried to save Juta.

Had Lydia been asked if Juta could work in the brothel, she would have needed to prove Juta was not a virgin to help her avoid this fate. We will never know if she succeeded, but the fact that Lydia was able to confirm to her superiors that Juta had already been selected for *Politische Abteilung*, the camp's administrative office, gives hope that she did.

Lydia found a cunning way of helping Juta avoid the brothels. She told the Commander that he himself had authorised this decision to let her work in the administration office. Lydia was lying, but her superior was drunk most nights and he often forgot what he had said or done. She persuaded him that Juta was perfect for the *Politische Abteilung*. She was pretty, spoke fluent German, and more importantly, Rudolf Höss – the king of Auschwitz – would love her.

Rudolf Höss was the Camp Commandant, the highest authority at Auschwitz: his fiefdom extended over fifteen square miles. He lived with his wife, Hedwig, and five children in a two-storey villa with grounds confiscated from a local Polish family on the edge of the camp. From the balcony, Höss enjoyed his kingdom, drinking an evening aperitif as he gazed over his gas chambers and crematoria. Now his kingdom was finished, but certain elements – the *Politische Abteilung* office and the brothel – were still functioning as normal. A new brothel was even opened in the final months.

When Auschwitz was at its apex, Höss entertained guests such as Heinrich Himmler and the esteemed doctor Josef Mengele, and in the summer, Höss threw concerts, played by the shaven-headed inmates from the camp orchestra. His wife once described her husband to their illustrious guests as 'God' in his own self-made 'paradise' of Auschwitz.

The staff in Höss's villa included cooks, nannies, gardeners, chauffeurs, seamstresses, hairdressers and cleaners. Many were prisoners who came to Höss's attention after gaining a position in the *Politische Abteilung*.

If you got a job there, you were halfway to joining his 'paradise'.

### 3 December 1944, Auschwitz

*After the war, my mother was able to obtain the following information about what Juta's duties would have entailed.*

On Juta's first day at work, she would have walked through the camp as an employee of the Nazis, passing less than a few hundred yards from her mother and sister, tilling the ground with hoes. She was on her way to the *Politische Abteilung*, and wore a brown skirt and a striped blouse, a modification of the pyjamas for prisoners. Juta was no longer a prisoner, but a *lager-dolmetscher*, one of the camp's translators.

There were between thirty-five and forty native languages spoken in the camp, all forbidden by the Germans. The main languages were Polish and Yiddish; Romani and Silesian,

French, Italian, Greek, Turkish, even Iranian, were all spoken as well.

Prisoners could only communicate with guards in German, and all paperwork and orders were in German. As a result, the SS needed *lagerdolmetscher* – and lots of them – to enforce their rules.

A huge proportion of the translators had initially been Jewish – well-educated, often multi-lingual. Jakub Maestro was a young Jew from Thessaloniki, so naturally gifted in languages that he interpreted for the Nazis from German into Greek, before moving on to French, Romanian, Spanish and Polish, all of which he learnt on the fly in the camp.

By October 1944, the month after Juta arrived, the last of the Jewish translators had been gassed to death. But even as the camp was falling apart, the SS still needed more translators, which is why Juta was chosen; she had avoided Puff and the new brothel, for now.

The *Politische Abteilung* was the administrative hub of Auschwitz. A staff of approximately a hundred and fifty ordinarily dealt with everything from registering new prisoners to supplies and allocation of accommodation. One hut was dedicated to policing the camp, which included surveillance of suspicious prisoners, and the interrogation, torture and execution of those planning uprisings, which were on the increase.

Now the camp was falling apart, the main job at the *Politische Abteilung* was destroying evidence. Juta had no idea what she was supposed to do and no one told her. She watched dozens of women, all dressed the same as her, patiently ripping up photographs and mountains of documents taken from filing cabinets.

There was a system to this eradication of the Holocaust. The ripped-up paper would be taken outside and carried to bonfires behind the huts. There appeared to be a system even to the bonfires, which were of varying sizes. Juta was taking in the scene, when she was interrupted by a man about the same age as her. He was wearing a civilian suit rather than a uniform.

'Would you like a cup of tea?' he asked in German.

'Thank you,' Juta replied, cautiously.

His name was Eric. He was a philosophy student from Bremen, who had chronic asthma and had been sent to Auschwitz three months before Juta to assist in the break-up of the camp. He had no qualifications for being there, he told Juta. He had been sent to two camps before Auschwitz and his job had varied at each.

At Ravensbrück, he had done little more than teach the camp commandant's children mathematics and algebra. At Chelmno, he had instructed several SS officers in basic Polish, so that they would blend into the local population when the Allies won the war.

At Auschwitz, people like Eric were brought in to destroy the business paper trail that led to the camp. Administrators spent hours on the telephone to dozens of suppliers, such as the arms producers Krupp and Siemens; food company Nestlé; Kodak, who supplied the film to document the prisoners; and Bayern, who supplied the Zyklon B. Other companies included IG Farben, who used slave labour from Auschwitz for their industrial plant in the Auschwitz sub-camp of Monowitz; Topf & Sons, who built the incinerators for the gas chambers; and even Coca-Cola, who created and supplied Fanta specially for the Wehrmacht and which the SS drunk by the gallon in Auschwitz.

Eric and the other recruits had been told by Camp Commandant Rudolf Höss that their task was essential. They were to instruct anyone they got hold of to destroy everything at their end: orders, invoices, receipts and contracts. There was to be no evidence linking any of these companies to Auschwitz.

'How's that going?' Juta asked Eric.

He laughed. 'The war is over. Everyone is saving themselves. You think anyone cares about some invoices?'

*December 1944, Block 73, Auschwitz I*

One day a Polish woman whom Olga and Alina had never seen before pushed her way into the hut. The *kapo* barred her way, but the woman, wearing a fiercely tight scarf round her head and gaunt, pinched features, brushed him aside as if he wasn't there.

'*Pane* Basiak?' she shouted down the length of the bunk beds.

'Here,' Olga shouted back. The woman gave Olga a scrunched-up piece of paper. It was a letter from Juta.

Olga carefully unwrapped the ball of paper. Within the ball was another scrunched up ball of paper. A letter within a letter. She and Alina stared manically at the words. The first brief letter had been typed in tiny letters, packed densely together, many clattering into each other from the crossed letter keys:

Dear Mother,

I trust this finds you well. I hope that you and Alencu are healthy and are receiving food. I am working as a translator in the *Politische Abteilung*. I am well looked after. I have made a great friend whom you will meet one day.

In the meantime, I will do my best to make sure you have everything you want. Please trust we will be together again when this is all over.

Juta.

Buried in the scrunched-up letter was the second letter, and this was far longer and more detailed than the first. It was written in pen in tiny, neat letters, so as to compress as much information as possible onto a single sheet. It was a diary of her experiences in Auschwitz in note form. It detailed Juta's journey from Pruszków to Auschwitz on the train, her arrival at the camp and some information on Lydia. She also described her escape from the disgusting SS commander, who she believed to be Hössler.

I'd always thought that Alina's great fear – a fear that had haunted her for seventy years – was that Juta had been handed over to the Nazis to work in the brothels. Auschwitz was a huge camp, and knowledge of the brothels was limited with prisoners. In reality, few women were ever identified definitively as having worked in them, but wider sexual abuse of women prisoners by the guards was rife.

From her letters, it seems the *aufseherin* Lydia had taken pity on Juta early on, and had determinedly steered her – with her language skills – towards working in the camp's administrative office.

However, what happened to Juta was the elephant in the room whenever I spoke with my mother about the war.

'*Do you think maybe she was covering up what was going on?*' I ask her one day. '*Telling you she was a translator in the letters, because that would have been easier to accept than her being forced to be a prostitute?*'

My mum becomes tetchy.

'*She wasn't a prostitute. You are obsessed with what happened to Juta. Even if she became a lulu, so what? Women were raped and attacked in Warsaw; and it was no different in Auschwitz. This is what happens in war. I don't think she was a whore, I've told you this a thousand times. Why won't you leave it? She told us she was a translator in that note. If I can accept that, so can you.*'

I decide to back off.

'*How easy was it for her to get the letters to you?*'

'*It would have been very dangerous in normal times, but as the system was collapsing, it was easier for her to get a letter to us. The written, not the typed one, must have taken time to write, and she had the means to write it.'*

'*A pen?*'

'*Exactly. This made my mother believe that Juta was in the administrative office, and was possibly in a position of some authority, maybe even able to get food to us. Olga prayed to God after that letter. I'd never seen her pray like that, so intensely. She sobbed and sobbed, and thanked God over and over again. For saving us all, and for Juta to have her job with the SS.'*

'*What did you feel when you read the letter?*'

'*Well, I was happy she was alive.*'

'*Do you think Juta was collaborating with the Nazis to keep you alive?*'

'*That's what my mother believed. After all, it is what she set Juta up for, telling the guard at Pruszków that she spoke German. She wanted Juta to be useful to the Nazis, because then she could save us all. I don't personally think Juta had the authority to get food to us. I don't believe it. I think we saved ourselves.*'

The fact that there were two letters from Juta, one hidden inside the other, showed either incredible naivety or supreme confidence on her part. The first letter was clearly a covering note should the messenger be stopped (allowing her to discard the second letter if necessary). The second letter – with explicit and compromising details about her job for the Nazis – appeared to be a needless piece of risk-taking.

My mother believes that Juta had no fear that her scrunched-up ball of paper would be intercepted. Working in the camp's administrative office, Juta would have known better than anyone how rapidly discipline was falling apart at Auschwitz. Even if found out, she must have believed it would result in little more than a reprimand. In the grander scheme of the camp's collapse, her letter would have meant nothing to the Nazis. For my mum and Olga, however, it confirmed that Juta was alive. It meant everything.

Nevertheless, Juta was taking a risk with the letters. It was still commonplace for Jewish and Polish women to be punished for the tiniest breach of the rules. Sometimes they were raped by groups of guards, from *kapos* through to the SS, under the pretext of a disciplinary misdemeanour. The women would then either have their breasts cut off, or would be shot so they could not speak about what happened to them. If they survived the attack and got back to their huts, the *kapos* would tell them not to speak of the rape to their family. For Jewish girls, the fear of *shanda* (Yiddish for 'shame') only intensified the pressure on them to say nothing.

Women like Juta faced immense danger simply by being in close day-to-day contact with the SS in the camp's administrative office, or working as a translator. SS guards formed infatuations, but they could quickly turn against their victims and have them killed. Shaven-headed female prisoners in pyjamas were considered too lowly and 'degenerate' to have sex with, so the SS would sometimes choose women from the office. They were thought to be 'cleaner' than the women forced to work in the brothels. This potentially made Juta a prime target.

Far more is now known about the brothels at Auschwitz than was known after the war. The brothel in Block 24 was so well organised, it even had its own photographer, who would produce stills of 'new girls' for the SS guards to choose from, complete with dramatic lighting. The women chosen were forced to pose as if they were Hollywood starlets and were given names like 'Rita Hayworth' and 'Mae West'.

Women who contracted venereal diseases, or typhus and TB, which rolled in waves over the camp, were replaced with new young women. They were selected not only by Hössler and the new *Oberaufseherin SS-Helferin*, Elisabeth Volkenrath, but SS officers who browsed the photos. Apart from the soldiers who visited Block 24 for their allotted fifteen minutes, other males were also coerced into having sex there: gay men, whom the Nazis believed could be converted from their homosexuality by enforced intercourse with women. Neither my mother nor I want to believe Juta would have been part of any of this.

After that first letter, Olga and Alina heard nothing more from Juta for several weeks, and then out of the blue, received a second scrunched-up letter, again delivered by a prisoner. To me, this suggests Juta had enough authority or insider knowledge from her job at the administrative office to make delivery of the letter into their hands successful. This one talked briefly about Eric and Lydia again.

*'Juta had help from the* aufseherin *Lydia,' my mum tells me, 'but the friend was Eric. The letter was on strange paper, official looking. Maybe to avoid drawing suspicion.'*

*'Do you think no one intercepted the letters because the camp was collapsing? It seems such a tremendous risk for Juta to be taking – she could have got you, your mother and herself killed, not to mention the people she named in the letter.'*

*'Probably, but no one had time to look for any hidden letters. I'll tell you why it was still a stupid thing to do, though, because prisoners were organising to rise up against the guards, so the Nazis would have been looking for notes planning an attack. Do you think they cared what Juta was doing? She could probably have arranged her own escape from Auschwitz and no one would have realised. Escaping was what most of the SS were planning anyway by then.'*

Juta said in her letters that she was a translator, and there were three types of translator in Auschwitz. A top tier of German SS officers and Silesians fluent in Polish, working in the *Politische Abteilung* and talking directly to Berlin. These were the most senior and trusted translators, because they were Nazis.

A tier below were Polish inmates like Juta, working as registrars (*schreiberinen*) or messengers (*lauferinen*). Initially these included Slovak and Hungarian Jews, who referred to themselves as 'secretaries of death', grimly aware of their complicity in the administration of the Holocaust. Their 'complicity' cut both ways. Many passed on crucial information to resistance members, warning in advance of shootings, beatings and changes to Nazi plans. One such translator, Raya Kagan, later testified against her SS 'boss' Adolf Eichmann at his trial in 1961.

The third group of translators and lowest rung on the Auschwitz ladder were prisoners singled out as interpreters for the huts. They were called *dolmetsche* and wore white armbands. *Dolmetsche* did not get privileges, nor were they excused from hard labour, but were expected to translate for the SS on behalf of their assigned *stalag*. *Dolmetsche* were expendable and continually replaced, and were often chosen by chance, overheard muttering some words or phrases in German and then assigned the job of translator on the spot.

The most famous was a phenomenally bright boy aged eight, nicknamed Zabko (Frog) by the Nazis. Zabko became a *dolmetsche* because he spoke bits of Polish, German and French. When he was caught shortening German sentences in translation for the sake of brevity, he was slapped in the face in front of his hut's inmates by the German guard he worked for. After Zabko explained patiently to the guard that the prisoners understood the meaning of most German orders anyway, since they were invariably one of three things ('come', 'stop' or 'go'), he was shot in the head for insubordination.

In our conversations together, I am coming to realise that the Auschwitz my mother inhabited is very different from the one I have in my mind, culled from the dozens of books and documentaries I have watched obsessively since I was a child, beginning with the brilliant *The World at War*, narrated by Laurence Olivier. For years, I was haunted by the gaunt face of the woman in flames in the title sequence, without ever knowing she was in Auschwitz.

I want Alina's account to conform to the agreed post-war narrative for the camp: its unique place in history as the acme of evil, devoid of all morality, but she resolutely refuses. It does not even occur to my mother to use adjectives such as 'evil' or 'unspeakable'. Auschwitz was simply what it was: another stopping-off point on her odyssey through the war. When I ask her to 'describe it', she winces.

It is summer 2020 and we are walking to the pub for a cider in the brief respite from Covid lockdown, and I decide to confront the problem.

*'You keep telling me that you were OK there; that you and your mother coped with the conditions. That can't be right. This was Auschwitz, for God's sake. Can't you bring yourself to tell me what it was really like?'*

*'What do you mean?' she says.*

*'Auschwitz. What was it actually like to be there? I have to step back sometimes and remind myself of the enormity of the fact that you were really there.'*

*'What do you want me to say? It was a relief after being in Warsaw.'*

I recognise that I need to stop trying to make my mum's experience fit what I want her to say and start listening to what she is really saying. When I do, it becomes apparent that perversely Auschwitz gave my mother and grandmother something that had been missing for them in the previous six years of war: a certainty of sorts. It was as awful as Warsaw, but in Auschwitz there was at least the grim relief of a bunk bed to sleep on and meagre, pitiful food. There was also the certainty that the Nazis were now beaten. They could smell the defeat of the Germans in the air, like the cordite of Russian guns. But because they were in Auschwitz, the threat of death continued to hang over their heads.

*'You could feel it the moment you arrived. You didn't need to see the gas chambers and crematoria to know that this place was about death. In the forest or in Warsaw, death was a flip of the coin. Chance. That uncertainty was unbearable, not knowing if you would die or live another day. In Auschwitz, the flip of the coin was taken away. It was a horrible kind of comfort, having the chance taken away. In Auschwitz, it was not if you would die, but when.'*

*'But the Russians were coming, so there was a strong chance you would live?'*

She laughs a hollow laugh.

*'You saw what the Russians did to us in Warsaw? Sat on the other side of the river watching Poles get murdered. You think liberation meant we would live? It offered more peril at the hands of the Russians.'*

*'So in a way there was no relief in being in Auschwitz, after all, even if it seemed a relief after the horrors of Warsaw?'*

*'We didn't think about it like this, in the way that you're talking about it. "Is this a relief? Is it better or safer? Will I live? Will I die?" We just carried on.'*

In Auschwitz, there was a community, cemented together by the unlikely glue of *Lagersprache*, a shared language that evolved in the camp, spoken by virtually every prisoner.

*Lagersprache* was unique to Auschwitz between 1940 and 1945. It never existed before Auschwitz and it died with the camp, constructed from a mishmash of Yiddish, Polish, German, Silesian and Hungarian. There were *Lagersprache* words for informers, food, vermin, the *kapos* and SS, the gas chambers, even for sex and regulatory indiscretions. There were dialects of *Lagersprache* spoken within the different camps of Auschwitz and some SS officers were known to speak it.

I had assumed before writing this book and in my ignorance that translators like Juta were basically accomplices to the crimes of Auschwitz. In fact, the vast majority were go-betweens who used their meagre position of power to help as many as possible.

Malka Zimetbaum was the most famous translator of all the camps. She walked an unnerving tightrope in her position, holding both the trust of her fellow Jewish prisoners and the SS. When Zimetbaum attempted to escape, it was ordered that she burn alive in the crematorium. It was a particularly sadistic and vengeful punishment, because the Nazis saw Zimetbaum (almost) as an equal; she had successfully won their trust and then pulled the wool over their eyes. Before she was killed, Zimetbaum drew a razor from her hair and slit her wrists, denying the Nazis their revenge.

Zimetbaum's male counterpart was the dramatically titled Count Wladyslaw Baworowski, a Polish aristocrat whom the Germans loved, responsible for translating the camp commandant's 'welcome' speech to new prisoners. When Höss pointed at the crematorium, saying that it was 'the only way out of the camp', Baworowski never failed to wince, knowing exactly what this meant.

Baworowski, like Zimetbaum, kept the enemy close. When a prisoner threatened to go to the SS hoping to gain privileges by betraying a group of forty Poles he had seen singing the Polish national anthem, Baworowski persuaded him not to. Baworowski's intervention saved their lives. The informer was later found kicked to death behind a hut. Baworowski never saw a thing.

Interpreters were generally far cleverer and better educated than their German masters. They could run verbal rings around their Nazi superiors, but dared not do it for fear of retribution. The Nazis did not want to be intellectually humiliated, least of all by Poles or Jews.

SS Unterscharführer Karl Broch summed up SS disdain for the translators, when he declared there was just one true language of the concentration camp: the whip.

'The whip is the best interpreter,' he said. 'It speaks all languages.'

How exactly Juta negotiated the collapsing camp is hard to pin down. She wrote only two letters in Auschwitz that managed to get to my mum and grandmother (the first letter-within-a-letter and the later handwritten one). She may have written more, which simply failed to get into their hands.

These two letters probably outlined as much as Juta could about her role and the people around her. She talked of Eric and Lydia, and she went as far as she could in detailing what they had told her – hoping, my mother thinks, not to incriminate them. Whether she succeeded is a different matter.

The Holocaust Museum has detailed records about prisoners and translators. Unfortunately, records fall apart from November 1944 to liberation in January 1945, before which the SS in the *Politische Abteilung* torched everything left: all remaining files and any last incriminating paperwork. They then shot the Polish women registrars who had been working for them.

Juta was almost certainly in this cohort of murdered women.

In 1993, my mum returned to Auschwitz to say goodbye to her sister. She had tried since 1946 to find out in more detail what happened to Juta, but was never able to do so. The records for those last women who worked in the camp's administrative office had been destroyed, probably by the women themselves, before they were murdered.

*   *   *

'She was a beautiful girl. I was so jealous of her.'

My mum is sitting in the pub garden, gazing at the clear summer sky. She has no photos of Juta, no keepsakes of her sister's, not even the letters. Nothing.

She smiles. 'I was jealous of her talent, and her ability to make anyone love her. People really fell in love with Juta. She was so magical, and I hated it! But even when I was in Siberia and Sweden, I missed her so much. She was my big sister. Then we were back together again for a short while, and I was so happy. And then she was gone.'

'So that's why you went back to Auschwitz in 1993? To say goodbye?'

'I couldn't face it before. Even stepping on Polish soil was very hard.'

'You went back to give yourself some closure?'

'If that's what you want to call it. I loved Juta, you know. She was my big sister.'

Whether Eric and Lydia were also killed by the Nazis for what they knew about the administration of Auschwitz is impossible to know. Juta's letters to Olga and Alina may have been intercepted by the *Politische Abteilung*, after all, and the information revealed by Juta about Eric and Lydia could have been responsible for their deaths.

I wondered what my mum thought about this: whether the letters were intercepted but allowed to be delivered. The Nazis sometimes kept tabs on interceptions in the hope those under surveillance would reveal better information down the line.

'No. No way. If those letters were intercepted, why would they let us even have them? They would have murdered Juta, there and then. She probably did her job and then was just shot. The SS were tying up loose ends. That meant my sister.'

'Do you think you ever received special treatment because of Juta's position as a translator?'

*My mum gets annoyed.*

*'You've asked me this before. No, I don't. Are we finished now?'*

*My mum goes off to get another drink and I decide to change the subject when she returns.*

Olga had paid a terrible price for trying to do what she thought best. Had my grandmother not told the SS officer at Pruszków that Juta spoke German, she would not have been singled out: whether to work as a Dolls' House prostitute or in the office at Auschwitz. Juta would have been with her mother and sister, sleeping in the same hut. Had Olga not gleefully advertised the fact that Juta spoke German, she might have lived, as my mum did.

Juta's life depended on a gamble taken in that interview in Pruszków before an inscrutable SS guard. Olga believed she played an ace card when she revealed that Juta spoke German. Instead, she had signed her daughter's death warrant. Ironically, had Juta gone to Auschwitz a year earlier, it is possible she might have survived too. She could have feasibly found a way to rejoin Olga and Alina, or never have been separated from them in the first place. As it was, she found herself in the *Politische Abteilung* at the very moment its employees were about to be liquidated. Her fate was sealed.

Olga and Alina never received confirmation that Juta had even been killed. In 1947, Olga, Alina and Kazhik went to Lodz to register with a service set up by the Polish government to help families of people missing in the Holocaust. They found nothing.

In the mid-1960s, Alina and Kazhik tried again. They contacted the records office at Auschwitz, but were told there was no more information on Juta than there had been in 1947. Even today, the Archive State Museum at Auschwitz, which is a fantastic research resource, was regretfully unable to help me any more than they could my mum sixty-odd years ago. The only reason Alina knew what she did was thanks to Juta herself and the two letters she managed to get to them.

The inquiry they made in the mid-1960s raised a terrible question my mother never dared ask before, nor wanted answered: had Juta been sexually abused by the SS, as were so many female translators in the *Politische Abteilung*?

They did not know. No one does.

My mother's abiding memory of Juta is not as she boarded the train for the camp, mouthing indecipherable words to Olga across a sea of people, but in the early summer light of Warsaw in 1939, her hands moving delicately across the piano as she played Chopin in their apartment, with a breeze blowing gently through the open windows.

Before they were all separated. Before the world went mad; before the war.

# 15

## *Little Bird*

*20 December 1944, Auschwitz*

My mum woke up on straw next to her mother. They were now on a bunk bed, which they shared, inherited from a sour Polish woman who died one night. There was no sense of sorrow at the passing of this woman. She was a thief and a snitch, Olga told Alina. Everyone in the hut hated her: she made up stories about the other prisoners and then informed falsely on them to the *kapo*.

One night, three prisoners tried to smother the woman to death with blankets whilst she slept, but she cried out and the *kapo* intervened. The three responsible were shot. After that, the horrible woman was deemed untouchable and made everyone's life hell.

Working on the assumption of keeping your friends close but enemies closer, Olga tried her fortune-telling charms on the woman, but to no avail; she informed the *kapo* that Olga was trying to spread witchcraft. When a boy of fifteen was taken ill in the hut with a high fever, the sour woman told the *kapo* that Olga had put the sick boy under a 'Russian spell'. Olga was beaten with a stick by the *kapo*, who ordered her to release the boy from her spell. After the beating, Olga decided to put a spell on both the *kapo* and the woman, who died shortly after.

It was a mystery how she had died. She was not malnourished, nor did she have TB, typhus or pneumonia. The prisoners were woken as normal for the roll call at 4.45 a.m., and in the sub-zero morning air, the woman was the only one that could not be roused. Her mouth was gaping wide like a cave, her eyes open and milky, fixed and unmoving on the ceiling.

'Stupid bitch,' Olga said. 'Serves her right for being so horrible.'

The other prisoners concurred, and shared her breakfast ration of oily hot water and stale bread. No one dared ask if Olga's spell had killed the woman and Olga didn't make them think otherwise.

After gaining the dead woman's bunk, life improved for Olga and Alina. They earned the grudging respect of their hut-mates. A certain group camaraderie made them suspicious of strangers, even other prisoners from nearby huts who came scavenging for food.

The Nazis continued to evacuate. The smell of the crematoria was replaced with bonfires: ID cards, death certificates and files detailing the minutiae of genocide – from the orders for Zyklon B to the weight of gold melted down from fillings taken from the gas chamber and turned into gold ingots used by Deutsche Bank. The Nazis documented everything; even the exact tonnage of hair shorn from the heads of Jewish women and children, used to stuff pillows for the Wehrmacht. It was all destroyed, thrown onto huge burning pyres by the fearful SS.

But one part of the camp continued as normal.

In 1966, my mum tried to conceive a child, but there was a problem and she could not understand what it was. She went to Hammersmith Hospital in London for tests and was seen by a young gynaecologist. He enquired about her medical history and when Alina told him she had been in Auschwitz, he asked if she had been experimented on.

Every concentration camp had a specific area of medical research. At Ravensbrück, it was bone and muscle transplants: prisoners had limbs removed without anaesthetic and bone marrow injected with disease to see how the body reacted. At Dachau, the Luftwaffe experimented with hypothermia, forcing prisoners to sit in ice baths for hours to simulate sub-zero temperatures at high altitude, then throwing them into boiling water. Dr Sigmund Rascher carried out live vivisections on the brains of prisoners who had survived altitude tests in low compression chambers.

At Auschwitz, Josef Mengele carried out experiments on twins, sewing them together and injecting or removing their eyeballs, which he kept colour-coded in a glass cabinet. These gruesome experiments were the tip of the iceberg. The vast majority of Nazi 'research' was carried out on thousands of women across the concentration camps of Poland and concerned fertility.

Mengele worked at Auschwitz under the direction of SS-Standortarzt (Chief Doctor) Eduard Wirths, who was appreciated and even liked by a large number of prisoners who came into contact with him. Wirths was responsible for halting a typhus outbreak across the camp in 1943. He even received a Christmas card from an Austrian in the camp called Langbein.

'In the past year,' Langbein wrote in his card, 'you have saved here the lives of 93,000 people. We do not have the right to tell you our wishes. But we wish for ourselves that you stay here in the coming year.'

Wirths saved prisoners not because he cared about them, but to keep Auschwitz functioning. Wirths' area of interest was sterilisation. Himmler tasked him with finding a cheap and efficient mass sterilisation programme rendering Jews and ethnic Poles 'biologically redundant'.

In Block 10 at Auschwitz, Wirths removed the ovaries and cervixes of young women and girls in surgery. He also used radiation, electric shocks, blood coagulation and intravenous injections of iodine and silver nitrate. Because of the high mortality rate, he continually sought new guinea pigs, preferably pubescent.

One morning in December 1944, a female SS officer came to my mum's hut. She was dressed like a nurse with a clipboard and asked the mothers if their daughters had been inoculated from the deadly diseases in the camp. She stressed the medical urgency and was very polite. Less than ten minutes later, a group of fifteen girls including my mum were standing awkwardly in a group at the behest of their concerned mothers.

On 1 December, Alina was taken to Block 10, a concrete building in the men's camp. Alina was struck by how much it resembled a real hospital. She was asked to stand outside and after twenty minutes, a female nurse in a uniform took Alina into a room with a cotton curtain for changing behind and a bed with a brown rubberised cover.

There were a number of young doctors present, each with pens and notebooks. They said nothing, they didn't even acknowledge Alina's presence. A young, handsome doctor came into the room.

*'He was very nice to me. Very polite. I didn't think he would do anything bad. He told me that he was going to give me some injections that would stop me getting ill. Sometimes I would be coming to the hospital, he said, and sometimes they would come to the hut. His voice was very soothing. He held my hand and the nurse injected me in my stomach.'*

My mum went to Block 10 twice more. She was injected, she remembers, nine times over a period of three weeks, between the beginning and end of December 1944. Sometimes she went to the block and at other times they came to the hut. On some occasions, injections were followed by an examination by the doctors, which Alina said was brutal.

Alina looked forward to seeing the handsome doctor again. He didn't come very often, but when he did, he made a point of paying Alina attention. He would ask how she was feeling and on one occasion, he even held her hand. He told Alina that she was his 'little bird'.

*The Covid-19 lockdown restrictions have eased a bit, and I sit with my mum a socially distanced width apart outside a local coffee chain.*

'That nickname …'

'"Little bird." It wasn't mine. I found out later he gave it to every little girl that came in to be injected. He had the same routine for all of us to make us feel reassured and calm. Stroke our hands, and tell us that we are his "little bird".'

'It is so strange,' I say, 'because that image of a little bird was also the one you saw on the wall as you stood before the firing squad in Warsaw. It became so important to you.'

'It meant hope. Whenever I felt trapped, I remembered that bird on the wall in Warsaw.'

*In Auschwitz, my mum was the little bird, trapped. She felt cheated when she found out that the doctor said the same thing to every little girl.*

'I thought he was this magical doctor who had chosen me, and chosen the name for me. He hadn't. He was just trying to make me calm so he could give me an injection to make me infertile. "Little Bird" didn't mean anything. It was a trick. There were thousands of "little birds", just like me, all thinking they were the only one.'

The doctor was following a programme created by the Auschwitz infertility specialist Dr Carl Clauberg. When Clauberg was released from a Soviet prison after the war, he continued to practise as a doctor in Germany, even apparently putting Auschwitz on his business card.

In the camp, Clauberg had injected formaldehyde into the uteruses of young women. Alina had no idea what Clauberg's protégé injected her with, but the suspicion at Hammersmith Hospital in 1966 was that it was something else, possibly one of the many other drugs they were trialling, and pretty ineffective.

My mum's problems with conceiving were psychological, not physiological, they concluded. The very trauma of being injected and believing she was sterile had prevented her conceiving. The moment Alina was told at Hammersmith Hospital that the Nazi doctors had failed in their attempts to make her infertile, she became pregnant. Had Clauberg and his subordinates been good at their job, I would not exist.

*25 December 1944, Auschwitz*

'Do you know what day it is?' Olga asked my mum.

'No.'

'It's Christmas Day.'

Alina perched expectantly on the ledge of their bunk at the end of the hut. It was dark and silent. Strangely, the *kapos* had not dragged them out for roll call that day. Alina had no idea what time it might be, but there was no moaning, no crying, no one muttering madly to themselves. It was deathly quiet and people were asleep.

My mum scrunched her eyes and tried to remember the Russian Orthodox church they would go to on Christmas Eve, with its bright onion spires in the forest. She tried everything in her power to recall every last detail of the wolves, and how they had nearly overturned the sled. Hard as she tried, she couldn't even remember last Christmas in Warsaw, with its sardines and Olga's attempt to make them remember the wolves. It all seemed a million years ago.

There were just the two of them left alive now. They had no belongings and no idea what had happened to Juta. The last letter had been some time ago. Olga was now certain that her two sons, Kazhik and Pavel, were dead, as was her husband, Michael; the only person she had left in the world was Alina. My mum stared out of the icy window and Olga held her hand.

'I'm sorry you have no presents,' Olga said. 'Or sardines.'

My mum smiled.

It had been Olga's intention to give Alina her battered tarot cards. A dog-eared collection of pentangles, harlequins, Death in a cloak, angels carrying clouds, handsome druids with faraway looks and bleeding hearts pierced by swords.

Olga had made every decision, major and minor throughout the war, consulting these symbols. The tarot cards had expelled the Nazis and Russians from the forest and kept them alive in Siberia. The cards told Olga to leave the safety and comfort of Sweden to return to the horrors of Warsaw, against the advice of every human being she spoke to. Yet the cards had always been right.

Now she was in Auschwitz, and the cards were gone. Olga didn't know if they were stolen; she hadn't the cards to ask. Everything got stolen in Auschwitz: clothing, food, keepsakes and, of course, the big fur coat she had hung onto doggedly for six years, with the jewellery and roubles sewn into the lining.

Olga had only one thing left to give Alina. She had hidden it in her vagina since the day they arrived in the camp, and on Christmas Day 1944, Olga decided that she might as well give it to Alina, for who knew if they would ever have another Christmas. It was a tiny gold ring.

Alina looked bemused. She held it up to the light as the other prisoners slept. It was so insignificant, and so delicate.

'Stupid!' Olga hissed. 'Hide it!'

Olga struck Alina's hand sharply and told her to keep the ring hidden under the blanket. They would be killed in a second for such a valuable object. Alina didn't even want the thing and gave it back to Olga.

'I want you to know that this might not feel like Christmas,' Olga said solemnly, 'but it is. Christ was born in a place like this, and that makes you closer to God here than you will be anywhere else, for the rest of your life. It is a privilege to be in a place like this. A religious place. Remember that.' Alina did.

It was the last Christmas anyone would spend in Auschwitz.

## 5 January 1945, Auschwitz

The camp began to unravel entirely. Fear is not an emotion associated with the SS, but they were scared. They could feel the distant Russian gunfire resonating in their boots now, the vibration of the advancing tanks shaking the shallow footings of Auschwitz.

Olga and Alina stayed in their hut, terrified by the random shootings. Anyone found in the wrong place, whatever the 'wrong place' might be, was instantly executed. Machine-gun fire in the camp was continuous and the cries of desperation incessant. The Nazis were killing anyone left. This was Alina's most fearful moment in Auschwitz: thousands of prisoners shot only days from freedom as the Nazis evacuated.

The logic of Auschwitz was impeccable: a killing machine with a life of its own.

The murdered of the Holocaust were being erased by the new recruits, who were in turn killed for what they had seen or 'knew'. Destroying the evidence of mass extermination required more death, and yet more new recruits to be murdered.

One morning, the *kapo* came to Alina's hut and told them the shooting had stopped and the German kitchens were abandoned; food was lying everywhere, waiting to be taken. Be quick, he said, before the other huts realise.

\*      \*      \*

*'It was a miracle because the food had stopped coming entirely. People were desperate. We had started talking in the hut about protecting ourselves from other huts if people attacked us looking for food. There had been nothing for days and I think the* kapo *knew we would starve. He didn't need to do it, but he did.'*

In the SS quarters, prisoners discovered meals abandoned half-way through the eating. Soup on tables, now frozen; beer tankards half-drunk; a cheeseboard with rats on it; and a chess game, half-played. Many prisoners loaded up with vodka and schnapps. In the first few days of January 1945, prisoners were seen drunk around the camp for the first time, violently sick, because they had not eaten proper food or drunk alcohol for four years.

Even as they abandoned Auschwitz, the Nazis could not let go of their brutality. Eighteen French Jews discovered by SS officers collecting food in sacks from an SS dining hall were shot in the head and dumped in the snow outside.

The free-for-all created by the Nazi exodus formed an inverted Darwinian pyramid: extinction of the fittest and survival of the weakest, epitomised by the 'death march'. On 15 January, the SS ordered 60,000 of the strongest and ablest surviving prisoners to be frog-marched without warning out of the camp. Some were marched north-west for 55 kilometres to Gliwice, where they were joined by prisoners from sub-camps in Upper Silesia. Others were marched due west to Wodzislaw.

The death march had no aim but to pummel the strongest surviving prisoners into the ground. Those who slipped in the sub-zero temperatures on the ice were beaten to death. On the Baltic, near Gdansk, a ten-day march from nearby camps ended when the 700 survivors reached the shore and were simply driven into the sea and shot.

In Auschwitz, Commandant Höss packed his belongings into his car and left the camp for good with his wife and children,

saluted by a line of SS guards. He turned back after a few kilometres, when he realised the road was blocked and he would be
captured by the advancing Russians.

*I asked Alina what she did as the camp was falling apart.*

'*My mother wouldn't allow me out of the hut. She said it was too
dangerous. She said the remaining guards were shooting anyone
looting. We thought they would liquidate the camp entirely. They
shot a hundred people outside our hut who couldn't stand or walk.
We were convinced we'd be next. So we kept moving from one hut
to the next, just like we did in Warsaw from basement to basement.'*

One of the last parts of Auschwitz to stop functioning was the
medical facility in Block 10. The doctors continued experiments
on patients until the very end, oblivious to the chaos outside. On
17 January, Dr Josef Mengele packed two boxes of specimens
from his experiments and left Auschwitz for the last time, escaping to Argentina.

*27 January 1945, Auschwitz*

A week before the Russians liberated the camp, the SS had
gone. Of the prisoners left, few had the energy or will to leave
the unguarded camp. On 25 January, Alina and Olga woke up to
find no sign of a Nazi anywhere.

'*My mother said it was a trick. They hadn't really gone. They were
waiting outside the camp and were going to machine-gun us all
the moment we tried to escape. But many prisoners started to leave
or began exploring the camp looking for food. So we knew it was
real.*

'*We had been taken just out of the camp perimeter by the Nazis to
work many times. But now they had gone, it was frightening. I know*

*this sounds strange, but the camp had given us some security and now that was over. Who knew what the Russians would do to us?'*

For two days before the Russians came, prisoners wandered through the camp in a daze. To people like my mother and grandmother, who had only been in Auschwitz a matter of months, the scenes of starvation beyond their sub-camp were hard to comprehend. Olga told Alina to stay near their hut; they were not to find out what lay beyond.

On 27 January, Alina bumped into a soldier. He came from nowhere; he was suddenly there, walking around outside their hut. He wasn't dressed like a German, he had a brown Russian uniform and was about Kazhik's age. Alina ran up to him.

The soldier looked at the little girl.

'*Svaboda,*' he said. ('Free.')

*'He said it as a question,' recalls Alina, 'as if he himself wasn't sure. Free from what? Seeing this? Who was free? Us? I went back to the hut and told my mother. There were five hut-mates still there. Some wept and others just stared at the floor. It was a miracle, but we were scared too, because we didn't know what this meant.'*

The Russians were baffled by the condition of the prisoners. Those who had come from the Warsaw uprising were relatively well fed. Prisoners who had survived since 1942 were barely alive. Liberation was different in different parts of the camp. For some, there was jubilation. In Birkenau and Monowitz, the survivors were living skeletons, unaware they had been liberated.

The Russian soldiers found 88 pounds of eyeglasses, 44,000 pairs of shoes, hundreds of prosthetic limbs. They could not understand the scene before them. They asked prisoners, 'What are you doing here?' The survivors were baffled by the question.

The prisoners looked so wretched and pathetic to the Russians, the Soviet soldiers were dumbstruck.

'What's over there?' they would ask prisoners, pointing northwards.

'The concentration camp.'

'And beyond that?'

'The concentration camp.'

'And beyond the camp?'

'The forest and crematoria. Beyond the crematoria, we don't know.'

Prisoners were 'liberated', but it meant nothing to many. They feared walking free through the gates more than anything else: the agoraphobia of the traumatised.

*'I don't get why, if the gates were open, you just didn't walk out?' I say to my mum.*

*'Where would we go?' my mum counters, annoyed that I find it so hard to understand. 'Where could we go, you tell me? You wanted to get out as quickly as possible, but there was nowhere to go. In the camp it was safe. My mother said we should stay put. We shouldn't trust the Russians. We were better off where we were. In our hut.'*

Alina and Olga stayed in Auschwitz for a further week. The Red Cross arrived, set up tents and started carrying out emergency triage on the sickest. People were suffering from frostbite, gangrene, bedsores, typhus and severe malnutrition, and 500 prisoners died in the first few days following liberation.

The Russian army had no particular interest in Auschwitz. They moved quickly onwards. The Allies, approaching from the west, liberated Majdanek, the first concentration camp they encountered. It was newsreels filmed at these first liberated Allied camps – Majdanek, then Dachau – that gave the world its pictures of gaunt figures behind barbed wire.

*4 February 1945, Auschwitz*

It was 8.30 a.m. when Alina and Olga walked out of the gates of Auschwitz. The honeymoon period of liberation was over; the news cameras had gone and the triage was packing up. There was an uneasy air around Auschwitz, as though no one knew what to do with this shameful place.

My mother and grandmother had nowhere to go. Olga had only one plan: to make the 500-mile journey to a village near Lvov in the forest, where she believed a cousin of Michael's lived.

It was a very difficult journey. Poland was a chaotic mess, with no infrastructure after six years of war. Mother and daughter stood on a rural platform with a dozen or so refugees sitting on broken suitcases.

'When the Nazis were here,' Olga said ruefully to Alina, 'at least you knew a train would come eventually.'

Alina could see her mother had no idea what to do. Without tarot cards to consult, jewellery to barter or the mission of finding her three missing children, she was lost. Olga thought that if Michael's cousin was still alive and in the same village, at least they would have somewhere to be, with someone to call family.

He was not there.

When they arrived, the village was only black ash; the whole place was razed to the ground, destroyed as the Nazis had retreated and discovered partisans. Olga sat on the ground defeated and looked up at the sky. She was out of ideas.

'Why don't we ask the government for a house?' Alina said brightly.

Olga looked at her daughter in amazement. She had the awestruck expression of a little girl given a birthday present.

'Can we do that?'

*12 February 1945, London*

Michael and Marcus were late. They ran from Oxford Circus tube station past BBC Broadcasting House to the Polish embassy on Portland Place. The red and white AK flag hung from the front. It was no longer a clandestine gesture, but the national flag of Poland.

Stanyslaw Mikolajczyk, the leader of the government-in-exile, who a year earlier told Michael his services were no longer required, had brought my grandfather back in from the cold. Michael could not believe this unexpected turn of events – now they would surely fight as one to free their country.

Poland was now under Soviet control. At the Yalta conference, days before Michael got the call, he and Marcus listened in horror to the BBC Home Service as it was announced that Churchill and Roosevelt had agreed to Stalin's annexation of Poland, on the condition he allow 'free elections'.

Michael did not return to Warsaw in 1944 as was suggested. He stayed in London, plotting with his friend Marcus and a group of exiled political dissidents to build what Michael called a 'genuine Socialist alternative to Soviet dictatorship'. There were a dozen such factions plotting in London and they were all called by Mikolajczyk to Portland Place a day after Yalta, to discuss what should happen next. Michael hoped the fate of Poland was about to lurch fortuitously in their direction.

Things did not go as he had hoped. Mikolajczyk was a small, underwhelming man; but his unassuming demeanour masked a shark-like instinct for survival.

He told the assembled factions that they must put their political differences aside and come together to do a deal with Stalin. In a few weeks' time, he said, he would be travelling to Moscow to discuss with Stalin the formation of a provisional government of national unity. As patriots of Poland, he expected them to support him loyally on this mission.

Michael could not believe it. Mikolajczyk was selling out Poland to the Soviets.

He was about to start a slow, sarcastic hand-clap, when he realised he was surrounded by Mikolajczyk loyalists wearing small enamel pins with the letters TRJN, the initials of the new Soviet-approved government. They jumped to their feet and began chanting, '*Niech zyje Polska!*' Long live Poland.

It was a done deal. Poland was Stalin's.

A few minutes later, Michael stood outside with Marcus, smoking a cigarette.

'What do we do now?' Marcus asked.

'Fight for Poland's freedom,' Michael replied. 'Except now we know who the real enemy is, and it's not the Russians.'

## 30 April 1945, Stalag X-B Sandbostel
### Internment Camp, Germany

Kazhik had been in a German POW camp for nearly a year. A week before Germany surrendered, British soldiers liberated Stalag X-B Sandbostel, arresting the few Nazis they found hiding in nearby barns and outhouses.

The camp was already under the control of the prisoners. On 21 April, the Nazi commandant, realising the war was close to over, had handed over authority to the most senior of the POWs, a French Colonel called Marcel Albert.

Stalag X-B was very different from a concentration camp. At Sandbostel, the POWs were initially treated by German guards as equals, but as the Nazi war fell apart, the food supply chain to the camp collapsed. Thirty-thousand starving, disease-ravaged civilians came into Sandbostel from other concentration camps, creating a humanitarian crisis. Lieutenant General

Brian Horrocks of the British Army enlisted local German civilians and medical orderlies to help treat the dying and bury the dead. Kazhik had never seen such a thing.

Before Alina and Olga left Auschwitz for the last time, they too saw something they never imagined possible: German prisoners of war – guards from Auschwitz – being captured by the Russians in the woods and surrounding countryside and sent back into Auschwitz.

It was an irony not lost on the remaining survivors, convalescing in the remains of the camp: their former tormentors were now separated from them by only a flimsy fence, a solitary Russian with a gun keeping them apart. The war was virtually over, but Auschwitz was still taking new prisoners: Germans.

One of the tasks given to these ex-Nazis was dismantling the rubber plant in the Monowitz sub-camp. The same guards who had forced Jews into the gas chambers were now POWs, sleeping in the huts they had once terrorised.

Local Poles descended as the fleeing Nazis were captured and taken back through the *Arbeit Macht Frei* gates, beating them with farm implements. Russian soldiers fired their guns to scare the villagers away, but some rushed into Auschwitz, tearing down many of the wooden barrack huts, and taking the planks home on horse-drawn carts for firewood.

On 7 May 1945, Germany declared unconditional surrender. Hitler had already committed suicide, shooting himself in his bunker, leaving Admiral Dönitz in command of the combined German forces. Peace was signed by General Alfred Jodl, a nondescript managerial type, who signed off on the end of the Third Reich like a grumpy bank manager approving an overdraft. The war was over.

# 16

## Lodz

Michael arrived at Okecie Airport outside Warsaw on a Douglas C-47, a military transport plane. The airport had been largely destroyed in the war, but a single cratered runway was patched up to bring vital supplies into the city.

He was followed from the airport, as Marcus predicted he would be. A tall man stood on the tarmac as Michael got off the plane. He followed Michael through the Nissen hut that amounted to the terminal and watched him get into a waiting car.

The tall man followed at a distance in a grey, unmarked car, all the way into Warsaw. He was an agent of the Polish secret police, driven by another agent who glowered over the wheel, keen that Michael understood he was being followed.

Michael was fully aware of the danger in returning to Poland. In March, members of the new 'council of national unity' were invited by a Soviet general called Ivan Serov to a conference in Warsaw. These were the talks that Stalin had promised Mikolajczyk, and he had announced so proudly in London.

Michael politely declined the offer to meet the Russians. The cortege that drove the delegation to the grand conference with Stalin included the AK's bravest heroes of Warsaw. At the airport, they were put in cars flanked by Soviet outriders, but instead of turning left out of the airport, they were taken straight to Pruszków internment camp.

When they got there, three of Michael's AK comrades, Leopold Okulicki, Jan Jankowski and Kazimierz Puzak, were arrested and beaten by the Soviet secret police. They were then flown to Moscow, where they were interrogated and tortured at Lubyanka prison. On 18 June, a show trial began, and the three men stood in a dock along with thirteen other Polish members of the wartime government-in-exile.

The situation was clear. The Nazis were defeated, and now the new war had begun: between the Soviet Union and the peoples of Europe they were trying to crush under their control. Those in the AK who had liberated Poland from the Nazis were now 'anti-communist' agitators – their reward for helping free Poland from Nazism, to be labelled as Nazi collaborators.

The charges against the men were risible, but designed in their ludicrousness to impress upon the Polish population the principle of Stalin's new dictatorship of their country: I can do what I like, with whomever I choose. They were to be examples to everyone in Poland, so that all understood the new rules.

Sixteen heroes of the Second World War stood in silence before Soviet Lieutenant General Vasili Ulrikh, the notorious judge (and jury) of the Great Purge trials of the 1930s, as he listed their crimes: 'collaboration with Nazi Germany'; 'intelligence gathering and sabotage of the Red Army'; 'state terrorism'; 'planning a military alliance with Nazi Germany'; 'propaganda against the Soviet Union'; and 'owning a radio transmitter, printing machines and weapons'.

Stalin was careful with the timing of the trial. It began at the same time as the Soviet-backed puppet government of Poland was installed in Warsaw. He was killing two birds with one stone.

No evidence was provided to the court of their guilt and the defendants were allowed no defence. The two most prominent were sentenced to ten years hard labour, but murdered in prison days after arriving. Mikolajczyk, who had told Michael and the

AK's many factions to welcome Soviet rule back in London, was spared a trial.

Luckily for Michael, he had been tipped off by Marcus that the 'conference' was a trap. He waited some weeks after the sentencing of his comrades to return to Poland and take up the cudgels of the fight. What he didn't know was that he was about to have his life turned upside down and run through with a sword.

### 4 July 1946, Kielce, Southern Poland

A year after its liberation, the site of Auschwitz concentration camp was falling in on itself. Many Jewish and Polish ex-prisoners, determined that it should never be forgotten by history and the collapsing buildings should be preserved for posterity, returned and got to work.

A Polish camp survivor called Kazimierz Smolen declared himself the first 'warden' of Auschwitz, protecting the site from looting. Initially, there was no attempt by the Polish government to save the remains of Auschwitz, which was perceived by President Bierut as a stain on the Polish communist state. Moreover, he could not publicly acknowledge the Holocaust even having happened on Polish soil. It certainly was not to be commemorated by a permanent memorial.

In spite of the best efforts of the returning survivors, Auschwitz became part open graveyard, part opportunity to plunder. Local gleaners and peasants sifted through the ashes looking for gold fillings and jewellery. Smolen and his small band of ex-inmates fought off looters, and began serving as informal guides for people who would turn up at the site, curious to be shown round. They were told about the gas chambers and the crematoria by the people who had survived it. These new 'guards' or custodians of Auschwitz had nowhere to sleep and occupied quarters once lived in by the SS.

Meanwhile, thousands of Jewish survivors, unwanted by the allied governments of Britain, France and the US, travelled to Palestine in anticipation of the creation of Israel. There had been 3.3 million Jews in Poland before the war, the largest Jewish community in Europe. By 1945, there were virtually none left. The few still alive who chose to stay in their native country witnessed anti-Semitism re-emerging. In Oswiecim, the nearest town to Auschwitz, Jews trying to find accommodation were told by residents, 'We thought the Nazis had killed you all off'.

Many Poles had already begun to blame Jews for their post-war problems. The old hatred of the 1930s was returning, this time tinged with the shame that they perceived Jews had brought on Poland for the fact of Auschwitz being there. Anti-Semitism was amplified by grim levels of post-war poverty and austerity. Jews were again to be blamed and punished.

On 4 July 1946, an eight-year-old boy called Henryk Blaszczyk went missing from his home in the town of Kielce. When he reappeared two days later, he told his family he had been held by a man in a basement. His father took him to the police station to give a description.

As they made their way, the boy pointed at a Jewish man he saw walking in the street. He was outside a large building at 7 Planty Street, home to 180 Jews, and owned by the Jewish Committee of Kielce. The residents were refugees, many of whom had survived the death camps. The building had no base-ment and had nothing to do with the boy's disappearance, but 7 Planty Street now became the focus of the kidnapping, and the Jewish man was the prime suspect.

With fears already growing in the building that something terrible was in the offing, the Jewish Committee of Kielce assured residents that after everything they had been through in the concentration camps, their fellow countrymen would surely not scapegoat Jews again. This time, they said, justice would be done.

Local police moved in to question the residents about the disappearance of the boy and rumours spread like wildfire through Kielce that he had been kidnapped by Jews in order to satisfy a 'blood libel': a Polish superstition dating back centuries that Jews abducted Christian children in order to sacrifice them as part of a religious blood offering. In the fevered imaginations of the people of Kielce, the boy had been taken to satisfy a practice on a par with Satanism.

A mob gathered outside 7 Planty Street. As Jewish residents came out to protect themselves, a scuffle began and the police opened fire. Instead of defending residents, they fired at Jewish families. Encouraged by the police, women and children were dragged into the square by locals and kicked to death.

Once the bloodletting began, the people of Kielce were in a frenzy. Jews were stoned and then hurled in the river, and a new-born baby was beaten to death with a rifle butt. Men came from a nearby metalwork factory with iron bars to kill anyone Jewish still alive.

It was a pogrom, the kind that had been carried out against Jewish communities in Europe since medieval times. Similar massacres of Jews took place in Krakow and Rzeszow, a year after Auschwitz was liberated.

My mum and her family never heard of the Kielce massacre, because it was not reported by Polish state news. They listened instead, as everyone else did, to Soviet-style propaganda relating tractor production figures and the triumphs of Polish gymnastics.

*October 1946, Lodz, Central Poland*

Poland was now entirely under Soviet control: a puppet state. Members of the Politburo suggested even going so far as to make Poland a district of the Soviet Union.

Olga and my mum wanted to go back to their beautiful country house in the forest of the Prypec Marshes, but they could not; the area had been 'de-Polonised' – erased of Poles. It was now part of the Ukraine, and of the Soviet Socialist Republic. It was deemed bourgeois to have owned a house, so there was no compensation, either for the house nor the flat they had owned in Warsaw. It did not even occur to Olga to apply for compensation.

Instead, they were offered a room to live in. It was on the top floor of a housing block in the city of Lodz, hundreds of miles from the forest.

Lodz was a large manufacturing city in central Poland, permanently swathed in a pall of sulphurous smoke from its factories. During the war, thousands of ethnic Germans moved there from all over Europe and it was renamed Litzmannstadt. After the war, the few ethnic Germans left were forced out, and hundreds of thousands of Polish refugees made homeless by the war were moved into the apartments vacated by the Germans. Olga and Alina's new home was a room on Piotrowska, or Principle Street.

In 1946, with Warsaw in ruins, Lodz became the unofficial new capital of Poland. When my mother and grandmother arrived, it resembled a huge building site. Cranes and lorries worked through the night to construct mile upon mile of new housing for the waves of Polish migrants moving there.

*'It was horrible,' my mum told me, 'but who cared? It was somewhere to live and it was like a palace after everything we had been through.'*

*   *   *

Olga and Alina lived in a pre-war block that smelt strongly of damp. They cooked on a gas camping stove, there was no heating and there were rats (*'bigger, fatter rats than any I'd seen before'*). The refugees either side of them came from Gdansk and Wroclaw. No one spoke to anyone. It was my mum's first taste of urban isolation.

Olga and my mum had survived Nazism and the prison of Auschwitz, only to escape and find themselves in a new, far bigger prison: communist Poland. This too had a tall electrified fence preventing escape, but the difference was that this prison was 120,726 square kilometres in size and held 24 million prisoners. No one was getting out.

Olga had never worked a day in her life, and never wanted to, but now she needed a job. She tried to get one in a laundry, but was turned down. She tried a local hospital, but for some reason she was told there was nothing available. Dozens of others who turned up on the same day were given work; it made no sense to her.

She sat in their one-room apartment watching the new brutalist metropolis of Lodz rise up around them. It went on twenty-four hours a day: concrete boxes were slotted together by day, whilst the deafening noise of drilling under floodlights kept them awake at night.

Olga knew how to do only one thing well: read tarot cards. She invested in a new packet and set up shop in their flat. At first, it was just people on their corridor who came, but after a few weeks, word spread throughout the block and a queue formed at their door, policed by Alina, who would also take their money.

Olga had always been fatalistic. Now her fatalism took on a doomy, apocalyptic tone. People like them, separated from family and hundreds of miles from their real homes, came to Olga searching for some hope and light at the end of the tunnel.

Olga was having none of it. Curtains were drawn and candles lit. She would clutch her victim's hand as though life depended on it and grimace, her eyes closed tight. Then she would sigh deeply and shake her head vigorously.

'No . . . no . . . no,' she would mutter darkly.

'What is it?' they would say.

'It can't be!' Olga would gasp.

'What is it?' they would say again, truly frightened. It was the terror of what the future might behold, and Olga knew exactly what that was.

'It's the Germans,' Olga would say at last. 'I see the Germans returning to this city. They will come here, take back their flats and kill us all. You must leave now.'

Alina would intervene at this point to break the spell momentarily, holding out her hand.

'Another fifty zlotys, please.'

Once the money was handed over, Olga would resume her doomy news, invariably telling them to prepare for the worst.

Olga believed it herself. Everything had been taken from her: three children, her terrible husband, her beautiful home and flat. What was the point of anything? When Olga was done with a day's psychic divining, she would sit in bed, eating *halva* with the curtains drawn.

*I have an admission to make. I have been writing this book primarily as therapy to keep my mum's memory working. Each day that goes by, her dementia shuts down another part of her brain. Getting her to talk about the war: remembering what the bearded smuggler in Siberia looked like; the smell of the basements in Warsaw and the wolves in the forest; the name of Kazhik and Juta's school mistress and the way Kazhik mimicked the crippled old Bavarian soldier crying. It all keeps the essence of who my mum is alive.*

*Alina phones and asks me if I am coming up today.*

'You asked me that half an hour ago,' I snap.

'Oh Christ, I am going mad, you know that?'

Her world has reduced to a nightmare of forgotten purses, misplaced glasses, bills that haven't been paid, friends that can't be called because they've passed away, or are so riddled with dementia, they can't be talked to.

'If ever I lose my mind, take me to Switzerland and have me put down,' she used to say. Thankfully, my mum has forgotten she ever said that.

## 8 September 1947, Mittenwald, Southern Germany

Kazhik had walked out of Sandbostel days after it was liberated, with a cotton sack over his shoulder. He was fifteen years old.

Lower Saxony was part of the British zone of occupation and Sandbostel became a rehabilitation centre for 'de-Nazification'. British soldiers sat patiently at desks with ex-SS, Gestapo and Wehrmacht POWs, showing them political textbooks about democracy and why it was such a good idea for the new Germany. Allied soldiers had been instructed by the British prime minister, Clement Atlee, to maintain 'a cold and dignified aloofness towards Germans at all times'.

Leaving Sandbostel to its new prisoners of ex-Nazi guards, Kazhik joined the thousands of Polish ex-POWs stuck in Germany. He had no reason to go home because as far as he knew he had none: no family and no plans.

Kazhik travelled to Hamburg with two Polish soldiers he had met in Sandbostel, called Marek and Andrzej. Their aim was to get very drunk and lose their virginity. They achieved the first of their aims on their first night out of the camp, when they stopped at a roadhouse owned by a fat German hotelier with a floppy walrus moustache and two questions for the boys: 'Are you British?' and 'How much money do you have?'

When Kazhik replied that they were Polish, the hotelier beamed. He held out his arms and hugged each of them in turn. The hotel proprietor came from Kiel, he explained, and had served as a merchant seaman on Polish cargo ships in the 1930s.

'I love the Polish,' he said. 'If you were French, I would have killed you,' he guffawed. 'If you were British, I'd be charging you twice as much for the drink and girls. As you're Polish, I can only commiserate. The Russians are doing to you what the British are doing to us – fucking you up the arse!'

In the bar of the roadhouse, Marek and Andrezj got into a fight with some German farmers. They were playing pool and the Poles challenged them to a game for money. A dispute over a moved cue ball led to a huge punch-up and broken chairs. The hotelier found this hilarious and ordered the farmers to apologise to the three Poles.

They couldn't afford a room, but the hotelier felt guilty and let the boys sleep in a laundry room on piles of fresh sheets. In the middle of the night, the farmers returned with metal bars, beating the three badly. Kazhik was lucky, escaping with little more than a few bruises.

Determined to achieve their second goal, to lose their virginity, they bought three stolen US Army motorcycles from a local garage and drove to Hamburg. The roads were now filled with German families on the move, their homes requisitioned by the Allies. Once it had been Jews and Poles who wheeled old fruit carts piled high with all their belongings, and now it was Germans.

Hamburg was a bombsite, flattened by the RAF. The brothels of the city were clustered around the old port and filled with British and American soldiers, drunk and still celebrating the end of the war. After losing their virginity to some veteran sex workers with mustard-coloured wigs, the three Polish boys went their separate ways.

Kazhik decided to head for the Baltic city of Gdansk, near the German border. During the war, it had been known as Danzig, but now the Germans were being kicked out, and Poles were heading there in their thousands to get work.

Kazhik bumped his motorbike along potholed roads and back over the Polish border to Gdansk. It broke down several times and eventually sputtered its last on the outskirts of the city. Kazhik sold the bike for next to nothing to a man selling farming implements by the side of the road, and hitched a ride into the centre of Gdansk from an army truck.

He headed for the port and got work almost immediately as a longshoreman, loading and unloading the British and Danish ships docking hourly, and paying for board and lodgings at a small hotel by the port that doubled up as a whorehouse.

In late September 1947, he decided to see if any of his family were still alive. He walked to the administrative office in the town and climbed the steps to the missing persons department on the first floor. The woman asked him to get himself a tea, and she would look under the name 'Basiak'. When he returned, she simply handed him a piece of paper with an address: Principle Street, Lodz.

'Good luck,' she said, and smiled.

Before making the journey, Kazhik needed to do something. He lay on his bed in his lodgings and rummaged through his sack of belongings. Buried at the bottom, he found what he was looking for: the wallet of Jonas Peter Becker, the German boy he had shot in Warsaw.

Jonas's *Wehrpass* and *Soldbuch* said he had come from Mittenwald in Southern Germany, near the Austrian border, over a thousand kilometres away. Kazhik used what savings he had from the job and bought a new motorbike the next day, a beautiful Norton 633. The following morning, he set off.

It took Kazhik nearly a week. By day, he bumped over country roads still riven with bomb craters two years after war. At night, he slept by the side of the road. When he got to an autobahn, he secretly thanked Adolf Hitler for the smooth tarmac allowing him to make up time through central Germany.

Kazhik booked in to Mittenwald's cheapest hotel – an Alpine chalet with low beams. He spent the next day exploring the picturesque Bavarian village surrounded by dramatic snow-capped peaks; he visited the pretty Catholic church and breathed in the cool mountain air. Late in the afternoon, he walked down a steep hill from the old town to a nondescript residential street near the bus station. An address he had committed to memory three years ago.

Kazhik walked nervously back and forth in front of the same house; a tidy concrete bungalow, with lurid orange curtains, and a neat lawn garden decorated with brightly coloured flowers. Finally he built up enough courage to go up to the door, only to lose his nerve at the last moment. He went to a bar and had a drink, and half an hour later, came back to the house.

Kazhik knocked. Even though the property had been built in the 1930s, part of the huge infrastructure drive by Hitler to expand the residential capacity of Bavarian towns, Kazhik noticed that the doorknocker was ancient: carved wood in the shape of a smiling cow.

A small woman opened the door after a few seconds. It was the exact amount of time you would give if you were waiting for someone to knock, but didn't want to give the impression you'd been waiting.

'*Bitte*,' she said. ('Please.')

Kazhik took it as a question, but it was an invitation to come in. She repeated the word, thinking perhaps Kazhik hadn't heard her.

'*Bitte*.' She gestured with her hand that he come in.

In the small living room, Kazhik, six foot tall, perched himself on a dainty sofa. The woman, wearing a cooking apron, sat herself slowly down in a single chair.

Kazhik had a prepared speech that he had gone over in his head thousands of times. It began with a detailed description of what happened; the moment he first saw Jonas moving between the panels of the barricade, through to him shooting Jonas and pocketing the boy's papers. There was one moment Kazhik knew he would not be able to describe – walking away from what he had done.

He was about to make his speech, when he was interrupted.

The woman began talking. She spoke in German. She said her name was Lilly. She leant unexpectedly across, placing her hand in Kazhik's. She said that she knew he would come. She had seen him outside; she knew who he was, and why he was there. Kazhik didn't speak much German, but he understood everything she was saying.

Kazhik asked about Jonas and what he was like. Lilly gestured for them to look at a photo album she had; there were no tears or awkwardness. They sat together on the sofa and Lilly took Kazhik through her son's life. His first day at school, the day he joined the army, holiday photos of the family together on a windy beach on the Baltic. Then Kazhik gave her back Jonas's wallet.

Lilly explained that Jonas had been her only child. Her husband Frank had died in the war of emphysema. She pointed at the photo with all three of them in it: Jonas, Lilly and Frank, dwarfed by the tree in the foreground. Kazhik looked out of the window at the same tree in the back garden, as ridiculously oversized as it was in the photo.

For the next fifteen years, Kazhik and Lilly spoke on the

phone once a week. He would ask Lilly what she had been doing and about her health; Lilly would enquire about Kazhik's life and his new family. He invited Lilly to visit him, but she never did. Kazhik returned to Mittenwald twice more before Lilly died in 1960.

When the local Catholic church organised Lilly's funeral and house clearance, there was very little to be removed. The house was largely bare of possessions, only a few pieces of furniture and some utensils in the kitchen. On the mantelpiece, they found two photos.

One of Jonas, and the other of Kazhik.

## *June 1948, Lodz*

Olga and Alina were in Lodz for two years. My mum celebrated her sixteenth birthday with her mother in the flat. The photo at the beginning of this book was taken on her birthday. Then one day there was a knock on the door.

It was her father, Michael.

He looked much older. His face was saggy with fatigue and running from the UB, the Polish secret police. He had heart problems. Michael was forty-one years old. Alina ran into his arms, and then turned and punched her mother in the arm as hard as she could.

'*Why did you do that?*' I ask.

'*She told me every day since the war started: 'Your father is dead, don't expect him to return' or 'He's abandoned us – he is a selfish philanderer living with his mistress in London'. Then he appears magically, when she said he never would. There he was, standing in front of me in the doorway. It taught me one thing – her tarot cards were bullshit.*'

'*How did you feel, seeing him there?*'

*'It was a miracle. The happiest day of my life.'*

*It seems too much to relive and my mum goes off to pour a glass of wine.*

Olga watched impassively as her husband embraced her only living daughter. She sat at the small kitchen table without saying a word. Michael handed Alina a present – a brand new doll still in its box. Michael had not seen his daughter since she was eight. He seemed to have forgotten that she hated dolls, but she thanked him for it.

Olga got up from the table and without saying a word, walked out of the room. She had her reasons: Olga had not been able to get a job, nor get Alina educated, because Michael was an 'enemy of the state'. He had suffered at the hands of the secret police, but now he had found a way to be reunited with his family, at a price.

The Ministry of Public Security of Poland (*Urząd Bezpieczeństwa* or UB) were the Polish version of the Soviet secret police, the NKVD. The UB took the NKVD's matrix of surveillance and torture and gave it a uniquely Polish twist. Michael was one of their first targets the moment he landed back in Warsaw.

The head of the UB was Stanislaw Radkiewicz, a slick party loyalist trusted by Moscow. Radkiewicz had extraordinary presence, looming imposingly over his subordinates. He wore flashy modern suits and looked more like a bandleader, with his slicked-back raven hair, than controller of the most extensive police state operation outside Soviet Russia.

Under Radkiewicz, 'the network' spread rapidly. His goal was to make every citizen of communist Poland a secret agent. He recruited 30,000 to spy on their neighbours and report 'un-Polish' activities to the UB. On Olga's corridor of the apartment block alone, there were three UB spies. Radkiewicz's web of informers reported to UB headquarters on Koszykowa Street in Warsaw, where they scuttled in day and night with information.

Radkiewicz's police state brought the underground resistance to its knees. The long-promised 'free' election was finally held in 1947, returning an 80.1% per cent communist majority; in some areas, the communists scored 120 per cent. The government offered 'anti-communist insurgents' like Michael an amnesty to come out from hiding and be part of the elections. It was a trick designed to draw out anyone still opposed to Stalinist rule, round them up and have them shot.

Michael was part of a resistance group called *Zrzeszenie Wolnosc i Niezawislosc* (Freedom and Independence) or WiN. One of the last refuges for anti-communist agitators, they initially had backing from the West, but were soon cut adrift and left to fight by themselves. WiN, though small, was a formidable fighting force, trained by many of the old AK guerrilla soldiers from the war. They attacked prisons and UB jails, bombed detention centres and even attempted a daring raid on the UB headquarters in Koszykowa Street.

In London, Michael had only ever planned attacks on the Nazis from afar. Now he was getting his hands dirty. In the dark days of post-war communist Poland, with hope of freedom extinguished, WiN appeared to offer people a chance.

Michael slept in barns with his guerrilla comrades, planted explosives and was once fired upon by UB operatives as he escaped in a car. WiN knew military victory against the might of Soviet occupation was impossible. The point was to fight and show the Polish people that resistance was not yet completely dead.

Then it all went wrong. In 1947, as part of the election amnesty, WiN's leadership were betrayed by UB double agents who had infiltrated the organisation. Michael, who had been on UB's hit list since the day he'd been followed from the airport, was arrested.

He spent four weeks in Mokotow prison. The cells were filled with his comrades from the war, chained to the wall and beaten with iron bars. They became known as *zolnierze wykleci*: 'the cursed' or 'doomed soldiers'. One of the prison's most famous enforcers was called Piotr Smietanski, a short, intense communist with short-cropped, brush-wire hair, and a profound love of inflicting pain.

Smietanski called Mokotow prison his 'palace of wonders'. He personally oversaw executions of the 'doomed soldiers' and would often force prisoners to torture one another. Smietanski executed the war hero Witold Pilecki, the soldier who had first gone in to Auschwitz in 1941 and alerted the West to the horrors of what was happening.

Michael was spared Smietanski. Instead, he lay in his own urine and excrement, unable to move beyond the semi-circle of stone floor circumscribed by his metal chain. The UB perfected psychological torture on the *zolnierze wykleci*. Guards would come in with a plate of stew, then kick it to the floor inches from a prisoner's face, just out of reach. Sometimes they would urinate in their face. Prisoners were tortured with electrical current and punched repeatedly in the genitals by UB guards that changed daily. Michael never saw who his tormentors were.

He was offered the chance to betray WiN resistance fighters in groups like the Polish peasants party and UPA (Ukrainian Insurgents Army). They also wanted to know about CIA agents now working in Poland to subvert the communist regime.

Michael said nothing for three weeks. Then one day, a UB guard came in, whose voice he had never heard before. He was an older man, perhaps in his mid-sixties, portly with a ruddy complexion and a book under one arm. He walked over to Michael, stepping over the filthy straw, and unbolted Michael from his chain.

'Come,' he said, sitting down on a wooden bench. 'Sit with me.'

The agent opened his book and asked Michael the name of his wife and daughter. Michael stared at the interrogator. He said nothing.

'Olga and Alina Basiak, that's right, isn't it?'

Again, Michael said nothing.

'Alina would be, what? Sixteen years old by now?' The guard turned over the pages of his book thoughtfully, as if examining a photo album.

'That's right,' Michael said finally. He was wary of where this was going.

'You must miss seeing your daughter very much.'

Eventually Michael spoke, slowly and calmly. 'My daughter is dead, my wife is dead. You have nothing to barter with. I won't be giving you any names.'

The interrogator stared into his book, then turned and looked Michael straight in the eyes.

'If they were dead, Michael, you'd be right. I wouldn't have anything to barter with. But as they're alive, I do.'

He shut his book quietly and patted it gently on the cover.

'I need names.'

Michael gazed at the filthy floor, then up at the small, grey oblong of cell window criss-crossed with metal mesh. He had never really examined this window properly until now, even after weeks in the cell. He wondered if perhaps he was hallucinating the whole situation: the prison, the interrogator, the news that his wife and daughter were alive.

The interrogator opened his book again and held the pen out for Michael.

'They're in Lodz,' he said flatly. 'Your wife and daughter.'

The interrogator had done this thousands of times before: sat calmly in front of a desperate prisoner. Often, they managed to withhold information in spite of being burnt with cigarettes, electrocuted with cattle prods and having teeth removed with pliers. None of it would break them, but then they would be dangled a last chance to see their family. It worked, virtually every time. The interrogator had no feelings towards this person before him, he didn't even hate them. He cared only for the information contained in the vessel of their body, and how best to extract it.

The interrogator pushed the book along the bench, and gestured to the pen again.

'The names, Michael.'

Days later, Michael was standing before his wife and daughter in their apartment in Lodz. Olga was lying perfectly still on the bed, her back to Michael. An ostentatious display of disdain for his return. Alina was holding the doll she secretly hated in its box. Inside, Michael was bursting with joy, as well as the shame of what he had just done. They were together again, but at a price.

# 17

# Michael

*June 1949, Lodz*

Michael had been free for nine months. In that time, he moved into a one-bedroom apartment on the other side of the city from Olga and Alina. He could not get work as an architect, because he was blacklisted by the communist government, so he worked as an odd-job man.

He continued to be followed by the UB. The Soviet NKVD had started using surveillance bugs and the Polish secret police were now enthusiastic adopters of the same techniques. They ran wires under the wallpaper of Michael's flat to transmitters hidden in light switches.

They monitored anyone who came and went or rang Michael's phone. An operative sat in an adjacent flat logging any phrases that could be construed as coded messages to Michael's friends in the underground. The UB records on Michael and the tens of thousands who were under state surveillance became public in 1993, four years after Communism collapsed. Ninety per cent of what they did was redacted.

Michael spent Thursday afternoons with his daughter Alina. They met at Klepacza Park in the centre, a botanical garden with a café and a huge, beautiful oak tree dating back 200 years, nicknamed *Fabrykant* (Factory Owner). Romantic couples would rendezvous there beneath its branches and walk through the spring flowers. Michael was photographed with his daughter by a UB agent.

*This is the only 'family photo' that exists: of my mum, grandmother Olga and my grandfather Michael together, taken shortly after Michael was released from prison.*

One afternoon, Alina turned up unexpectedly with her mother, Olga. Olga was wearing a dress for the first time in a decade and she had a thin outline of lipstick on. Michael and Olga walked slowly round the park together. After a while, they tentatively held hands, as they once had in the Jardins du Luxembourg, courting in Paris twenty years earlier. Alina skipped gleefully ahead of her parents, as if she was nine again.

Michael was mopping the floor of his flat one morning when the phone rang. The UB operative in the next-door apartment hastily put on his headphones, scrabbling for a pencil.

'Michael?' a female voice began uncertainly.

'Who is this?'

'Marta.'

They met in a busy café a mile from his flat, chosen carefully because there was enough noise of crockery and conversation so as not be overheard.

'I thought you were dead,' Michael said, pouring sugar into his black tea.

'I thought *you* were dead,' Marta replied. They laughed. She looked much older, just as he did. It was only five years since they had been lovers in London, but it felt like fifty. Marta's long revolutionary hair had been cut into a bob, the odd strand greying. She was still as beautiful as ever in Michael's eyes, maybe more so.

'Where are you living?' Michael asked.

'Lodz.'

'What a coincidence,' he said coolly, not believing for one minute it was a coincidence.

'I was in Katowice. Then the war ended and I moved here,' Marta said casually.

The question was 'why?'. Instead he asked another question. 'What are you doing here?'

'Teacher, in a primary school.'

'No ring on your finger,' Michael observed, with a laconic smile.

'What do you want me to say, Michael? I loved you.' She touched his hand gently. 'I *love* you,' she said, correcting herself.

Michael was right that it was not a coincidence. Marta had been arrested by the UB in the 1947 amnesty and told that if she wanted her career as a primary-school teacher in Katowice to continue, she needed to work as a double agent.

Two men in sharply cut suits came to her dingy studio flat and gave her Michael's address and phone number in Lodz. Marta was told she had to move to the same city; she was given a six-month lease on an apartment, where she was to resume sexual relations with Michael. She was to find out whatever the UB needed from these meetings and report weekly to their headquarters in the north of the city.

In the uncomfortably hot summer of 1949, Michael came to Marta's flat on Andrzeja Struga and they made love for the first time in five years. As they sat afterwards on the unpacked boxes in the living room, Marta confessed everything without any prompting. She explained how the UB first approached her.

They wanted to know what the survivors of the 1947 purge were planning. Michael pointed at the walls without opening his mouth, as if to say it was a bad idea to talk there.

Marta laughed. 'The UB are decorating my flat next week. They will install the bugs then.'

Marta was incredibly open about being a double agent, as if she enjoyed the fact that in confiding in Michael, she had now become a triple agent. She told Michael that the UB had a detailed file on him, believing him to be an ongoing danger to security. They knew about Michael's activities in the WiN; his falling out with the AK in London; and his confession in Mokotow. They also believed, she said, that Michael was weak, and could be turned to their side. They would use Marta to do it.

'Of course, the fact that you have a wife and two children still alive . . .'

'What did you just say?'

Marta looked puzzled, and repeated herself.

'You have a wife and two children. Alina and Kazhik.'

Michael ran from the apartment. His heart hurt and his bones were like toothpicks that could break at any moment. He wanted to kiss every human being on earth. His son was alive.

He caught a bus to the government missing persons agency in Gorniak, a large office in the centre of the city created after the war to help families reunite with relatives. He leapt two stairs at a time up to the third floor, where a woman with spectacles on a string went to a filing cabinet and searched for the name 'Kazhik Basiak'.

'Prisoner of war, Sandbostel. Released 1945. Whereabouts unknown,' the woman said matter-of-factly.

'Thank you,' Michael said and kissed the woman on both cheeks.

The following morning, Michael was sitting in Olga's flat, at the kitchen table.

'Kazhik is alive,' he said, expecting the heavens to open and a big hand to come down.

'I know,' Olga replied dispassionately, stirring a large pot on the stove.

'What do you mean, you know?'

'Of course he's alive' Olga said. 'The cards told me.'

Michael didn't know what to say. He was beaten to it, as always, by his wife.

'The cards told me you were alive,' Olga continued. 'They told me to go back to Poland and find my children, our children, when everyone was telling me they must be dead. Why would the cards not tell me that Kazhik was alive?'

Michael had to take his hat off to this woman.

'Where is he, then? Our son?'

'I have no idea,' Olga replied curtly. 'But he will come back to me.'

The cards also told Olga that Michael was sleeping with another woman again. When he left the flat, Olga told Alina to follow him.

She hid behind a newspaper kiosk as Michael waited at the bus stop. When he boarded the bus, Alina ran as fast as her legs would carry her alongside. At the next bus stop, she squeezed on board. Michael was so engrossed in his book, he didn't glance up.

The bus passed into a part of the city Alina didn't recognise. Mile upon mile of the social realist dream: concrete slabs of apartment blocks, standing an equal distance apart, like unfeasibly huge dominoes. What people in the capitalist West considered the drab monotony of communist architecture was a dream come true to the people of Lodz, after six years of brutal war.

Many residents tried to personalise their identical apartments by tearing out pages from banned Western magazines like *Life* and sticking them to the walls: pictures of people in bikinis on holiday; brightly coloured sports cars; even unobtainable luxuries such as cakes and pastries, giant blancmanges with cherries on top and Black Forest gateaux.

Michael got off at a wide intersection with a brand new petrol station. Alina darted out of the bus doors at the last moment, frightened she would be spotted, but Michael continued to read his book even as he weaved between the cars. He didn't spot his daughter.

Alina followed Michael into one of the huge apartment blocks labelled 'D'. The concrete dominoes stretched from A to O, receding into the distance. There were no trees and no people. A boy kicked a ball against a wall, but besides the boy, there was nothing.

Alina watched Michael climb the stairs and hid like a UB agent behind a wall. When he moved on to the next flight, she followed. Each landing, she would do the same thing. Eventually, Michael reached the sixth floor and walked briskly along the corridor. Alina waited to see which flat he would stop outside. Then a woman appeared suddenly and embraced Michael, kissing him passionately and holding him for what felt like an age.

The couple seemed frozen in time. Alina was numbed to the spot. She was transfixed by the surreal image and its lack of connection to her. This man before her was a stranger and everything about his life was suddenly alien to Alina. The kiss seemed merely an anointment of her father's distance from Alina; the final dramatic act of two lives lived separately for six years. Michael was as real now to his daughter as Father Christmas.

Alina returned to the flat, where Olga was turning over tarot cards as usual by the radiogram, a large piece of polished wooden furniture that she had bought on hire purchase from a department store. It was playing funereal government-approved music.

'Well?' Olga said. 'Who is she?'

'There isn't anyone,' Alina said. 'He returned to his flat.'

Olga – or perhaps it was the tarot cards – was right about Kazhik finding them. One morning, there was a knock, and it was a mirror image of what happened in Warsaw. This time, her son was behind the door. Olga opened it, frailer now than she had ever been in her life: she was only forty-one, but felt a hundred. The pain in every limb fell away as she embraced her boy. He held his mother tightly and they said nothing.

Kazhik sat at the kitchen table and finally, he opened his mouth to his sister.

'It's been a long time,' he said.

'You found us,' Alina said. 'Thank you, brother.'

They embraced, and Alina told Kazhik about their father. That he was alive, that he had been in London with the AK, and was now with the anti-communist underground. Oh, and by the way, yesterday she had followed him to the apartment of a woman stranger. Kazhik shrugged.

'He's trouble for us.'

'Don't you want to see him? Your father?'

Kazhik shook his head slowly and resolutely no. 'That man is no father. He abandoned us to war and he's abandoned us again now. The only thing he cares about is his bullshit, help-the-poor-peasants socialism. Not us. Now there's a communist government, he's not even happy. Leave him be.'

Secretly, Kazhik had no intention of leaving his father be. The following day he left the flat at 5 a.m., got on his motorbike and found his father's address. Kazhik sat outside Michael's block for two hours, unable to go up, yet unwilling to leave.

As he was about to ride off, Michael appeared from the front door with a book under his arm. He walked nonchalantly down the street to a local café. Kazhik dismounted the bike and followed him. The café was largely empty. Michael sat with his back to the door at one of the tables, reading his book with a black tea beside him.

Kazhik stood for an age behind his father. They looked like two models in a life-drawing class, asked to hold stilted poses. Michael sat still as a stone reading, whilst Kazhik was frozen behind him, unable to move. Michael was so engrossed in his book, he would never have noticed his son. Eventually, Kazhik leant forward clumsily to touch his father's arm to break the spell, and at the same moment, Michael turned. Their movements coincided, and they crashed into one another. Michael spilt the tea across the table and drenched his book.

'Kazhik,' Michael said, mopping up whilst gesturing for the boy to sit with him. Michael had exploded inside, but appeared calm. He was trying to do everything simultaneously, but had no idea what to do.

'Kazhik,' he repeated breathlessly, unable to get beyond his son's name. He couldn't compute the fact that he was standing before him.

'Father,' Kazhik said, sitting on the soaking chair beside him. They looked at one another. They were two grown men: Kazhik was nineteen and Michael was forty-three. They reached out and embraced one another. They didn't say another word. As quickly as he had appeared, Kazhik got up, wiped tears from his eyes and walked out, determined not to turn around, or ever see his father again.

Marta and Michael lay in bed together. They had booked a hotel room where they could meet, because both their flats were riddled with bugging devices.

Michael had reconnected in Lodz with Marcus, the underground resistance friend he had known before the war. Marcus had introduced Michael to a group of anti-communist agitators, who were forming a cell in the city to print an underground *samizdat* newspaper.

The UB were following Michael, knowing he was up to

something, and Marta was under pressure to give information on him to the secret police.

'If I don't give them names of some of the people you're working with,' she told him, 'I'll lose my job as a teacher.'

'Tell them I'm working alone on a newspaper,' said Michael. 'That will throw them off Marcus and his group. They will search my flat and carry on following me. They'll find nothing.'

'They don't need anything to put you in jail, Michael.'

'Actually, they do. They need an excuse. But it would probably be better for everyone if I *was* in jail. Olga can't get a job. Alina can't go to college. You will never get your teaching job back. And Kazhik . . .' His sentence trailed off. Who knew about Kazhik anymore? Their lives were all on hold, Michael said, because they were fatally connected to him: an enemy of the state.

Michael and Marta both understood the purgatory of life in Poland's surveillance state: perpetual limbo for anyone attached to someone like Michael. If he was jailed, he said, they would all be freed from this purgatory. He knew what he had to do.

Michael met with Marcus at Muzeum Sztuki in Wieckow-skiego, the museum of modern art in the old grand palace. Michael chose it deliberately, because it was such an obvious rendezvous spot for a clandestine meeting, and he could easily be followed by the UB. Sure enough, one of their agents shadowed him badly, hobbling from behind one plinth to the next.

Marcus met Michael by the big fountain in the grounds, the sound of rushing water drowning out any conversation. The UB agent, realising it was impossible to get closer, had disappeared, probably to get a coffee.

'You know about the new cell?' Marcus said. 'Four leaders, no one knows who they are. That's deliberate, of course.'

'You're one of them?' Michael said.

Marcus said nothing.

'The plan is simple. We set up cells in the main cities – Warsaw, Krakow, Katowice, Lodz. We then coordinate an assassination plot against the leaders of the communist dictatorship in each city at the same moment.'

'It's a CIA plot,' Michael said. He knew the CIA had infiltrated dozens of insurgency cells in Poland.

'No. No CIA. I give you my word.'

'What do you want me to do?'

Marcus said he wanted Michael to do what he had done in London during the war. Pinpoint the weak spots on the railway bridges on the Lodz-to-Warsaw line.

'We need to get it right, because we're going for him directly.'

'He' was Bierut. The President of Poland.

'The bastard will be blown to pieces,' Marcus said.

The men stood silent for a moment, as if paying their last respects to the hated dictator of the puppet communist Poland, whom they were about to assassinate.

Boleslaw Bierut was the instigator of the 'silent terror'. Following the rigged elections of 1947, Bierut took full political control of the country. His first action was to order the UB to arrest anyone remotely construed as against the regime. It didn't require much – if you so much as breathed the same air as a traitor, Bierut said, you were a traitor.

Six thousand people were rounded up by the UB and either tortured or executed in the first months of 1948. The WiN was reduced to a band of thirty renegades hiding in the forest near my family's old house in the (now) Ukraine.

Bierut was a cast-iron Stalinist. He had been loyal to Moscow throughout the 1930s and served his time dutifully as a member of the Comintern. He was dull and efficient, and lacked the intelligence for treachery, Stalin told Beria, which made him perfect for erasing Poland of people like Michael and Marcus, once and for all.

Marcus's new cell was created in 1949 as the last stand of free Poland. It was aimed at bringing down the puppet government and ridding Poland of Soviet oppression. It was led by grizzled veterans of the AK wartime government-in-exile in London and members of WiN who had somehow avoided being rounded up and thrown in jail by Bierut.

Battered and betrayed, there was no one left after the 1947 communist purges to fight more battles. Marcus turned to Michael not because he wanted to, but because he had no choice. The elephant dancing round the fountain as they spoke was Mokotow prison.

'I know it was you,' he told Michael.

'I had no choice, Marcus.'

'We all had a choice, Michael, and you chose to betray your comrades. To give up their names. Men and women died because of you.'

'It was that or my family,' Michael said coldly. 'There was no choice for me.'

Marcus didn't respond. 'Just do the right thing now,' he said, and walked away from the fountain.

## 3 October 1950, Lodz

Alina spent night after night in the one-room flat in Lodz poring over the pages of *Architectural Review,* a magazine from the West she had bought on the black market. It was like a fashion magazine, filled with glamorous images of bold, white modernist structures being built across the world, photographed at dynamic, heroic angles. The architects featured – Le Corbusier and Mies, Aalto and Frank Lloyd Wright – were profiled as the new gods of this post-war Western utopia. Men in polo necks and swept-back hair treated as visionaries, shown staring meaningfully into the far-off distance with a look of futuristic mission.

Alina was smitten. She wanted to become an engineer and an architect like them, to escape to the West and be part of this brave new world. In their cramped flat in Lodz, it seemed impossible. She applied to architecture school in Warsaw and Lodz, and was turned down.

Meanwhile Olga refused to get out of bed anymore. She did not even have any enthusiasm for her tarot cards.

'You're losing customers,' Alina told her.

'Where is my daughter?' Olga asked, distractedly.

'I'm here,' Alina said, convinced that Olga's spirit was fading.

'No,' replied Olga. 'My beautiful daughter, Juta. Where is she? And where is Pavel?'

At night, Kazhik began poring over the architecture magazine with Alina; it was their new obsession. However, if they could not escape Poland and become world-famous architects, Alina and Kazhik made a pact to dedicate themselves to another goal: finding out once and for all what happened to their brother and sister, Pavel and Juta.

They scoured the records of missing persons made available to Polish citizens by the government, which did not amount to much. They approached the dozens of tracing bureaus that had sprung up across Poland, including the Red Cross, Jewish Relief Unit and ITU (International Tracing Service). Some were charities and others charged a fee, but even these organisations struggled with any information on Poland's 'missing millions'.

Alina and Kazhik sat for hours in different waiting rooms. They were told by someone behind a desk that yes, they had found a description matching Pavel or Juta; but no, the date of birth didn't match. The SS who had abandoned Auschwitz in 1945 had been as ruthless in destroying records of the Holocaust as in making genocide happen, extending the torture of the victims' families for years to come.

One afternoon, Alina and Kazhik were stopped in the corridor of yet another missing persons agency by a woman with pockmarked skin and a knitted shawl.

'Excuse me,' the woman began, 'but I couldn't help overhearing that you are looking for your sister?'

'And?' Kazhik replied wearily, exhausted by another long day getting nowhere.

The woman extended her hand formally. Her name was Ursula, she said, and she had been in the same block as Juta in Auschwitz. She said that if they wanted to go for a coffee, she could tell them everything she knew.

They sat in a dirty coffee bar on Bratyslawska and the woman fiddled nervously with a tissue. She said that Juta and her had worked together in Auschwitz cleaning toilets. Juta had been very kind and had arranged for her and her family to receive food. She was beautiful, Ursula said, and a kind soul.

'Do you know if she lived or was killed?' Kazhik asked impatiently, cutting to the chase.

'I think she escaped with Soviet soldiers in 1945. I believe she told another girl that she wanted to look for her family, and was going to head towards Warsaw.'

The woman leant across and held out her hand.

'I'm sorry to ask, but please may you give me some money? My family have no food.'

Kazhik rummaged in his pocket and gave her a handful of scrunched-up notes.

'Thank you, sir. Thank you. If you want, we can meet tomorrow and I can tell you some more about your sister and what I know?'

Alina looked sceptically at Kazhik.

'No, it's fine, Ursula. Thank you.'

Back in the municipal offices, the police officer on the door told them that 'Ursula' was a well-known scam artist and moved on rotation from one missing person's bureau in Lodz to the next.

'Be careful,' he said. 'There are plenty more like her, and far worse. Fake private investigators who will claim they'll find your sister and take all your money. Watch out.'

He nodded solemnly, touching his nose conspiratorially with his finger, satisfied that his words had been heeded.

## 14 January 1951, Lodz

Police smashed Marta's door at 5.45 a.m. and Michael was taken in handcuffs to the train station and from there to Warsaw. There was no need to smash the door, Michael told the arresting secret police.

Michael had done exactly what Marcus instructed, and spent weeks at the architectural association of Lodz, examining the elevations and cross-sections of bridges along the Lodz-to-Warsaw railway line. On his way to prison, the train passed over the bridges that Michael had planned to blow up.

Marta knew the arrest would happen and even the time, because three days earlier she went into UB headquarters in Lodz and told them what she said she knew about Michael's plan. But Marta betrayed only the information Michael told her to betray.

The script they concocted together went like this: Michael was organising an attack, and no one else was involved. There was no mention of the target being Bierut, nor Marcus's involvement, nor blowing up the trainline. Michael hoped it would buy Marcus and the plot valuable time: he was making himself a sacrificial lamb, though he expected no one to thank him for it.

The real reason Michael was doing it was to free Marta and his family from the purgatory of the communist state: the surveillance, the paralysing fear of arrest hanging constantly over them, and the endless blacklisting from jobs and university. Alina was now twenty, yet had failed to be accepted on any architecture course. Kazhik, equally enthralled by Alina's copies of *Architectural Review*, wanted to become an architect too, like their father, but he was rejected as well. The reason was obvious: their connection to Michael.

After his arrest, Michael was taken straight to Mokotow prison, a jail he knew well. He was tortured and interrogated by UB agents, and confessed that he was a member of *Kraj* and planning to assassinate Jakub Berman, Bierut's second-in-command. It was all part of the script he had concocted with Marta. Berman was a shrewd choice – he did not figure in *Kraj*'s real plans and was a curve ball to send them off Marcus's scent.

Michael was marched to a courtroom and stood alone in the dock before Mieczyslaw Widaj, a notorious show-trial judge. Michael had no defence and nothing to say, and Widaj took thirty seconds to sentence my grandfather to twenty-five years without parole, the first ten in solitary confinement. When Widaj handed down the sentence, Michael shouted 'Long live Poland!' and was taken handcuffed to the cells.

Alina and Kazhik were in the flat when the phone rang. It was Marta.

'My name is . . .'

'I know who you are,' Alina said.

'Your father. He's been jailed.'

Alina fainted. Kazhik lay his sister's limp body on the lurid orange sofa in the middle of their flat. When Alina came round, they sat in the kitchen together for two hours. They agreed that they should meet Marta. She was the only thread now connecting them to their father.

It was not hard to make contact again. Alina retraced her steps from the day she had followed her father to Marta's flat. She put a note through Marta's door. The following day they met in a café. Marta told them about their father in the war and how he had organised AK missions against the Nazis. She told them about Michael's plan to get Olga and Alina out of Siberia. Marta told them also how they met again after the war and how she had betrayed her father to the UB.

Kazhik sat silently and stared at Marta, stirring his tea thoughtfully.

'He must love you,' Alina said, when Marta had finished.

'He does, and I love him.'

'What happens now?' Kazhik asked.

Marta said she would try to find out more about their father's situation and would contact them as soon as she knew anything.

'I will post you a letter with a time and place to meet.'

Kazhik and Alina agreed with the plan. As they both left the café, he asked his sister, 'Do you trust her?'

'No,' Alina replied.

'Neither do I,' Kazhik said. 'But we have no choice.'

They were right to be suspicious.

Michael spent six months in solitary confinement. Food was brought to his cell and passed through a hatch. He was allowed to exercise in a small yard, where he could hear the sound of children in a primary school playing over the wall. The UB questioned him further about his plan to assassinate Jakub Berman and appeared to believe him when he said he was acting alone. That, or they knew it was all a pack of lies. They had bigger fish to fry anyway – the real plot against Bierut. For whatever reason, Michael stayed in solitary.

On 1 March, seven of WiN's bravest and most loyal resistance fighters were executed in Mokotow, the prison where Michael was held. They included the leader, Lukasz Cieplinski, and WiN's elite '4th Headquarter' commanders, Karol Chmiel and Adam Lazarowicz.

They had been sentenced months earlier, prior to Michael's arrest, and kept in a large communal cell with eighty other suspected WiN 'terrorists'. The charge was 'plotting with the Nazis against Poland'. Whilst awaiting trial, they were tortured and beaten so badly, Cieplinski had his legs broken and had to be carried in blankets by his comrades to the courtroom.

The night before their execution, Cieplinski, a devout Catholic, swallowed a small depiction of the Virgin Mary in a suicide attempt. The next day, the men were taken to the boiler room in the basement. The executions began on the stroke of 8 p.m., happening at ten-minute intervals, with a single bullet fired to the back of each man's head. The only one to resist was Karol Chmiel, who ran down the corridor screaming, 'They are murdering us!' He was shot in the back, falling on a pile of coal.

In his cell, Michael heard the WiN prisoners banging metal soup cans and chanting the old AK mantra, 'Kill The Nazis! Fuck the Russians!' followed by the Polish national anthem. Even though prison guards threatened to shoot the remaining prisoners, they continued to shout the names of the dead late into the night, the sound echoing around the prison.

*Kraj* never achieved their goal of a mass assassination of the Polish government's top brass. They avenged the Mokotow executions with the killing of a radio propagandist called Stefan Martyka, who broadcast to the nation with graphic tales of the anti-communist 'traitors in our midst' and how they had been trained by the Nazis in the war.

Michael and Marcus were two of the last of the London AK renegades still alive in communist Poland. Michael was in prison and Marcus was free. They never saw each other again.

# 18

## Redemption

*5 September 1951, Lodz*

Alina and Kazhik received letters on the same day. They sat at the kitchen table and stared intensely at the envelopes lying beside one another. On the front of each was the distinctive lion and black eagle stamp of Wroclaw Technical University. Kazhik opened both with a flourish of his knife; Alina could not contain her excitement and dug her fingers into her brother's arm, unable to look at what they said.

They had been accepted on the prestigious architecture course at Wroclaw on the fourth attempt; successful now because their father was in jail and – to use the UB euphemism for executed or captive 'enemies of the state' – neutralised.

Michael knew his imprisonment in solitary confinement was the price that had to be paid for letting his children start their lives. It was this, not political idealism, that drove him to be deliberately captured and arrested.

When it was time to leave for Wroclaw Technical University, Olga kissed Alina and Kazhik primly on the cheek and said goodbye. They manoeuvred their big over-stuffed leather suitcases out of the flat and the door slammed. It was the first time Olga had ever been alone. She sighed deeply and pulled the curtains, then took a pack of fresh tarot cards from a drawer and arranged them face down in front of her on the table. She planned to go back into business.

Alina and Kazhik had a fantastic time at university. Alina dyed her hair bright red and smoked a pipe in lectures 'to get noticed', whilst Kazhik turned his energies to climbing. At weekends, they headed to the mountains with a group of friends. They used ropes and crampons to climb the steep rock faces, peppered with nails hammered into crevices.

In 1953, Josef Stalin died suddenly from a brain haemorrhage. Alina was having a lecture on steel load-bearing when the whispered news cascaded through the hall.

Suspicion for Stalin's 'murder' fell on his long-term sidekick, secret police chief Beria, who was rumoured to have boasted to his fellow Politburo member Molotov that he 'took him out'. It was nonsense, a ruse in the power struggle to discredit Stalin's friends and loyalists. But it worked, Beria – who had first come up with the idea for gassing people in vans later adopted by the Nazis – was executed. Nikita Khrushchev became the new Soviet leader, and life was about to change for my family forever.

Alina returned frequently from university to see her mother, whose tarot card business was thriving once again. There were queues down the corridor.

'Do you need money?' Olga asked her daughter.

'I'm fine. But thank you.'

At night, Alina began frequenting the Honoratka coffee bar. It was in the student area of Lodz and the hub of the bohemian and intellectual scene. Lodz had a famous film school and prestigious experimental theatre, where people would dress all in black and sit on metal chairs, making barking sounds as a critique of capitalism. Lodz had taken over from Warsaw as the destination for bright, young intellectual Poles to go and make their name.

One night, Alina met a tiny intense man who was very full of himself. He told Alina that his name was Roman Polanski, and he was half-Jewish. He was surrounded by a group of fellow students from the film school. They organised screenings of experimental films in a wine cellar, and Polanski invited Alina to come.

*       *       *

'*He was sort of a showman, very enterprising and full of ideas,*' my mum remembers. '*I recall one of his films included footage of Nazis marching backwards. The Nazis had become a kind of cipher for the communist regime. It was ideologically acceptable to make fun of the Nazis, but the authorities didn't realise it was their regime that was being lampooned in these films. Every time artists used Nazis in their work, they were really making the comparison with communism. The authorities were just too stupid to see it.*'

'*Did Polanski become your boyfriend?*'

'*God, no. We were friends, but he was very short. He wasn't my type, but I remember he was very confident about getting any woman he wanted. He'd say, "If I want to get Gina Lollobrigida as a girlfriend, I will get her." He got the next best thing, the actress Barbara Kwiatkowska, who was the Polish version.*'

In 1954, Alina returned to Wroclaw architecture school for the start of her third year. She was crossing the quadrangle to the lecture theatre when she was stopped by a man blocking her way on the path.

'Excuse me,' Alina said, attempting to pass him to one side.

'I know who you are,' the man said, refusing to move.

'You're Alina Basiak.'

Alina's blood ran cold. When she had applied for university, she and her brother had used their mother's surname, Bialonoga-Szahovska.

'*I knew it would be impossible to get in if I used my father's name. We'd had rejection after rejection. You needed to be a workman or a peasant to be accepted on a course. You had to have the best proletarian credentials because the bourgeoisie were hated. I said on my application form that my father was jobless, because they wouldn't be able to check that. I forged his signature and my references. It was the only way to get in, and it worked.*'

\*       \*       \*

Someone had found out. He was a second-year student, and now he was standing in front of Alina on the path, threatening to destroy her future.

'What do you want?' she said, as calmly as possible.

'Ten thousand zlotys.'

'I don't think so.'

'You think the rector will be happy that you lied your way into university? And your father is in prison?'

'Go fuck yourself. Now, get out of my way.'

Alina was bullish, but in truth she was terrified. She spent two nights lying awake in her room, praying that he would not go to the university authorities. He did.

Alina was summoned to the rector's office four days later. She sat in a deep leather armchair, a grandfather clock ticking loudly behind her. Alina's eyes scanned the rows of heavy books on the shelves, thinking desperately what to say. She knew it didn't matter; the game was up. She would be expelled. Alina could even go to prison, like her father, and her mother lose her flat.

A man with longish greying hair and a heavy old suit lumbered slowly into the room, glancing quickly at a gold watch hanging from his pocket-chain.

'This won't take long,' he said. 'It's Alina, isn't it?'

'Yes. sir.'

'Alina *Basiak*.' He enunciated her real surname.

'I'm afraid so, sir. I can explain everything, my mother didn't . . .'

The rector raised his hand.

'Alina Basiak,' he said again. He mulled the name over, as if tasting a complex wine. 'Tell me. Does your father still have that annoying habit of cracking his knuckles in a self-satisfied way every time he gets a question right?'

'I don't know, sir. He's . . .'

'Yes, I know. In prison.'

Alina twiddled her thumbs and stared at the bright red shoes she had on, which now seemed frivolous in the circumstances. The man took an age to speak again.

'I knew your father at architecture school,' he said, eventually.

This was unexpected. Alina looked the man in the eye.

'Will you be . . .?'

'Expelling you? No, Alina, I will not be expelling you.'

My mother let out a huge exhale of breath and slouched back in her chair, not so much relieved as utterly exhausted. Then a new anxiety bubbled up in her brain.

'The boy, sir.'

The professor squinted at Alina. 'What about him?'

'I forged my application, sir.' She felt the need to remind the rector of the reason she was there.

'Yes. I know.'

'Doesn't that mean you could get in trouble for refusing to expel me?'

The professor mulled this over for a minute.

'Probably,' he replied, finally. 'I should, but I won't. Here's what's going to happen, Alina. You are going to complete your studies at Wroclaw, and when you have graduated with first-class honours as an engineer, you are going to become a world-class export of Poland's. Just like your father.'

Alina didn't know what to say, so she limited her response to a polite nod.

'I'm not guaranteeing I'll get a first-class honours,' she said, smiling at last.

'No,' the rector replied, 'nor am I,' and they shook hands.

*21 November 1956, Mokotow Prison, Warsaw*

Two women visited Michael in prison. One would come on a Monday, and the other on Thursday.

'That woman has been here again,' Olga would hiss across the same trestle table. 'Who is she? Tell me.'

Michael would sigh and look up at the ceiling. 'Have you anything else to say to me?'

'No, you bastard. I haven't. Who is she? Alina lied and told me she doesn't exist. I know she does.'

'Let me guess,' Michael replied, 'the cards told you.'

'They did, and I trust them a damn sight more than I'd ever trust you.'

Michael had an entire speech ready for Olga, one he had rehearsed in his cell: how he had arranged Olga's escape from Siberia; found them again after the war in Lodz; and now sacrificed his freedom for their future. It was a disingenuous speech, because Olga was right. There was another woman and Michael loved her, not Olga. So he never made his speech. He merely sat and waited for Olga to stop. What he didn't consider was that Olga's compulsive jealousy was the only way she could show her love for Michael. It was her version of passion: Olga's own prison.

In March 1956, the hated Bierut, who had put Michael in jail, died abruptly from a heart attack. The conspiracies around Stalin's death started all over again: this time it was Bierut who had been poisoned by modernisers trying to wrestle power from the old guard, just as Stalin had been. No one in Poland cared what the truth was. Bierut was dead.

Alina and Kazhik were now both five years into their six-year architecture and engineering degree. Alina's dream of graduating and moving to the capitalist West had been made real by the rector's speech to her. It actually seemed possible. *If he believed in me*, she thought, *then so will other people*. On a practical level, Alina knew it was still a hopeless dream, but the timing of Bierut's heart attack could not have been better. The man who stopped anyone having a life in Poland was dead. But Alina had no idea how fast his fatal coronary would change everything.

Bierut was replaced by Wladyslaw Gomulka, a popular elder statesman of the Polish communist party, who had fallen out of favour in the last years of Stalin's rule. Gomulka was not a boring *apparatchik*, nor was he loyal to Moscow. He was a razor-sharp operator, hungry to get his chance to give Poland greater independence from the Soviets.

Gomulka used the liberalising changes under Khrushchev in the Soviet Union to suggest a 'thaw' in Polish culture too, allowing small businesses to start trading and society to begin opening up. He also sought more Polish 'autonomy' from Moscow. Most importantly for my family, he wanted to pardon political prisoners.

On 23 June 1956, Gomulka got the boost he needed. A revolt in Hungary against the communist regime by students in Budapest quickly escalated into the most serious crisis for the Soviet empire since its creation. The Hungarian government collapsed, free elections were announced and thousands of people filled the streets celebrating the imminent end of dictatorship.

In Poland, 100,000 people marched on the communist head-quarters in Poznan with home-made banners saying, 'We Demand Bread!' buoyed by the Hungarian uprising. Gomulka used the Poznan protests to plan his 'Polish October', the announcement of far-reaching reforms. He told Moscow it was the only way to save Soviet rule from an imminent proletarian revolution. Gomulka did not need to point out to his Soviet bosses the irony of what he was saying – that they needed to be saved from 'the people'.

Khrushchev reluctantly agreed. In November, whilst he sent in tanks to crush the Hungarian uprising, killing 3,000 protestors, Khrushchev let Gomulka make his reforms in Poland.

'My priority now,' Gomulka told the UB secret police, 'is to release the political prisoners rotting in Mokotow.' If they stayed in prison any longer, he said, they would become martyrs for the increasingly restless crowds outside.

Michael was released without warning on 21 November 1956. He was in his cell reading a book when a UB agent came in with a prison guard. Michael assumed he was about to be beaten and tortured again, but instead the UB agent gave him a pen and a piece of paper.

'It's a discharge notice,' he said casually. 'To say you are happy we have returned your valuables in good order.'

'Sorry?' Michael said, getting up from his bunk.

'You have been pardoned by the Polish people. You have fifteen minutes to vacate your cell.'

The UB agent turned on his heel and walked out. Michael had been in solitary confinement for five years. The prison guard, who had known Michael his entire time in jail, smiled.

'Go quickly,' he said, 'before they change their mind.'


*22 November 1956, Mokotow Prison, Warsaw*

Marta was waiting outside with flowers. They took the bus to the station and the train to Lodz.

*'Why weren't you there?' I ask my mum. 'For his release?'*

*'Why aren't you here?' she counters, on the phone. 'I haven't seen you for weeks.'*

*'Because of the virus. The Covid lockdown has been extended. I'm not allowed to travel more than five miles from my home ... for exercise.'*

*'Exercise? Really? Is that what they're saying? You have to travel five miles for exercise? That's exhausting. What did you ask me again?'*

*'Why were you not outside the jail when Michael was released.'*

*'No one told us he was being released. And even if they had, Marta was the one he wanted to see.'*

\*    \*    \*

Michael woke suddenly at midnight in Marta's flat, a habit of imprisonment. He wanted a hot bath. The water in the flat was tepid at best, so Marta brought kettle after boiling kettle to fill up the bath. Steam filled the tiny space until Michael was invisible in the fog. He had never been so happy.

Alina and Kazhik were informed by the police of their father's release and returned home immediately. They telephoned Marta and spoke briefly to Michael, arranging to meet the next day to celebrate at U Milscha (At Milscha's), a fancy restaurant in the centre of Lodz. When Alina got off the phone, Olga asked suddenly and without precedent how her husband was.

'He's fine, he's well,' Alina said brightly, surprised by her mother's question.

'Is that woman with him?'

Kazhik laughed.

'Yes, she is,' Alina replied patiently. 'And will be, I imagine, always.'

Alina decided to change the record. She told Olga about the Gomulka reforms. Her mother never watched the news or read newspapers. 'The news is rubbish. It's all what happened yesterday, in the past,' she would say. 'My cards tell me the future'. For all Alina knew, Olga still believed Hitler was alive.

She thought it a good opportunity to tell her mother about her dream: to go to the West and become a world-famous architect, perhaps one day afford to buy her own flat. Olga laughed so much, it hurt her ribs.

'Why are you laughing?' Alina said indignantly.

'My girl! What is the point of doing or owning anything in this world? Go to the West? Why? Own a flat? My darling Alina, my family owned half of Russia. We were rich. Then the Bolsheviks came and took everything. So I married your father, who put me in a miserable house in the forest. Then the Nazis came and took that. Now I am in this shithole in Lodz. One day someone will come along and take this away from me too.'

'Well . . .' Alina said, unsure how to respond.

'You want to go to the West?' Olga continued. 'How are you going to afford that? And who's going to allow you to leave Poland?'

'Gomulka is letting students travel there now, if they go soon.'

'Huh'. Olga grunted dismissively. 'Where would the money come from? Because I certainly don't have any more jewellery to conjure from my coat.'

Alina liked this new nihilistic Olga. In spite of what she said, Olga seemed to care nothing about the future, even if she could foretell it, because anything good would be taken away from her anyway.

Olga continued to make a small amount of money reading tarot cards in the flat, and at a café near the hospital; it was her only means of income. Kazhik disliked his mother's hocus-pocus enterprise. He said that Olga was preying on the emotional vulnerabilities of families awaiting news on their dying loved ones, but Alina said it was all she could do. Besides, she had noticed a marked change in what Olga told her clients.

Instead of telling them what their cards foretold, Olga now told people what she believed to be the right advice to give. She no longer cared what the cards said, nor whether people even liked her advice.

The old props – dim lighting, the clairvoyant curtain – were now simply a way of hooking them in. Thereon out, she relied only on perception; what people in the West might call 'therapy'. Against every fibre of her being, Olga had reluctantly developed an ability to empathise and even, on rare occasions, be kind.

U Milscha was a grand and ornate restaurant in the centre of Lodz. Michael arrived early and was nervous; he wore a neat suit and was freshly shaven. Marta had straightened his tie before leaving the flat and told him he looked very handsome.

Kazhik and Alina were fashionably late and looked every inch the cosmopolitan young Poles that they were. Kazhik was now twenty-six. He had grown very tall and filled out substantially. Alina said he looked like 'a fat banker' with an expense account for lunches. In fact, he was a talented architect on the cusp of graduation; glowing reviews from his tutors had earned him offers of work at three big firms in Warsaw and Krakow.

At twenty-five, Alina was less self-assured. Behind the bright red, extrovert hair and affectation of smoking an old man's pipe (of which she secretly hated the taste), Alina carried the memory of Juta everywhere. Her elder sister had never been found. There was little chance she had survived Auschwitz. Even though there was no evidence to suggest it, the idea that she had 'compromised herself' (as my mum put it) in order to keep Alina and Olga alive continued to prey on her mind.

'Why else did we receive food in the camp?' she would ask Kazhik. 'How come we avoided the hard labour detail given to everyone else in our hut?' (questions, seventy-odd years later, my mum no longer torments herself with). Juta had been watching over them from the administrative office, Alina was sure of it. My mum didn't want to think about what else Juta might have been forced to endure.

The war-crime trials of female SS guards like Irma Grese and Maria 'The Beast' Mandl revealed the daily and routine sexual exploitation of female translators and secretaries in the camp administrative office. How likely was Juta to have avoided this? It was not what Alina wanted to think about when she thought of her sister, but she couldn't get it out of her head.

When they arrived at the restaurant, Kazhik and Alina greeted their father as if nothing had happened: not war, nor his imprisonment, nor the absence of their two siblings. Instead, a warm hug and a present for him: a copy of a P. G. Wodehouse novel, which Michael loved because it reminded him of his time in

England. They ate ox tongue and caramel sauce, trout with parsley sauce, pig's head with an apple in its mouth. The Polish food of celebration.

Alina told her father of her plans to get to Europe. There were pats on the back and many toasts of vodka for Alina's escape ambitions, and for Kazhik and his job offers. When Kazhik had last seen his father, he had walked away from him in that café vowing he would never see Michael again. Perhaps nothing much had changed between them – they were still awkward figures unsure how to be with one another – but the world around them had changed considerably, and this had inevitably altered their relationship. Kazhik and Alina were no longer in the planetary pull of their mysterious larger-than-life father. They now had their own orbits.

Michael was so inexpressibly proud of his children and relieved to see them alive, he could have wept. Instead he laughed and joked that they were useless children and unworthy of such a great father.

Three days later, Alina heard the phone ring. She was deep in sleep and the only one in the flat. She wasn't sure how long it had been ringing, but the tinkling sound had invaded her dreams in the form of distorted cow bells and air-raid sirens. She jumped out of bed, freezing cold, and leapt across the flat. The phone continued to ring as she snatched at the receiver.

'Hello?'

'Alina?'

It was Marta.

'Your father. He's dead.'

Alina dropped the phone and slumped to the floor. She was in the same position when her brother returned two hours later. They sat together on the concrete with their arms around one another, neither saying a word.

*December 1956, Lodz*

The funeral was on a Tuesday in an empty cemetery on the outskirts of Lodz. There were eight people present, most huddled under umbrellas in the rain. Michael's two surviving children, Alina and Kazhik, his old friend Marcus, and another comrade from the London days of the AK, whom no one recognised. Marta was there too, at a distance. She was too embarrassed to come nearer, fearful of Olga being there too. She stood in the trees, with a small bunch of damp posies.

There was a thin, beaky priest, who stood impatiently at Michael's graveside, his cassock drenched from the rain; and two large men in flat caps smoking cigarettes a respectful distance away, waiting with shovels to fill in the hole.

Michael was a devout atheist and he had only ever been concerned that his children remembered him as a good man. When Alina asked her mother if she was going to her husband's funeral, she knew the answer already.

'That woman will be there. I have better things to do.'

Olga was nevertheless already dressed head to toe in black. She would continue dressing like this for the rest of her days. Olga was in mourning for her own life, Kazhik said, as much as Michael's death. When Alina and Kazhik returned from the funeral, Olga asked Alina to come and sit beside her.

'I have been doing some research,' she said, pouring them both a cup of boiling mint tea.

'On what?'

'How to get you to the West.'

Alina looked in amazement at her mother, who for all her faults, never ceased to surprise her.

'How on earth do you think that might happen?'

Olga smiled and pulled out a newspaper, which she had folded in half on the sports pages.

'Here,' she said, jabbing at the football results.

'Here *what?*' Alina said, weary now of this nonsense.

'I have been studying the football pools,' Olga persevered. 'You have to predict the results of the matches and if you're right, you win money. A lot of money.'

'I see, and you think your tarot cards will predict the results for me and we'll all live happily ever after in the West?'

'It's not as hard as you think. You don't need tarot cards, you just need to understand the strengths and weaknesses of the various teams.'

'If it was that easy,' Alina said, 'everyone would be doing it. And anyway, what the hell do I, or you for that matter, know about football?'

'I know this much, my dear, I've been doing this for six weeks now, and I've been right in twenty-eight out of thirty-four matches.'

Alina sat with her brother.

'Do you think there's something in it?' she whispered to him.

Olga had dozed off and was lying in a rocking chair in her mourning veil, with a plate of *halva*, a vodka and the sports pages of the newspaper spread out like a blanket across her shoulders.

'I once heard of a parrot that could predict football results,' Kazhik said. 'Perhaps she's using the same system.'

They laughed and thought nothing more of it.

*I am driving round a ring-road with my mum, late for an appointment to sort out the cataracts in her right eye.*

*'Thank you so much for coming up and taking me,' my mum says repeatedly.*

*'It's no problem. I just need to work out where the car park is. Does this look familiar?' I ask, pointing at a huge, multi-storey attached to a shopping centre.*

'I have absolutely no idea,' Alina says laughing. We spend an hour driving round in circles, but it really doesn't matter. My mum is in full flow, talking in huge detail about long-gone conversations with Kazhik, Juta and Olga.

The present to my mum is now a giant ring-road of forgotten tasks and chores she travels round in circles all day long. But the past of her childhood is vivid with colour, smells and intricate details: the forest and its wolves; Tallinn and the fishing boat; the children she played with in Sweden. The more she remembers, the more new doors into the past are unlocked. As her present disintegrates from dementia, this past comes ever more sharply into focus. Sometimes it is so sharp and overwhelming, my mum bursts into tears.

The fact is that seventy-five years of her life were not lived in the trauma of war, the Warsaw Uprising or Auschwitz, but in the north London suburb of Stanmore, where she worked as an engineer, architect and then a tour guide and classical concert organiser.

Like everyone who has dementia, she is not in essence the person she is today. My real mum is the woman I have been talking to in this book. The person that lives in the retelling of her story.

A whole life was there before the memory loss – working in West Africa and Switzerland, meeting Bob Marley in Jamaica, and swimming with basking sharks off the coast of Wales. Loving opera and literature, going to a football match (just once) and having a glass of wine (every day).

Everything that happened to her, she tells me weekly, was an unexpected bonus after surviving that Nazi firing squad in 1944. It was 'extra'. A life she never expected to live.

For many survivors of Warsaw and Auschwitz, the experience made or broke them. Some felt guilty for living when others died and never recovered from their misplaced guilt. Others, like my mum, went on to live amazing and fulfilling lives in spite of their experiences.

*Her answer, as theirs, was to live life to the full. A duty to the eight million who died, Jew and non-Jew alike. An obligation to pick up the baton left behind by the fallen and run with it.*

### 15 March 1957, Lodz

Regardless of her children's disdain, Olga continued to study the football results of the Polish league, predicting the outcome of matches with uncanny accuracy. This was not down to luck, but a quirk of Polish football that Olga had serendipitously stumbled upon.

After the war, as a result of territorial boundary changes to Poland, a large number of Poland's best teams, such as Lechia Lwow and Smigly Wilno, were now part of the Soviet Union. Conversely former German teams found themselves in the Polish league.

Olga scrutinised the results of these teams intensely and came to an epiphany.

Polish football had been turned upside down by these territorial changes. Newcomer teams to the league (like the German teams) often blew everyone else out of the water. The all-Polish ties invariably played out as dull draws, just as they always had.

By mixing and matching predictions of big newcomer wins with draws between evenly matched Polish sides, Olga found she could predict the results. Olga had in effect built her own football crystal ball. She no longer used her mystical powers, just crunched the stats, and was about to put her expertise into action.

One Monday morning, Olga was frantic with excitement. She sat Alina down and showed her the coming fixtures for the weekend.

'Look,' she said.

'What?' Alina replied, annoyed that her mother was still banging on about this.

'The circled games are the ones you need to bet on. I have given you score-draws and no-score-draws. There are three games I predict heavy wins. 5–1, 4–1 and 6–nil.'

'What on earth are you talking about? You think I'm going to bet on football matches?'

'I do, yes. I've worked it out.'

Olga tore the page out of the paper and pushed it into her daughter's hand. Alina couldn't believe all this nonsense. She walked out of the flat and joined her brother, whom she had arranged to meet in a nearby café and who was sitting with a beer.

'She is still talking about the pools,' Alina said, sighing.

Kazhik took a newspaper from a bar stool and opened the sports pages.

'OK, what does she predict?'

Kazhik was football crazy, ever since he had lived in Warsaw, where big games continued until 1943, and even as the city collapsed. He knew the name of every player in the league. Alina took out the crumpled-up sports page and pressed it flat in front of her brother on the table.

'I have no idea what any of this means,' she said exasperated, and went to the bar to get herself a glass of red wine. When Alina returned, Kazhik was studying the fixtures and looking at Olga's predictions next to them. His face was ashen.

'This is good,' he said. 'Very good. Remember when you were in Sweden and everyone told mother it was madness to come back to Warsaw and find us? She was right then, wasn't she?'

'That was a hunch about her children being alive, this is blind guesswork about football teams she can't even pronounce properly.'

'What harm will it do? Come on Alencu.'

Alina looked cautiously at the newspaper.

'Give me a pen,' she said spontaneously.

Kazhik fiddled in his jacket and handed her a fountain pen once owned by their father. Alina looked at the fixtures, and circled the first five games on the list.

'What are you doing?' Kazhik said, his mouth open. 'They weren't her predictions! Are you mad?'

'What difference does it make? I'm doing my own version.'

'That's ridiculous,' her brother replied. 'No one ever wins by just circling the first five games. When have the first games on the list ever been draws? It doesn't happen.'

'Well,' Alina replied, finishing off the last of her wine, 'at least you can all shut up about the football pools when I lose.'

Alina forgot about it and went climbing with her brother in the mountains with friends. It was an incredible weekend; there was not a cloud in the sky and the cliff face they scrambled up seemed like child's play to her.

Kazhik held the rope as his sister ascended the boulders swiftly, Alina's hands and feet drawn as if by magnets to precisely the right ledge or crimp. Everything she attempted went right for once. Instead of looking down fearfully to her brother far below, Alina's eyes were focused on the summit.

She pushed through her fear and kept going, climbing higher than she had ever gone before; the valley below was peppered with the tiny dots of people, cars and houses. She brushed pine branches aside from her face and breathed in the deep, rich mountain air. It was so clean, it hurt her lungs.

Suddenly, on an exposed outcrop of rock, she stopped. The air had gone cold, the change in wind direction evaporating Alina's confidence in an instant. She hung uncertainly to her only good hold, a solid 'jug', her fingernails digging into a tiny pocket in the rock, one foot hanging in the air whilst the other pressed into a small crack; the only thing preventing her from falling. She could feel it slipping and then she looked down.

For the first time, Alina's brain began to compute where she was. A tiny figure with scant climbing experience, clinging to a near vertical rock face with nothing but a rope between her and death. Her brother was 150 feet below and shouting wildly for her to continue. Her climbing partner, another student, was pulling tight on the belay line to keep her taut and safe, but it didn't make Alina feel any better.

At moments like these, Alina went back to her memory of the firing squad in Warsaw. The little bird on the wall, the finch without a care in the world, had become her lodestar: a talismanic comfort for her to be used in a crisis. She had summoned the little bird as she stood at her father's graveside, unable to weep. She had briefly imagined jumping into the hole with her father and the ground swallowing them both, but the finch flashed into her mind, taking flight from the wall, and she stopped herself.

On the rock face, she tried to remember her thirteen-year-old self, lying still in the midst of those corpses. The translucent hair of the woman beside her, perfect as if she had just been to the hairdresser. The indecision of the SS officers – unsure whether to stop shooting or kill them all – and the little bird on the wall, oblivious to it all; tweeting merrily to itself and flying off suddenly.

Alina shut her eyes on the mountain as the fear took a grip. She tried to take herself back to the familiar horror of the firing squad one more time, but she couldn't do it. Alina saw nothing. No bodies, no woman's hair; no little bird. Her lodestar had never failed her before, but that day, on the cliff face, it had gone forever.

All she knew was who she was right now: a twenty-six-year-old woman with the wind blowing in her face, and a job to do. To reach the summit. Alina stretched her arm up to a tiny crack in the rock above, and pulled herself with all her might. In fifteen minutes, she had reached the top. She lay on the grass and looked at the sky.

# 19

## *Paris*

*25 March 1957, Lodz*

The first Alina heard about it, she was sitting at the kitchen table, eating a piece of bread with cheese. She heard her brother's shouts in the corridor outside. Kazhik was hyperventilating, barely able to catch his breath as he fell over himself through the doorway, a heap of limbs and sweat. He had clearly been running all the way up the street.

There was nothing coherent coming from his mouth, only a string of non-sequiturs.

'I . . . it's . . . I . . .'

He sat on the floor, his eyes gazing serenely at the ceiling, as if he had just seen a vision of heaven. He was, for once in his life, speechless.

Alina got up from the table and looked pityingly at her brother.

'Would you like to tell me what's going on?'

Kazhik held in his left hand a copy of the morning newspaper. He seemed unwilling to be separated from it, so Alina took his fingers and prised it free.

She sat at the table and her eyes scanned the headlines: tractor production up (again) – Soviet Union performs atmospheric nuclear test – Cuban people rise up against the fascist dictator Batista.

'Look at the sports pages,' Kazhik said, once he had calmed down. Alina went to the back of the paper.

The football results were laid out in a box. There was a 2-2, a 0-0, then a win, another 0-0 and a 4-4 draw.

'And?' Alina said, confused.

'Four *draws*,' Kazhik said. 'In the first *five* results. Don't you see?'

'No, I'm afraid I don't see.'

'You circled the first four games in the pools . . . as draws.'

Then Alina froze. The penny had dropped. She tried to focus again on the page, but the text was a blur. Alina shut her eyes, reopened them and re-read the results, her eyes moving slowly across the characters, one by one.

2-2, 0-0, 5-1, 0-0, 4-4.

Kazhik nodded slowly.

'That's right,' he said smiling. 'You've won.'

But Alina was suddenly confused. 'I don't think I have. You need *five* draws to win money.'

'No, you need five draws to win the jackpot – ten thousand zlotys. But *four* draws and you are a runner-up – that's two thousand five hundred.'

Kazhik was enjoying this. He felt like a television announcer; he should have been wearing a bow tie.

'You've won Alencu!' He jumped up and picked his sister clean off the floor, spinning her round in circles. Olga limped into the room and Kazhik dropped his sister and picked up his mother. She was so heavy, he could only manage a perfunctory hoist, before easing her gently back down onto the sofa, where he sat exhausted beside her.

'I imagine this calls for a celebration,' Alina said. She had never celebrated anything in her life. 'Kazhik, go and buy champagne from the black market shop. Buy three bottles. One each!'

My mum had won the Polish equivalent of £500. In 1957, that would buy you a quarter of a house in London. It was enough to buy Alina and Kazhik a one-way ticket to the West; a year of accommodation; and enough money aside for Olga to keep her in tarot cards and *halva* for the next twenty years.

\*          \*          \*

*Alina did not go to a real football match until 2018, when I took her to see Arsenal v Chelsea, which she enjoyed thoroughly.*

'*I wish I'd done this earlier!*' *she said, as we left, jubilant.*

'*Did you never think of going to one before, given that football was your ticket to the West?*' *I asked, as we exited the stadium. She looked utterly mystified.*

'*Why on earth would I do that?*'

*She was still shaking her head incredulously at my question as we walked to the Tube.*

'*My coming to the West had nothing to do with football,*' *she explained.* '*It was a gift from my mother. She knew I'd choose my own numbers and ignore hers. It was Olga's way of making me decide my own destiny.*'

*She smiled.*

'*And it worked, didn't it?*'

Alina used the money from the football pools to travel with her brother Kazhik to Paris, where Michael and Olga had first met in the 1920s, émigrés on the run from the Russian revolution; followed thirty-five years later by their children, running away from its consequences.

This is Kazhik and Alina in Pigalle, at the beginning of their new lives. They knew no one in Paris so they lived like millionaires, eating at La Coupole and playing roulette at the Aviation Club. Within weeks, the money had virtually run out, but they didn't care. They were alive and whatever they did with their lives, it would be a ludicrously fortuitous gift that neither had ever imagined possible: 'extra' after the war they had survived.

In this photo of my mum, she is looking at her reflection in a shop window. As a child, I was intrigued by this photo, which sat on the piano. I wondered what might have lain on the other side of the glass. My mum is looking not at the camera, but back to something out of frame; Orpheus gazing into the underworld, to a place beyond reach. Maybe she's gazing back to the war, and the questions that were never answered, or into the unknowable future.

I never asked my mum about the photo until we started to work together on this book. We were in Cartons coffee shop in Stanmore one day, having a sausage roll, and I plucked up the courage, thinking it absurd to be asking something so strange.

*'What were you thinking when that photo was taken?'*

*'Which photo?'*

*'The one on the piano.'*

*'Oh, I seem sad, don't I? I wasn't. I was happy. My brother and I were in Paris. It was just after the money ran out and we had no idea what would happen next.'*

*'I was wondering if perhaps in the back of your mind you were thinking back to everything that had happened? Juta and Pavel; your father; maybe the love you never got from Olga?'*

*'Christ, all this analysis. I wasn't looking back, I was looking forward. To everything I couldn't yet see. To having a child, marrying and knowing that all that had happened in my life and everyone I'd lost, would be with me always. I was happy, and do you know what? I never stopped being the happiest person alive.'*

Later we take a walk through the forest near my mum and dad's house. It's a beautiful autumn day. I want to ask my mum something that I never felt I could before, but now suddenly seems appropriate.

*'Would you like to know what happened to Juta and Pavel? To have the truth, even if it was something terrible, or would you prefer to remain ignorant, if the truth proved too horrible?'*

*'Does it matter?' my mum says to me. 'Does it really matter so much what happened to Juta?'*

*'It matters to me to know.'*

*'Well, it doesn't matter to me and I'm her sister, and I was there.'*

*We pass through the empty autumn trees. It is not as pleasant as I thought it might be. There is supposed to be a clearing ahead, but it* is thick with brambles and the sky has gone cloudy. My mum does not seem keen to go any further. She stops beneath a huge oak.

'You can't know everything,' my mum says. 'That is something you learn as you get older. Life is full of holes, and it's better to accept the gaps as part of the story. The holes are what make the certainties – who you love and the memories you have – even more important.

I can tell you something. I thought I knew everything when I was thirteen: I was harsh and judgmental. Now, at ninety, I realise I know nothing.'

We stop to take in the silence, except for the trees in the wind.

'Every day I wake up, the world never ceases to be a wonder to me,' my mum continues, peering up. 'The war taught me that. All its horrors. It taught me to be fearless. Life is an adventure, and it's exciting! Don't be afraid of it, and remember to forgive. Always, always forgive. Because forgiveness is empowering.'

'What did you think of the book?' I ask. 'Have you read it?'

'Which book?'

'The book I've been writing about you and Juta, and everything that happened.'

'Is it published?'

'No, I gave it to you to read first.'

'Oh, no. Sorry. Did you give it to me?'

'Yes, I gave it to you three weeks ago.'

My mum looks embarrassed, and then she laughs. We stand together in the woods and I give her a hug. I never did this when I was a child. It never seemed possible for either of us, as though we were separated by the pane of glass in the photo.

'It doesn't matter,' I say. 'Maybe read it when you have time.'

'Thank you,' she replies. 'I'd like that.'

# Epilogue

A week later, I am in a doctor's surgery awaiting the results of some tests. I am called in and the doctor asks me to sit down.

'We've had your DNA profile back,' she says briskly. 'Can I ask, is there any dementia in your family?'

'My mum has dementia.'

'That makes sense. You have what I'd class as a moderate to strong chance of developing it too, I'm afraid.'

An orchid sits smugly on a window sill, mocking my diagnosis. I go to the pub and my friend Johan tries to be reassuring.

'Everyone has a chance of developing dementia,' he says. 'Don't worry about it.'

I smile. 'Some of us have more chance of developing it than others,' I say.

Dementia is a twenty-first-century disease. No one in history ever lived long enough to get it, but now human beings can prolong their lives into their nineties and hundreds, they invariably find the brain fails first.

I wish I could say I am not scared of what will happen to me, but I would be lying. Even though I have inherited some of my mum's bravery, embracing adversity without fear, I still struggle with the idea that I have also inherited her dementia.

*'What's it like?' I ask her, one wet afternoon.*

*'What's what like?'*

*'Dementia. What's it like?' I pause. 'You know, having it'.*

'*Oh, it's not so bad. You forget the things that don't matter and remember better the things that do. Then you begin to forget the things that do matter, and realise that they don't matter either.*'

We laugh.

'*So you live in the present,*' I say,' *because you have no choice?*'

'*You live in the present in the most profound way. You live like a baby.*'

'*I will probably develop dementia,*' I say. '*Just like you.*'

'*Then you'll get a chance to infuriate someone else, just as I infuriate you!*'

My mum lived through the most momentous of events, and this book has been written in momentous times too: in the tumult of the Covid pandemic. Obviously, it was not anticipated, but when I began to tell my mother's story to other people, I found that they were less amazed by the extraordinary events than in drawing comfort from her resilience and unbreakable enthusiasm for life. Something they could use for themselves.

My mum would be the first to baulk at the idea of drawing a parallel between the two events (whenever I mentioned the dangers of Covid, she dismissed it contemptuously with a wave of the hand), but I think you can: my mum survived, and thrived, and so shall we.

Alina dropped any certainties she had about life the moment she stepped into war. In spite of witnessing unimaginable cruelty, she remained kind and open towards everyone she met throughout her life, even Germans. In the mid-1950s, she travelled across East Germany to understand better the people and country that had murdered her sister and brother. She learnt the language and made friends that she kept for the rest of her life.

After winning the football pools money that allowed her to go to Paris, she moved to London in the early 1960s, and began work for the London County Council, working on some of the biggest social housing projects of the post-war era, including the construction of the Westway. Every time we pass over the concrete section above the Edgware Road, my mum says, 'I built this bit'. It was at the LCC that she met my father, Peter Peretti, who was also an architect. They travelled together to Sudan, Senegal and Mali in West Africa, where they worked together on the construction of dams and clean water projects.

In 1967, my mum became pregnant with her only child, me. She travelled to Poland to see her mother Olga in Lodz. Olga read her tarot cards for the unborn foetus and placed pebbles on my mum's belly, just as she had the pregnant woman in the Siberian camp twenty-five years earlier. My mum returned to London, happy that she would have a successful birth, but Olga died before I was born.

My mother and grandmother were reconciled with one another on that journey back to Lodz, shortly before Olga's death. My mum says she felt sorry for Olga, for the first time. Everything Olga did, Alina realised, was ultimately to try and keep her children safe, and she was demonised by them for it.

'She was a strange woman, but aren't we all strange in our own ways?'

In spite of what Olga believed about her shamanistic special powers, she had no gift. Her trinkets were comforters, like rosary beads. But what this delusion of paranormal foresight really gave Olga, my mum says, was the courage to face anything thrown at her.

Olga lived long enough to see her two surviving children, Kazhik and Alina, travel to the West. Her parting gift to them was to provide escape from communist Poland, setting them free to live their lives.

Against expectation, Kazhik returned to Poland and became a famous and successful architect in Lodz, marrying Mirka Adamiak, another feisty architect. Mirka was so tiny and Kazhik so huge, when they drove together in their Fiat bubble car, it leant preposterously on to Kazhik's side. They had a son called Martin, whom I met only once, on holiday in Kazimierz when we were kids. He later emigrated to the US and became an architect too, like his father and grandfather. In the early nineties, I was in New York on work and Martin tried to make contact with me, but I failed to return his call. I regret that now.

Kazhik died of a heart attack in 1980 at the age of fifty, just as his father had. It happened on the nineteenth floor of the Hotel Forum in Warsaw, where he collapsed suddenly. The lift didn't work, so paramedics had to climb fifty-seven flights of stairs to get to his room, by which time Kazhik had stopped breathing. It was the kind of wryly cruel turn of events that I like to imagine he would have found amusing.

Kazhik and Alina both stayed in touch with their father's lover, Marta, for several years after leaving Poland, without Olga's knowledge, after which their correspondence abruptly ended. They never knew what happened to her. Kazhik always said that it was out of loyalty to Michael, because Marta was 'the one woman our father really loved'.

In one of their last conversations, Marta confessed to Alina that 'Marta' wasn't her real name, it was Alexandra. Marta was a codename that had been given to her by the Soviet secret police in the war. She had always been a communist spy, even when she met Michael, supplying information on the AK in London to the Stalin-backed government in Lublin. It made no difference to the fact she had loved him. After Michael died, she remained alone.

Alina's story has a happy ending. My mum travelled the world, learnt six languages, and after retiring as an engineer and architect, became a tour guide and classical concert organiser. The only place she declined to take a tour around was Auschwitz. She never made it through the gates again, no matter how many times she tried. She just couldn't do it.

Her life was joyful and filled with adventure. Her openness meant that she made friends everywhere she went. In Germany, Alina met the opera singer Jessye Norman (pictured) after organising a concert for her there in the 1980s. They remained lifelong friends.

My mum never stopped hating war and guns. As a child, I was forbidden from playing with toy soldiers, hence my obsessing over the Second World War. In 2003, Alina was detained by police on the London march against the war in Iraq (pictured). Her hatred of authoritarian communist Poland did not stop her becoming a staunch defender of revolutionary movements across the world, as her father had been. She also became tremendously nostalgic for the Poland of the 1950s that she had left behind, and returned often.

More surprisingly, she became a huge supporter of Queen Elizabeth II. This is her (with my dad seated) saluting throughout the entire duration of the Queen's Christmas speech in 2019.

Dementia, like war and Covid, is not feared by my mum, but treated simply as another wave to be sailed over, with a fair wind in her sails.

Her story is not set in the distant past – in a foreign landscape of snow, spotter planes and wolves hiding in the forest – but in the now. She describes the traumatic events in Warsaw and Auschwitz as a blessing not a curse, enabling her to live the life she wanted to live. In spite of me forcing her to look back for this book, the truth is that my mum never looks back. She faces the challenges each day brings, overcoming them without drama; because to her, it is natural to triumph over adversity.

The people my mum loved dearly – Juta, Pavel, Olga, Michael and Kazhik – are ever-present for Alina. They are not distant ghosts but a living presence, as alive to her now as her grand-children, or as they were when she was a child. There is no past, present and future for my mum, only a single experience, lived wholly with wonder and curiosity, inhabited by the living and the dead; the ensemble cast of her life. Just as it is for all of us.

My mum is now becoming a child once more, as I was when I first heard my mum talking in tantalising snippets about her own childhood. At the time, these stories were no more than glimpsed pieces in the jigsaw of her life. It has taken me my own lifetime to put those pieces together. I am glad I did.

It began with a conversation. All that was needed was to press 'Record'.

*Jacques and Alina in 2021.*

# Acknowledgments

There are several excellent books giving context to the events covered here. Alexandre Richie's *Warsaw 1944* is a comprehensive account of the uprising, rich in detail and political background, to which I am indebted.

*Auschwitz: A History* by Sybille Steinbacher is a slim volume about the concentration camp, shorn of drama, simply the numbers and facts, which speak for themselves.

I found also *Interpreting in Nazi Concentration Camps*, edited by Michaela Wolf, and *Das KZ Bordell* by Robert Sommer, on the translators and camp brothels, respectively, illuminating on the context Juta may have found herself in at the camp.

I never expected anyone to publish this book, so I want to thank Rupert for seeing something here; Robert, for his cheery encouragement; Barry, for putting it all in order, being so sensitive to the material and so patient with my tracking phobia; and Vic for her swingeing use of the marker pen slash-through.

Thanks also to Hannah, for her honesty and for banishing doubt; my dad, Peter, for keeping my mum on the straight and narrow; and my children, Theo and Esme, for encouraging me in the first place to speak to Alina about everything that happened. I would like finally to acknowledge all those whose mothers, fathers, brothers, sisters, uncles and aunts passed in the camps, and who have kept their memories alive through the determined retelling of their stories to their own families. It is, as my mum would say, 'important'.